W9-BPM-676

Zen *Confidential*

Zen *Confidential*

CONFESSIONS
of a
WAYWARD
MONK

Shozan Jack Haubner

SHAMBHALA
Boston & London
2013

Shambhala Publications, Inc.
Horticultural Hall
300 Massachusetts Avenue
Boston, Massachusetts 02115
www.shambhala.com

Portions of this book have appeared in different form in *The Sun, Shambhala Sun, Tricycle, Buddhadharma, Utne Reader, The Best Buddhist Writing 2010* and *2011*, and *Pushcart Prize XXXVII*.

9 8 7 6 5 4 3

Printed in the United States of America

♾ This edition is printed on acid-free paper that meets the American National Standards Institute z39.48 Standard.
♻ This book is printed on 30% postconsumer recycled paper. For more information please visit www.shambhala.com.

Distributed in the United States by Penguin Random House LLC and in Canada by Random House of Canada Ltd
Designed by Daniel Urban-Brown

LIBRARY OF CONGRESS CATALOGING-IN-PUBLICATION DATA
Haubner, Shozan Jack.
Zen confidential: confessions of a wayward monk / Shozan Jack Haubner.—
First edition.
pages cm
ISBN 978-1-61180-033-3 (pbk.)
1. Haubner, Shozan Jack. 2. Zen Buddhists—United States—Biography.
3. Buddhist monks—United States—Biography. I. Title.
BQ962.A85A3 2013
294.3'927092—DC23
[B]
2012048993

For Papi-san
Who feels the tree branches swaying in his gut

Great things are done when men and mountains meet;
This is not done by jostling in the street.

—WILLIAM BLAKE

A Zen master's life is one continuous mistake.
—DOGEN

Contents

By Way of a Foreword

This is the best account I have ever read of the education of a Zen monk in America.

I was ordained a long while ago. Shortly thereafter my teacher let me know that I was a "pretend monk." That was true. I was in it for the robes.

Shozan Jack Haubner has trained for more than nine years with a teacher whom I love, on a mountain that I know. Difference is, he is the real deal. He stuck it out while (many years before he arrived) I escaped.

But now this punk of a monk, who should be tending to his own affairs, has decided to infect the real world with his tall tales, and worse, to let the cat out of the bag. And what a sly, dangerous, beautiful, foul-smelling, heartwarming beast it is. We can almost forgive him.

If you are interested in these matters, this is a book you will enjoy. If you want to go a little deeper, this is a book you will need.

—JIKAN LEONARD COHEN
APRIL 1, 2012

Acknowledgments

A chance not to take a bow before your favorite readers, but to recognize your cowriters:

My dharma aunts, uncles, brothers, sisters, nieces, and nephews. You are the bravest people I know.

Tom Tom, my legal eagle; Markus, for carefully nosing his way toward the notes that matter; Jikan-san, who dropped a hand from above when I needed it, and gave me a yank; the inji, without whom I would be growing immature in direct proportion to the increase in my chronological age.

Dave O'Neal: a good editor makes you realize you're not as good as you thought you were, and then makes you better than you were before.

The editors at the *Sun, Tricycle,* and the *Shambhala Sun,* especially Andrea Miller, Rod Meade Sperry, and Melvin McLeod—the brilliant guidance of this powerful trio puts a lump in my throat and tears in my eyes.

The Baldy boys, from every generation—you keepers of the flame, you mechanics in the mensch factory!

Pops, Mom, Mona, Helen, Beth, Andrew. My people, now and forever. *Baboo!*

My mentor.

My teacher.

Zen *Confidential*

1

Confessions of an
Angry Young Monk on the
Cusp of Curmudgeonhood

AN INTRODUCTION/AFTERWORD

A Zen Buddhist monastery is a laboratory where you are discovering the natural properties of your true self. You are both the subject and the observer of an experiment that often gets ugly. There are explosions, nasty messes, volatile interactions, strange smells, more explosions, and finally, fascinating, unpredictable results. Something new is born—or rather, uncovered—from all of this experimenting. That something is you: your fundamental nature as a human being.

Training at a monastery is simply the organic process whereby you learn to get out of your own way so that the life you were meant to live can fully emerge. I can truthfully say that this approach to spiritual work has utterly transformed me. It has also nearly driven me batshit with frustration and despair. Although I've been doing this work full-time for close to a decade now, I am no "religious expert." I am simply someone who has had his resistance to reality thoroughly worn down by spiritual techniques.

A year into my stay at the monastery, in an attempt to process everything I was going through and to share the experience with others, I began writing personal vignettes dealing with the more mundane, nitty-gritty realities of spiritual work. With my missives from the mountaintop I hoped to leave my mark on American Buddhism, like a teenager stealing through a parking lot, leaving behind a row of elongated, mushroom-shaped "items" drawn in the dust on the car windows.

And so it begins: a penis joke within the first three paragraphs of the book. I see a hand rise from the back. "Why the obscenity?" you ask. "Are you trying to shock us or show off?"

In the pages to follow I hope I'm not showing off so much as taking off and revealing. A Zen monk, I feel, is someone unafraid of being bare. He leaves himself exposed, spread-eagle, always. And so you are witness to the most intimate workings of the human spirit. His approach may be crude, but it is the exact opposite of pornography, so much so that an analogy is inevitable: he strips himself away, layer after layer, to reveal your own image and likeness, the one we all have in common, staring back at you from the space where he used to be. The private is made public, universal.

Put more modestly, all work that seeks that which is fresh and true is "dirty." And monastic work is dirty. And so I will try to undress before you in the pages to come. I will get shy and excited. It will get a little weird at times. I'm warning you. But I'm trying to bring us closer together, to remove artifice, to break down barriers: between you and me, the sacred and the profane.

As for the feral feel of these essays, the reading of which I'm afraid may necessitate regular shower breaks, it can be traced back to stomping, snorting, horn-locking spiritual rutting sessions with my Zen mentor (the wild spirit who eventually introduced me to my Zen teacher) that began more than a decade ago and are still going strong today, both of us still trying to mount the same

Truth from different angles: he through logic, I through poetry, and after we fail at both, by way of humor. Typically I write in a flurry of ecstatic inspiration, especially if, as a central metaphor, I have something involving a bodily function; my mentor—that greatest of gifts: a compassionate critic—then eviscerates whatever I've written, and (to my mind) castrates it for good measure. I then issue a few ethnically charged epithets in reference to his Irish heritage and set to rewriting, gradually incorporating most of his ideas as though they were my own (sometimes tweaking details and events to disguise my peers and, frankly, to improve the narrative). My mentor insists that this process is a subtle Zen lesson delivered through the back door of writing. I counter that it is a clever tactic on his part designed to leave me feeling obligated to pick up the tab in the tequila-soaked settings of our most passionate dharma encounters.

It's my biased opinion that the spark of Zen is at the core of every spiritual path. That said, full-time monastic living ain't for everyone. The hours are endless, the food gives you gas, the outfits are hot and itchy in summer and cold and cumbersome in winter, the pay is nonexistent, and the people drive you berserk. There's never enough sleep, protein, petty cash, privacy, or affirmation of any kind. It never ceases to amaze me, then, that *Zen* continues to be a catchall in popular culture for a kind of balmy, glassy-eyed minimalist aesthetic and little more. The word itself has become a synonym for spiritually infused apathy, à la the Dude from *The Big Lebowski,* with his golden tresses shaved, in Zen robes instead of a bathrobe, sipping green tea and not White Russians. "It's, like, yoga for people who don't like to exercise," an LA eyelash-batter once informed me, answering her own question: *What is Zen, anyway?*

For so many of the Americans that I meet, Zen equals trickling waterfalls, *shakuhachi* flute music, and placid Japanese monks with vaguely lobotomized grins raking out anal-retentively pristine rock gardens. I daresay that if you lift the robes of these monks—monks who, by the way, exist only in certain Westerners' minds—you discover not human genitals but black censorship bars or a yellow smiley face blocking your view of anything interesting.

However, if Zen clichés paint the practice as placid and benign, the homeopathic version of Prozac, there is some excuse, as the Far East has mostly been an enigmatic unknown to the Western mind. Unfortunately, stereotypes about our actual homegrown monks are even more condescending and confused. In my experience, Americans see the monastic—Buddhist, Catholic, or otherwise—as a marginal, slightly spooky creature. His skin is pale, his genitals unused. When's the last time he had a martini? Like a troll of the inner world, he inhabits spaces and places most of us aren't quite sure even exist: subconscious caverns, dens of silence, ineffable realms—nameless, shapeless, formless interiors.

Where do people get these ideas? I once met an ancient dust-colored poetess at the Lost Souls Café in New Mexico who elucidated the problem with aplomb nearly as withering as her cappuccino breath: "We just don't have a strong and storied tradition of wise-men-dropping-out-of-society-and-living-in-the-hills in this country." She picked at her teeth with the blade of a jackknife and thought about it for a moment. "Grizzly Adams and the Unabomber. These are the guys who drop out of society and live in the hills. Oh, and those incestuous sodomite brothers from *Deliverance*."

To summarize her position, then, when Americans hear the word *monk*, they think: "Squeal like a pig!"

Such formulations all point to one common misconception: that the Western monk has no relationship to this world. He is of no help to it (and sometimes a harm). He is totally removed from it, removed from everyday life. These are incorrect assumptions, as I will show after I return from my afternoon levitation. . . .

Life was not meant to be easy. We all know this instinctively. The problem is that as a culture the solution we offer to this suffering is lies, a complex network of lie upon interconnected lie—always the lie of "more": work more, eat more, buy more—as opposed to one or two hard, indisputable truths. Truths like the First Noble Truth in Buddhism: life is suffering. Start here, the dharma sages tell us. Instead of relentlessly pursuing a life tailor-made to sating each of your needs and desires, accept that you are not meant to chase happiness. You have a higher purpose, which connects you to everyone else on the planet, and which you must live up to, and which will require a great deal of you. The message of the old masters is the same as that of the new ones: you are meant to grow into a true human being. Right now you are to a human being what an acorn is to an oak tree. A good start, that's all. You've got a long way to go, baby, and you're not going to grow into your full potential sitting in front of the laptop, bag of Cool Ranch Doritos in one hand, dick in the other, anime porn boring a hole in your corneas and consciousness. Just a thought.

An Afterword, Beforehand

I fear I've already gone too far, lost too many readers. I'm banging out this shaggy introduction after having just finished writing the last page of the book. It is 2:30 A.M., and I have to be up serving tea in the *zendo,* the meditation hall, by 3:15. I'm writing by candlelight at my desk, as I've written so much of what you're about to read, at odd hours and with little sleep. This is my last chance to put the finishing touches on my first book, and dammit I want to shout here in plain English what the pages hereafter only imply.

It's been a long journey getting here, to this introduction of my life as a Zen monk. I started out Catholic, I'll have you know. For so many of us, the religion we were born into is like a birthmark or even a deformity: either we've kept it and learned to live with it or we bear the scars from its removal. I was lucky enough to graft a new spiritual practice in Zen onto the open wound my lopped-off Catholicism left behind before the gaping gash could harden over.

Yet I still feel my childhood faith twitching in the emptiness like a phantom limb. It is into this emptiness that I toss these words, the final ones I am writing for a book you are about to begin. Sitting beside me here in my room is myself, a decade ago, and each word I scribble is another plank in a rickety old bridge extending back to him.

But I can't reach him. I can only reach you, and that is good enough—better, in fact, than I could ever have hoped for. For so many years I just talked to myself in an empty room, writing, thinking, and living for no one but that ghost in the mirror. It is a blessed thing to finally have some company. It is you who are sitting in this room here with me now, as I am sitting in your room, in your mind, in your heart. I hope that our meeting gives rise to an experience akin to lovemaking, a relationship wherein something new is born, a bridge between two minds, two hearts, two spirits.

To this end I offer you stories from my life as a monk, and in so doing, I offer you myself. For so long my self was the problem. Now I know it is also the only bridge between the two of us. It is all I have to offer, and I gladly give it away. Clung to, it rots. Given away, it flourishes, and nurtures your flourishing.

I am not an expert in Buddhism or Zen. In the end I am really only an expert in my own screw-ups. And so I have great sympathy for screw-ups like me. But screwing up is not the problem. Even the founder of Buddhism himself, old Shakyamuni, met his unfortunate end after mistakenly gulping down a mouthful of bad food. A real life begins with finally accepting that we can't run from our problems. Once this is done, the endless challenge then becomes to merge, over and over again, with the beating heart of rapture at the center of every moment of time, good *or* bad, up to and including our last, often very messy breath. Believing fully in this is what the word *faith* means to a Zen Buddhist.

I imagine a reader, then, who is someone like I was a decade ago (someone slightly less high and more intelligent, however). I want to tell him: There is a way out of the materialism, nihilism, and—in response to the first two—religious fanaticism that are endemic in our age. There is eternal light within the infinite black hole of human suffering. I want to grab him and shake him and cry: Idiot! The reason you're having prostate problems and you're not even thirty yet is because you just can't stop playing with yourself. I would have killed someone for this information when I was twenty-five. In fact, I nearly did kill someone—myself. When you're truly desperate and confused, you mistake the self-destruction that you crave for the self-negation that you truly need.

Fortunately, I discovered Zen monasticism, which has been my antidote to globally capitalistic, ultraindividualistic, überalienating megachurch and minimall McAmerica. (Monks, as you can imagine, make lousy consumers. I suspect this is another reason that contemporary mainstream society finds us so damn creepy.) In Zen you don't chase after things, people, or ideas. You give up the rat race state of mind entirely, denuding yourself of material possessions, intellectual certitudes, and religious comforts. You give up your schemes and dreams. Ultimately, you learn to even give up yourself, that is, the delusive constellation of ideas, emotions, and beliefs whereby you come to feel cut off from a universe that, in fact, you are plugged into via a kind of invisible umbilical cord with nutrients and energy running both ways, in a circle. (For, as the French mystic Simone Weil said, "The circle is the symbol of monotony which is beautiful. . . . Only the cycle contains the truth.") And then, after giving up yourself, you learn to give up giving up yourself. And that's when you are born again, along with the whole world around you.

The seed of the universe, my mentor once told me, is that space where the out-breath ends and the in-breath begins, but we can never witness its germination, as it is we ourselves who lie dormant within that seed. Sound complicated? Take a deep breath. It's no more complex than inhaling and exhaling, which is why we do so much conscious breathing in Zen.

One of the reasons that Zen is such a subversive practice is that it's so simple. "The truth has few moving parts," my Zen master has said. There is simply the principle of "not self"—*anatta*, in Sanskrit—and the putting of this principle into practice: through openly giving and receiving but never taking. When practiced correctly, even a handshake or a hug demonstrates this principle perfectly, which explains why much of early Zen practice with a qualified master consists of simple, basic human physical contact. Any time you stray from putting the fundamental principle into practice, the Zen master is there to whack you or hug you or shake you back in line.

The Zen master I trained with came to the States five decades ago with, as the legend goes, a Japanese-English dictionary in one sleeve and an English-Japanese dictionary in the other. I'm partial, but I feel there is no one like him left on the planet. He was born in 1907 and recently passed his one hundred and fifth birthday. He has said, "A Zen master is not a saint," and has proven it time and again in his own career here. He has also said, "but sometimes it helps to imitate one," which is always how he has behaved toward me, and it is, for better or worse, that side of him that I present here, so that we can all glimpse a flawed spiritual teacher at his highest. When you are at your lowest, however, know this: the greatest among us are no better than us—or, if they are better than us, they are also a great deal worse. This paradox is at the heart of my work with my teacher. You will not hear of him directly until the end of this book, but every page along the way is informed by his presence, every sentence haunted by the only literary advice he has ever given me: "Words are lies."

I'm no Zen master (more of a Zen monster, actually), but I hope the following "lies" whack you, shake you, hug you, and if you need it, stroke you a little. I've tried to include the spirit of Zen in these pages, which are rife with intimate details. Please be embarrassed for me. Share my idiocy and know that you are not alone in yours. In my experience, too many Buddhist books focus on the lotus of enlightenment, as it were, and skip the muck from which it arises. In fostering convenient and naive misconceptions about the spiritual life, we abdicate any responsibility for having one. "That monk gets to sit up on a mountaintop with his thumb up his butt all day," we think, "but down here in the real world we can't afford the dubious luxury of a detour into the meditative ether. We've got bills to pay and mouths to feed!"

What we have forgotten as a people is that a spiritual life is vital for having something other than "the world" alone, with its genocide, starvation, environmental destruction, religious wars, and boy bands to serve as our compass; something to interweave the trillion trajectories of our personal and professional byways into one momentum-gathering life path, a path that leads inward to our deepest selves, out toward the hearts of others, and ultimately to the recognition that both places are one and the same.

And so, as I overshare, in pitiful and horrifying detail, my struggles and failings as a full-time Zen Buddhist monk, I hope to provide a friend as you encounter similar challenges on your own journey toward self-transformation and completion. It's amazing how much we can learn from the spiritual mistakes of others. And in this, I have much to teach. In these self-dissecting pages, I humbly offer myself as your Zen guinea pig in the monastic experiment. The book I've struggled to craft here is the book I desperately searched for when I was lost, angry, and twenty-five. It is the deeply felt journey of a young man who crawled out of the anus of his own self-absorption, suffering, and despair . . . and lived to tell poop jokes about it.

2

Growing Ground

It began as a fine plan: replace the primitive outdoor toilets at our rural, monastic-style Zen Center. The head monk at the time was a charismatic and idealistic German (look out), and he made the final call to install composting toilets. CTs are based on a beautiful principle. It's a principle with great metaphorical as well as practical value. The way the toilets work is, you crap down a long narrow chute and it accumulates in a large plastic box. Once a week you shovel a bag of wood chips into the box. Eventually heaps of rich, earthy soil appear. This manure, or "humanure," makes primo fertilizer for your gardens. What you took from the earth in food, you return to it as food. Beautiful, right?

I'll admit, I got jazzed about the project. It sounded great on paper, with its universal themes straight out of an animated kids' film. I could almost see little Pixar "poo people" singing Elton John numbers about the circle of life à la the *Lion King*. "We take a journey from your butts to your plates / We compost your garden, acquiring whole new tastes!"

The problem is, the lease we have on our land from the forestry service strictly prohibits us from planting anything—fruits, vegetables, flowers, trees. We probably can't even legally grow Sea-Monkeys up here. So here we are, twice a year, stuck with a thousand pounds of human-based fertilizer and nothing to fertilize. As a solution, the board of health makes us periodically jar up a pint or two of the compost-in-progress and bring it to them so they can test it. When they deem it fit for burial, we have to stuff all one thousand pounds into special plastic boxes, bake it in the sun for a week to kill the pathogens, carve out mass graves six feet deep in the mountainside, and put every last, useless morsel to rest.

The German head monk has recently returned to his homeland, where he is no doubt enjoying precision-engineered flush toilets. Our new head monk hails from the streets of NYC's Hell's Kitchen and harbors none of his predecessor's romanticism when it comes to playing Professor Higgins to our craps' Eliza Doolittle, transforming turds into topsoil. The CTs are again packed to capacity, and his solution is decidedly American: "I'm no fecal alchemist, a'right? Let's just get these friggin' things pumped."

The task falls to me and "Rose," the gruff, grandmotherly sewage sorceress we've hired from the village a thousand feet below to make this mess disappear. Rose is kind, sweet, and patient; she is a mountain woman with an earthy naturalness that puts this city boy to shame. She is also exactly the kind of woman you'd expect to find on a job like this. She looks like André the Giant in drag. You can look for her breasts, but you won't find any, unless you're looking somewhere near her navel, where she's got them tucked into her tool belt. She sports a flattop haircut, her neck is as thick as her shoulders are wide, and she's got the vocabulary of a trucker with Tourette's. In her left earlobe is a single diamond earring, an almost ironic nod to her ostensible gender.

This potty-mouthed, lantern-jawed Lady of the Loo muscles the side hatch off one of the compost tanks and leans forward,

pensively stroking her chin and screwing up her chiseled face.
Several moments pass in silence as the "stool whisperer" psychically tunes in to the situation.

Then she turns to me, problem diagnosed, solution at the ready: "We're gonna hafta make poop soup."

Crammed into each of the three bins are dense, towering shitbergs. The plan is to soak them into a thin gruel of sewage, which Rose will pump into her twenty-five-hundred-gallon truck tanker. I spray the manure masses with a garden hose while Rose—Slayer of Fecal Dragons—hacks them apart with her shovel. A grueling hour passes. We switch jobs. If there is a trick to impaling the increasingly gelatinous heap and removing the shovel without producing a suction-like back slurp of shit spray, I do not learn it.

"You really *do not* have a feel for this kind of work," Rose says. She tries to smile encouragingly, but her eyes betray her real thoughts: *Whither the man who can whip up a batch of poo-brew?*

I am embarrassed and ashamed. How could I have gone my whole life without learning how to liquefy a nine-hundred-pound boulder of human defecation? Clearly I have lived a Paris Hilton–like existence of sheltered luxury. Like the monomaniacal Captain Ahab sighting the great white whale, I harpoon the shovel into the murky depths without mercy or pause. Finally Rose raps me on the shoulder, sweat clinging to the hairs haloing her mouth. Her eyes are wide and full of life: *You done good,* they say.

"See?" She grins, sloshing the shovel around inside the bin like a muscular, mustachioed witch churning her pot of poison. "Poop soup."

If there's an anal stage of spiritual development, I'm in it.

When I first moved to the monastery a year ago, I had delusions about a Zen center's being some kind of bliss factory. *There's no smog up here,* I noticed upon strolling the grounds. *The air is clean. I'm going to get clean up here too.* I felt special, chosen. I convinced myself that all of my various failures in life were inevitable steps on the path to this higher calling. Then came my first intensive *dai-sesshin* retreat: I remember hours beforehand peering down the open lid of a compost toilet and suddenly getting the sinking feeling that, like a reader of coffee grounds, I was divining my future in the dark and ominous shapes below.

"That's a lot of shit down there—it's not, like, piling up, right?" I asked, naively hoping that it was just sort of taking care of itself, politely decomposing into the earth, checking out of the game without too much hassle.

"You think you can take a dump in a hole and it's gonna just somehow disappear into the ether?" roared the monk from Hell's Kitchen, bleaching down a urinal nearby.

"I've been doing it my whole life," I cried. "I just go in a bowl, push the metal lever, and it's gone. I don't know where it goes, but I know *I* never see it again. You've been out of civilization too long."

He chuckled, sizing me up. I was still wearing clothing from my former incarnation as a wannabe LA scenester. While great for camouflaging my straightness at gay dance clubs and giving me a certain Ryan Seacrest-y savoir faire, my wardrobe was not quite suited for the rigors of mountain living.

"You came here for the Zenima, didn't you, to get flushed clean of all your crap?" he sighed. "But it doesn't work like that—there's no guru or godhead to carry your shit away in a golden box. You have to learn to deal with it—to *work* with it—yourself."

He leaned in, confidentially. "Listen, Fancy Pants, you're gonna have to get dirty up here."

Back then he was *shoji*, the *zendo* mother figure who is also in charge of work assignments. He escorted me to the concrete bunker beneath the compost toilets and assigned me the weekly task of shoveling wood chips in with the waste. "See if this doesn't help you get to the bottom of it." He grimaced, handing me a turd-encrusted spade. "Dig deep."

I tackled my new responsibility by ignoring it completely. Then one day I sat down on a toilet seat only to discover that my worst nightmare had come true: a midget had shinnied up the toilet chute and was tickling my butt cheeks with a feather. I leaped off the toilet seat—only there was no gap-toothed leprechaun grinning up at me. Instead, a bonfire of silvery flies sparked up from the malodorous abyss. Trillions of them were breeding and feeding and otherwise setting up shop in the festering fecal metropolis below. They were probably already on Facebook, "liking" different varieties of turds and plotting to overtake the whole bathroom. I grabbed seven large bags of wood chips and dumped every one into the bins until the infernal buzzing abated.

"First you ignore the problem, now you're burying it," the monk from Hell's Kitchen growled, and he could have been talking about the reason I scaled this mountain in the first place: to address a certain malodorous air that had been fouling my inner life, which indicated that I had a lot of personal shit festering deep below. He rested a hand on my shoulder and tried to remain calm: "How 'bout you deal with it?"

And so, for two hours every other day I geared up in a pair of goggles, a breathing mask, and a dung-freckled hazmat jumpsuit; grabbed my heavy-duty Appalachian Special spade; and went to work in the stool mine. During winter we're often cursed with fifty-mile-per-hour winds so sharp they all but swipe the stubble off your shaved head. One day I accidentally left all the hatches off the tanks, creating vicious wind tunnels that funneled air from under the poorly insulted CT bunker door right up the toilet chutes. It was Rohatsu, our most intense and serious retreat of the year. One by one students, monks, nuns, and priests sat down on the toilets and broke silence for the first time that week with a goose-pimpled gasp. Imagine a bidet with frigid air instead of warm water greeting you at 2:30 A.M. on a twenty-degree morning. Sometimes when you tossed your soiled toilet paper down the chute, it blew right back up in your face, flapping around the room like some special breed of albino mountain bat.

It was the beginning of my long chilly winter of trial and error in the compost-toilet-hell realm (or, forgive me, poogatory).

By the first irises of spring I had nailed the proportions— twenty parts waste per one part wood chip. I became a matchmaker, a yenta, contriving to mate the starchy Mr. Wood Chips with the teeming potential of Ms. Shitpile. Under my careful midwifery, Humanure was born. The stench in the compost toilets transformed into a complex, husky poopourri, and the burly, gelatinous mounds assumed a moist, spongy texture not unlike cake in a Duncan Hines commercial. Once they get going, wood chips and waste have the kind of chemistry and connection that puts most human couples to shame. Mix them together and they literally turn themselves inside out for each other, to be within each other, to become each other. They meet in some bottomless place neither science nor religion nor philosophy has yet mapped and emerge as one, rippling with receptivity. To use Yeats's phraseology, "Love has pitched his tent / In the place of excrement." When a nun dumped a thatch of seemingly dead vegetation down the women's toilet, mushrooms miraculously popped up between fecund compost clods, their little bobble heads nodding to greet me every time I yanked a hatch off one of the bins. Bacterial heat from the compost "cooking" process warmed my rear whenever I sat down on a toilet. I felt proud, like a mother hen atop her egg, life slowly taking shape beneath me.

"Nice work, Fancy Pants! You've got quite the 'brown thumb.'" The monk from Hell's Kitchen beamed, observing my progress in the tanks one morning. "You're growing ground. You're birthing earth."

Making compost was just one of multiple things I loathed during my first winter at the monastery, including 3 A.M. wake-ups; taking care of all of my personal business in a series of blink-and-you-miss-them breaks; and not wearing socks, blowing my leaky nose, or even so much as twitching a limb in the meditation hall (although you're free to burp and fart: go figure). The environment at our Zen center is simple, strict, and clear: it's the perfect mirror for your condition, constantly throwing you back at yourself. Any color or personality, any fullness of self, stands out in stark contrast to this blank backdrop of black robes, identical mudras, and impersonal rules. Deprived of your comfort zone, you hammer inward. You see exactly what you are; all your shit comes up.

You deal with your shit in Zen by sitting with it. By breathing right into it. You don't try to ignore it with pleasant thoughts or lofty ideas, and you don't try to bury it with solutions. You deal with it, you work with it, one breath at a time. You hold it right there, in your *hara,* or breathing center. You don't try to breathe it out; you don't try to breathe it in. You keep it suspended in your diaphragm like a burning-hot coin. Your problems won't change; only you can change. That's the point.

My work in the CTs helped me see that growth requires discipline the way compost requires carbon. The festering raw material of your inner life, all of your personal shit, dissolves into the self-negation of your spiritual practice the way waste dissolves into wood. Gradually, over time, you feel a softening inside, a ripening. You cultivate rich, fertile, living ground for insight and compassion—for deep human feeling and wisdom—to continually sprout and take seed. It's a natural process. You can't force it. You simply set the right conditions in motion and then get out of the way. The same principle is at work in our universe whether you're mixing wood chips in with waste or practice in with your problems.

I could write a best-selling toilet book about it: *Everything I Know about Love I Learned from Composting Crap.*

3

A Funny Thing Happened on the Way to Enlightenment

At seven thousand feet, the Zen monastery where I live is level with the clouds, which should give you some idea of where my head usually is—not to mention the heads of those who visit our grounds. Let's talk about them. Occasionally, college students from the basin below appear through wispy nimbi on our gravel driveway. I first catch sight of them via their hairdos—which are dazzling and neon, like art projects—bobbing spikily through the dull gray mist. They travel in brightly colored, body-buttered, scantily clad, cologned and perfumed packs, like wolves with iPods. They are everything I'm not: still in their twenties, hopped up on caffeine and red meat, and eager to talk about Zen.

"Tell us about meditation!" they implore, pens poised over spiral notebooks like cub reporters on the enlightenment beat.

Sharing my experiences as a Zen monk is a great opportunity to take inventory of everything I've learned in my three-plus years on the mountain, and I avoid it like the plague. Not because I haven't learned anything but because the lessons I've learned have been mostly negative. Which is to say, I've *unlearned* things during my tenure on the mountain. You could say I've wised up a little: I don't listen to myself so much anymore. I don't take that voice in my head completely for granted. I try to follow my heart, which has no mouth. I've never heard a word out of it, yet it's never steered me wrong. Nowhere is its muteness felt more strongly, however, than when someone asks me to speak about Zen.

Isn't it shameful how you start to sound exactly like those experts in your field you've never understood when talking to someone whom you're pretty sure understands less than you? Nothing inspires confidence in a so-called specialist like ignorance in others. I listen to myself holding forth on Zen practice and I want to puke. Who is this fraud? I think. What the hell does he know? Last time I checked he was still putting his *hakama* underrobes on inside out and backward. Yet I can't very well tell these diligent seekers the truth, can I? I couldn't bear the disappointment on their innocent, curious little faces. They want to hear that Buddhism is the *answer* to all of their problems, not a big fat arrow pointing to the *source* of all of their problems: ego.

One thing I've discovered is that when people ask you about meditation and you pause to frame your reply, they usually waste no time in answering their own question. As it turns out, everyone's an expert in the stuff that no one really knows how to talk about. People visit our grounds and a little bit of the Zen ambiance sinks in, with blue jays gabbling, the sun cutting affable arrows of light through the treetops, and a bald guy in black robes cross-armed before them, and suddenly it's open season on the ineffable.

"Buddhist meditation is always like, relaxing and mellow, right? Kinda like soaking in the Jacuzzi but while reading a spiritual classic like *Jonathan Livingston Seagull?*" This charming description of what in no way resembles my meditation practice came to me recently by way of a bespectacled English major. She was brand-new to thinking. You could tell. She had that facial sheen that college students sometimes have, as if their mind were a child playing with a brand-new toy. For a moment I envied her: so young; so unencumbered by common sense, life experience, and logic.

"It is the Middling Way," I quipped, but my pun was met with earnest nods.

"Now, what's my mind supposed to be doing during meditation?" a student they were calling "Colonel Ralph" asked, winking as if I were a used-car salesman and he was letting me know that he appreciated my efforts and just maybe I had a buyer on the hook here. Days later, as I struggled to focus during our morning sit, the colonel's still-unanswered question had assumed mythic proportions and was all but hunched before me on scaly, roiling haunches, glaring into my eyes and passing its forked tongue over my sweat glands, sizing me up for lunch. Why didn't he ask me what his mind is *not* supposed to be doing? I mused. Then we'd have a conversation starter. It does no one any good to harbor illusions about this path, I concluded. You need to know what you're getting into. You need to go headfirst through the windshield of your expectations.

I decided then and there to sit the next group of students down and give them "the talk," speak directly from my own experience about the facts of spiritual life. "You're old enough to know the truth," I'll say. And like a sex-ed teacher showing bubbly and clueless teenagers sobering medical photos of STD-riddled genitals, I will lay bare the scabby underbelly of serious spiritual discipline and so challenge them to deeper, more realistic religious views.

For starters, deep and meaningful meditation often behaves like a love interest who's out of your league, or a cat. The more ardently you pursue it, the more contemptuously it ignores you. One instant you're almost shivering with insights, the kind you're sure would send a jealous Eckhart Tolle back to his park bench, and the very next you're wondering if you put deodorant under only one of your armpits that morning (*again!*), and you waste the rest of the sit trying to subtly sniff yourself to find out. Or you've got that song stuck in your head, the last one you heard on the radio before the retreat started—the one your kindergarten-aged niece can't stop singing, about her booty or some drug deal gone bad. Occasionally, you even catch yourself counting lifetime sexual partners. (For some of us this is a swift game. It barely eats up five minutes of a twenty-five-minute sit. The trick is, count them out of order. This makes it harder to catch yourself when you "inadvertently" double up on a partner.)

Deprived of external stimuli, you discover that your mind has a life entirely its own. And between the two of you there is no real consensus on where it ends and you begin. You try to get to the bottom of yourself, to catch your mind in the act of coming up with you, or vice versa, and it's as though you've wandered into an M. C. Escher sketch of a house of mirrors, the subject lost in an infinite regression of reflections. This leads to a kind of mental vertigo, and so you compulsively raid your inner life for something solid to grab on to, some tangible insight, belief, or mantra, as though if you just kept pumping quarters into the inner jukebox, eventually you'd find the perfect track, which you could then keep playing in your head, over and over, grooving out to self-generated bliss. You'd never walk into the forest with the radio blasting and expect wild animals to appear by your side. Yet it never occurs to you to unplug the inner jukebox and get quiet inside so that a natural, organic state of mind can reorganize you and your life from within.

It's paradoxical game we hunt from the cushion on our sitting safaris. Shakyamuni Buddha and his peers tried to put us on its scent with core injunctions like "Follow your breath." The sages of the ages in their most prescient moments, however, would never have imagined the world we live in and the kind of mental baggage we lug into our meditation practices. Just look at the culture that surrounds you—the Hollywood blockbusters, the Washington spin machine, the Madison Avenue schlock, that Google-headed distraction hydra: the Internet—then look at your inner life, which reflects it. Sit still for five minutes, and far from watching your breath, you find yourself a captive audience for the relentless stream of self-propaganda within.

This flurry of thoughts, emotions, and story lines, wherein you explain yourself *to* yourself, endlessly, is generated by what we might call the Ministry of the Interior, a dubious and clandestine entity whose sole purpose seems to be to convince you that you are still the grinning, winning general of the "Army of I," despite a lifetime of evidence to the contrary. From somewhere behind the closed doors of your mind, there issue forth endless reams of "innertainment," starring a much more intelligent and morally exacting version of you, someone with capped teeth and a rear end as round and symmetrical as a pair of cartoon eyeballs. To take your seat in the *zendo* is to discover the packed marquee of fantasies playing on an endless loop in the backwoods multiplex of your imagination.

I can blow three sits daydreaming about the eulogies at my funeral alone. The praise I insert in the mouths of family members, former girlfriends, and an assortment of celebrities, not to mention the image of me in my casket—the shut eyes, face pallid and eerily tumescent, like a massive gourd—never fails to bring tears to my eyes. I linger on the scents and sounds and wend through pockets of guests like the camera in a ten-minute tracking shot that reeks of early Scorsese. Satie's melancholic yet wistful "Gymnopédie No. 1" gently tinkles on an unseen baby grand. Many joyous tears, much heartbreaking laughter. Fruit baskets from the Dalai Lama and Richard Gere. Finally, dead, I am the life of the party.

Perhaps, as the young girl dreams of her wedding, the young monk dreams of his funeral (that celebration of the "final extinction"/nirvana by default). What will I wear?! I wonder. Classic black *hakama*/kimono combination, or my mesh summer *koromo* with ceremonial whites underneath for that luminescent effect? God, I leave a foxy corpse. I can see it now: the lack of flowing blood and the subtle onset of decay make me look tragic, cute even. This is a body that appears to have been pleasantly exited. Death makes anyone look sophisticated. Such is its charm.

Believe it or not, there are days when deep, focused, fantasy-free meditation comes easily, as though getting in touch with my true self were actually what it's supposed to be—the most natural thing on the planet. From a simple sitting position, I completely plug in to the world around me. It's like being wired for DSL. Other days, I sit down and I wait. And I wait and I wait and I wait. Finally I get a connection, but it's weak and I keep losing it. These are the dial-up days, when meditation is not just trial and error. It is error after error.

Unfortunately, the Ineffable tends to be pretty tight-lipped when it comes to feedback. Which makes the spiritual path a great investment; a great risk. You're surrendering to the Unknown. Talk about potential for rejection! What if it doesn't want you; what if you're unknown to *it;* what if you're just not what it's looking for right now, but good luck with the Known? You chant, light incense, spread statues across your altar like peanut butter on a mousetrap. You try to trick the Unknown out of its natural habitat. And when that doesn't work, you try to trick yourself.

I've learned to question any Big Insight I have on the cushion if I become convinced of its wisdom only to the degree that I can convince others of it. This is the evangelical mind-set. If I'm already, seconds after having it, framing its future presentation as The Experience for friends and family, then I need to head back to the drawing board. Beware of putting things to words in your head that you haven't fully experienced yet, reflecting on conclusions you have yet to truly reach. There's a difference between an experience so deep and profound you can't talk about it and an experience so deep and profound you can't *stop* talking about it.

The latter is usually accompanied by a semilobotomized grin and the need to hug others for about thirty-five seconds longer than the absolute outer limits of what they're comfortable with even on their most touchy-feely days. Perhaps you've been the recipient of one of these New Age or born-again hugs. It ends with her extended, soft-focus study of your face as she slowly nods her head, her expression reading either "You *too*?" or "You *will*," depending on how she gauges your spiritual progress. If religious fanaticism is one pole in our spiritually confused age, the "transcendent experience" fetishist is holding down the opposite: religious dilettantism.

Oftentimes it's hard to tell whether I'm faking my practice or just plain getting it wrong. With each new era of personal growth, I laugh at what once passed for insight. Present selves mock past selves, and future selves lie in wait. Meanwhile, the problem of "self" itself goes ignored. "What was I thinking?!" I chuckle and head off on some new ridiculous tangent. Alas, I've spent much of my life trying to change who I am, such that who I am has in many ways become a person who tries to change himself. And how do I change *that*? My practice often feels like a head-on collision between the classical apophatic self-negation taught by the world's greatest religious mystics from all traditions and the self-help of affirmative contemporary secular manuals like *I'm OK, You're OK*. I want to negate myself, it seems—I just want to feel good about it.

Sometimes I merely trade one mode of distraction on the cushion for another. I mistake a change of scenery for a change of heart and swap inner distractions for outer, mental for physical. During a recent retreat, I went from being completely preoccupied with "adult innertainment" and sexual fantasies during meditation to being utterly hypnotized by every pair of bare feet that waltzed by my cushion as monks and nuns left the *zendo* for private meetings with our teacher. Oh, the parade of confused, semiformed pinkie toes like little aquarium stones! I learned a lot that day, like how hard it is to tell whether a foot is actually deformed or simply idiosyncratic. There are legions of bizarre and frightening feet out there, and you can waste a lot of quality time on the cushion interpreting bunches of toes as though they were Rorschach inkblots containing key information about their owners. Other times, you simply think you're seeing toes where there are none. This is called *makyo* in Buddhism, or practice-based hallucinations: *Did he have six toes on one foot? Does she? Him? Her? I must find a six-toed person! For the love of God do not ask why, I simply must!*

Not surprisingly, the longer you sit the less seriously you take yourself. Fear and desire become like two formerly imposing parents who have begun to lose control over their fourteen-year-old. After a while there's nothing they can tell you that you haven't already heard. They still boss you around, but their threats are more like nagging, their logic reduced to "because I said so!"

Unfortunately, by the time your mind—your outlook—starts to lighten up, your body begins to fall apart. Worse still, the most impressive-looking sitting positions are always the most painful. As such, whenever I take my seat in the *zendo,* I like to grimace and squint like Saint Sebastian receiving that final volley of arrows. I make a great show of grabbing my foot and yanking it back as though I were planning on resting the heel on top of the opposite hip socket—or lodging it between a rib, yogi that I am. In reality, all I'm doing is lifting the foot up, moving it around a bit, then putting it back exactly where it was, in the most basic cross-legged sitting position, obscured under my robes from any would-be admirers. In a practice that allows little to no opportunity for showing off, it's important to capitalize on every opportunity to "get a leg up" on your peers.

Our bodies are all unique and respond to sitting practice differently. Mine often shocks me with new and humiliating possibilities for pain. Invariably I get into position, with my legs pretzeled, spine arched, and hips rotated forward—ready to go!—

only to find that I'm sitting in such a way that my ability to one day sire offspring feels compromised. The *inkin* bell rings, the sit begins, and everyone goes into motionless silence. I could, with a simple yank, deal with the problem forthrightly, but the thought of addressing this crisis in public is too much to bear. So I wait it out, a cruel parody of the princess and the pea, that horrific stomachachy sensation making my eyes cross.

When you began meditating, did you ever imagine running into a problem like this? The ancient sutras, koan work, Pema Chödrön audio cassettes—nothing prepares you for this contingency. The spiritual calling is truly a solitary one. And you start to wonder, perched there, squirming, if your sole contribution to the cause will not be discovering entirely unique ways to fail miserably at it.

When I was a twelve-year-old boy, I awoke one morning to discover that one nipple had ballooned to nearly twice the size of its neighbor. It was as though someone had stuck a bicycle pump in my nipple hole and inflated me overnight. A red ring—a scarlet O—had recently appeared around that promontory of my personal geography that, with its unchecked growth, renegade mind-set, and separate set of rules, seemed to be trying to secede from the rest of my body. Previously a smooth, lucid Sahara, I was becoming hot, wet, and tropical, with tangles, bulges, odors, and urges. *Surely,* I thought, *my adventures in self-abuse have precipitated a physiological imbalance not unlike prolonged exposure to radiation.* Soon to follow: a third, rheumy eye! Groin goiters like shrunken heads! Like the scientists in some 1950s nuclear disaster horror flick, I had disturbed God's natural order. My fluids had leaked out into the countryside, and now there was hell to pay.

It was a time of great confusion and uncertainty—and weirdness. Fortunately, my father swept into my bedroom one evening, and with characteristic sensitivity and depth he cleared the whole matter up for me. "Pretty soon some junk's gonna come out of your wiener," he said. "It's gonna look like shampoo but it'll smell like bleach. This makes babies. Any questions?"

"It's an awkward stage," my mother admitted, inspecting my freakishly oversized nipple, like the one eye of Marty Feldman staring back at her. "Growing pains," she sighed.

As your body breaks out, swells up, elongates, and fills in during puberty, so your mind, your very *being*, acts out, recoils, rages, and rebels on your path to spiritual adulthood. It's an awkward stage, as any stage must be where you're coming up out of yourself, where you can no longer hide what's going on inside you. Puberty manifests in tits and zits, outward changes, but spiritual growth is an inward process. Thus we imagine we can control it with the right mantras, prayers, and intellectual efforts. But spiritual change is precisely a process that is *bigger than you*. You don't control it. You surrender to it. You don't reinvent yourself through spiritual work. You face yourself, and then you must let go of all the ghastly things you find. But there is no end to these ghastly things. They keep coming. The ego is a bottomless pit of suckiness. And so you finally let go of the self that clings to itself (one definition of ego). True freedom comes when ego goes.

During college I spent a semester in Rome, where I took a theology course offered by an old Cistercian monk we called Father Fester because of his spectral bald skull and a fresh-from-the-crypt leering quality. I bought an *Addams Family* T-shirt featuring the large, green-gleaming head of Uncle Fester. I wore it every day to Father Fester's class, where the old priest's spirits tended to drop whenever my hand went up.

One day I interrupted Father Fester's exegesis of Aquinas's *Summa Theologica* to ask, "What's the most important thing a person needs for the spiritual path?" This was, of course, a question he had been asking and answering in one way or another all semester, when I had been busy studying my female classmates out of the corner of my eye and trying to determine if their breasts were still growing.

"What's the most important thing a person needs *for* the spiritual path?" He put a finger to his mouth as though considering this question for the very first time in his forty years of priest-hood. Then he squared his shoulders and studied me evenly, much like the bull eyeing the matador. He was a large man with a waistline that would get stuck inside a hula hoop. As I recall, his eyes were no more than a millimeter apart. When he focused them on you they became, in essence, a single eye.

"The same thing you get *from* it," he finally growled, giving the answer I now give students when I get this question: "Humility."

This reply elicits the same unmistakable look of admiration and wonder from my student visitors that I gave Father Fester that day. And the look I give them back is the same knowing, mysterious look he gave me. Only now I know what it actually means: "If you only knew . . ."

4

Shitty Monk

On the mountain where I live, there is but one season. Winter. You are either recovering from it, preparing for it, or God forbid, *in* it. This past December, as the temperature shriveled along with my remaining illusions about Zen practice, the great wheel of dharma turned once again here at the monastery and I rotated into the officer position of *jikijitsu*.

The *jikijitsu* is the badass father figure in charge of making sure meditation in the *zendo* is tight, strong, and clear. He shouts corrections: "No moving!" "Breathe quietly!" He carries a big stick and hits people with it. He leads all of the sits as well as walking meditation and formal meals. Don't F with him. His is the most distilled embodiment of the spirit of Rinzai, or samurai, Zen.

Rinzai Zen practice can be brutal, savage even. It is designed to bring you to a crisis within yourself, to trigger a dark night of the soul. Zen attacks that one last thing you hold dear: your precious self-conception. It unravels any notion of a freestanding, unconditional "I" and shows it to be a lie, a fabrication, a construction. True realization, the old masters tell us, takes bone-crushing effort. We pulverize the very skeleton of ego—upon which the meat and skin and organs of our illusions hang—and we do it through intense, hurtle-yourself-off-the-cliffs-and-into-the-chasm practice.

To prepare for my training as *jikijitsu*, I decided to get tough with myself. I loaded up daily on protein drinks and vitamins, threw away that Anne Lamott book I was reading, quit e-mail cold turkey, and prohibited myself from partaking in all pleasures of the flesh, self-induced or otherwise. I was going to need a backlog of strong, masculine chi energy. I was like a boxer who steers clear of his girlfriend before the big fight.

"You're a train wreck of overzealousness," decided my mentor. He was living in LA at the time, and I'd contacted him by phone. "You've got a little power now. Don't abuse it. The primary ass you should be whipping in the *zendo* is . . . ?"

"The big fat collective ass of those clueless students?" I tried, smacking my fist into my palm.

"Your own," he growled. "Don't bring your personal shit into it."

The following weekend I was patrolling the *zendo* when I passed the meditating form of Tico, our most eccentric student and the worst kind: the kind who is convinced that his eccentricities have spiritual significance. That morning he had tried to shave his head, but he'd left patches of soft, curly, gray-black down, which gave him that *One Flew Over the Cuckoo's Nest*, fresh-from-electroshock look. He was quivering and shaking, his eyes rolling back into his head, his mouth open and frozen in an Edvard Munchian silent scream. Clearly, he was convinced that he was in the throes of spiritual-mojo overload. How much, I wondered, do you let people drift into their own flames, like moths, before you shake them and say, "Enough!"?

In a shamanistic culture Tico might be revered for the trances he slips into. Ours, however, was a shared environment, and he was rupturing its equanimity by deviating from the etiquette. It's not about your own little personal trip. The body of practitioners is your body, and you really don't want to be that one area of the body that's an irritation, the inner-ear itch or belly rash. This is the reason for the rules. We move as one, act as one, function as one, and as one we beat our egos down like the redheaded stepchildren they are.

But I began to develop a creeping ambivalence about the inexhaustible ferociousness of this style of Zen. "Eyes down," I grumbled incessantly. "Don't sniff." "Wake up!" I began to feel like a priest from some Mike Leigh film about 1950s working-class Ireland. "Keep yer hands in *gassho,* boyo, or I'll rap 'em!" "Erin McMurphy, did I see ya dippin' yer fingers in yer green tea at breakfast now? I know yer mum. Ya weren't raised in a barn!"

The truth is, like many underweight, overread *sensitivos,* I've always seen myself as an outsider, a nonconformist. My heroes have always been the rebels, the applecart upsetters—Nietzsche, Ikkyu, Cool Hand Luke. It's ironic that so many of us who are attracted to a tough, no-nonsense discipline like Zen also happen to be repulsed by the practice's endless formal punctilios and ornamented, brocaded behavior.

The battle between these two opposing sides of me—*zendo* cop and irreligious rebel—began to take its toll. This is the monk-in-training's challenge. The middle way isn't all nicely laid out for him, like an insurance plan, as though to be enlightened is to sign on the dotted line—"Here ya go, here's my desire, my self-interest: Take 'em all. They're my down payment on satori!" No, he has to establish the middle way within himself by testing the extremes. He has to put himself out there constantly. This is the true meaning of that religious catchall "self-sacrifice." The monk puts himself on the altar, or else he's a liar and a fake.

Which is what I felt like as *jikijitsu*—a liar and a fake. I felt wimpy half the time, sadistic the rest. I couldn't strike the right balance. I couldn't be *strong.* The truth was becoming clear: I'd been a rebel my whole life not because I was idealistic or original but because I simply didn't have the guts to stand *for* anything— only *against*. Ikkyu? Nietzsche? Please. Try Eddie Haskell meets Woody Allen. I was a coward. A coward and a bully.

Full of self-hate and self-pity, desperate for warmth, for a warm body, I did what we all do when we don't want to face ourselves in the *zendo*. I fell in love with a new student. She was a carrot-topped, foggy-skinned Dane who had buoyed her smile with some recent cosmetic dental work. It was a welcome diversion, this dharmamour. We made love on every continent, grew old together. She got a dramatic disease; I stood over her fresh grave with flowers. Then I deeply regretted our time together and considered myself fortunate for having lived it only in my head for several sits, the downside being the arousal that made it awkward to take my rest periods standing up.

One evening she visited me in my cabin, where I cracked open a bottle of Jack Daniel's. "When I got ordained," I said, laughing over my shoulder, trying to be worldly-wise and charming, "all the junior monks got me books and all the senior monks got me booze. What does *that* tell you about this path? *Ha ha ha!*"

Alas, she had no interest in me except as a sounding board for various reconciliation scenarios revolving around her estranged boyfriend. The evening ended with her backing out of the room while thanking me for the drink after a charged silence I had foolishly hoped would lead to a kiss.

I had barely crawled under my quilt with every intention of breaking my pleasure fast when my new roommate—a Frenchman—arrived. For the month.

"A-loo!" he chirped, his air-travel BO filling the room as he took in its dimensions. "Tiny!" he said, whistling and looking askance.

Jacques-san is no doubt someone's idea of a tall, cool drink of water. Sinewy and athletic, he stripped to his Skivvies, hit the lights, lit a candle, and started in with what were to be his ritual nightly asanas, standing on his head and scissoring those graceful, giraffe-neck limbs, which practically touched both walls. I rolled to my side and pretended to sleep. Blown up on the wall in monstrously immense proportions just inches from my face, the bulging shadow of his manly midsection bobbed up and down in the candlelight. It was like a soft-porn image dreamed up by some cigar-chewing cinematographer.

Even in my bed, facing the wall, there was no denying that I was trapped on a macho, male-heavy mountain with a squad of spiritual Green Berets. I fled my cabin for the monastery's small library, a rundown cottage nestled in a womb of conifers. My eyes flitted across the shelves, where the spiritually desperate (but always literarily sensible) had for more than forty years buried their intellectual discards. My fingers paused over a slim, turquoise volume by Pema Chödrön. I'd once perused an essay in which she was gracious and respectful toward Zen but not without leveling a subtle criticism, which I would paraphrase as "Geez, lighten up. You guys can be really asshole-ish!"

Pema Chödrön was just what I needed. Even her author photo on the book back was encouraging. First off, she was grinning. "Come on in," she seemed to be saying, "the water's warm. I'll be your dharma momma and I'll scrub you clean." Second of all, she had a sensible haircut. Short but not shaved raw to the skull, not revealing every crinkle and crease, every bony flaw, like the lack-of-hairdos in our Zen tradition. Pema was even showing a little bit of her bare shoulder in the photo.

Wild! Take me to your buddha breast, Earth Mother!

Like a little boy perving on *Hustler*, I crawled under my covers that night, clicked on a book light, and pored through *The Wisdom of No Escape*. "If you are alive, if you have heart, if you can love, if you can be compassionate . . . then you won't have any resentment or resistance," Pema purred. "Loving-kindness is the sense of satisfaction with who we are and what we have. . . . Fear has to do with wanting to protect your heart: you feel something is going to harm your heart, and therefore you protect it."

Surfeited, I laid the book aside and trembled with satisfaction. Were a cigarette handy I would have blown smoke rings and played with my chest hairs. But the following morning, bitterly ashamed, I vowed never to touch her tome again. It was schmaltz, I told myself. A onetime thing. I was perfectly happy with the husky-voiced, thick-ankled Zen practice I'd taken vows to honor. I returned the book to the library—only to furtively yank it from the shelf again that evening.

And so I began an affair with her lush, seething dharma, cheating on my frigid-but-loyal Zen practice. On the cushion, supposedly steadfast in my *zazen* meditation, I was really thinking of paramour Pema's vivacious birdsong prose and rich, voluptuous metaphors. "Go ahead," I thought to the students, my *jikijitsu* practice going to seed, "move around all you want. Have a good cry while you're at it!" Pema hit my G-spot: *gentleness*.

And yet it was the great soft one herself who ultimately sold me on the rigors of Zen life. Toward the end of her slim volume of talks, she extols the virtues of inconvenience. "Opting for coziness, having that as your prime reason for existing, becomes a continual obstacle to taking a leap and doing something new, something unusual, like going as a stranger into a strange land."

"Stick with one boat," one practice, she suggests, and let it "put you through your changes." If you continue to "shop around," you learn a lot about different religions but very little about your true self.

Inspired, I redoubled my efforts as *jikijitsu,* refusing to don my skullcap during walking meditation one evening as moonlit frost crunched under our sandals. By the time the last winter retreat rolled around, I'd contracted the dreaded flu-cold and achieved great enervation instead of great enlightenment. This, combined with my militant new desire to do everything by the book, set off a chain reaction. It led to the low point in a quota-busting winter of lows, when forty of my peers witnessed—to hearken back to my mentor's warning—my "personal shit."

During the evening bathroom break of the final retreat, I didn't doff my outer robes and try to navigate the sea of students and their teeming bladders. Instead, I sneaked down into a dank and grungy storage space beneath our *zendo*. I made for a dusty corner and hiked up my robes to relieve myself.

After a few preliminary squirts, I had an ominous, involuntary sphincter contraction, and instantly my priorities changed. I needed to get to a stall. There was no denying this call of nature; no single-pointed Zen concentration would make it go away. This point was driven home with the first round of wet gas.

"Oh, you gotta be kidding me," I cried inside. "You gotta be friggin' kidding me."

I looked at my watch. The ten-minute mark! Everyone was in the *zendo* right now, waiting for me to start the sit. Via a bow-legged crab walk—an embarrassing proposition to begin with but made all the worse by my heavy, multilayered big-deal Mr. Important robes—I awkwardly exited the storage shed into a flood of harsh winter light.

I contracted and released the appropriate muscles. But there seemed to be no denying it. I'd shit myself. A man's life is made up of choices like this: right, the *zendo*. Left, the bathroom. The bathroom, I decided, will have to wait.

I can handle this, I told myself, slipping my boots off on the *zendo* porch. The *shoji*—the *zendo*'s kindly mother figure—opened the door for me, and I took my seat with alacrity next to the co-*jikijitsu*, effectively corking my bottom on the cushion beneath me. That's cool, I thought. I can sit this out, then dash to the can during the next break. Before my co-*jiki* peer rang the bell to start the sit, however, she turned and gave me a small bow.

No. *No!* It was my turn to carry the *keisaku*. During sits before koan meetings with the master, a member of the *jiki* staff patrols the room with the *keisaku,* a long, thick, ruler-like stick tapering from handle to end. When he comes to a student or monk who looks too loose—or too tense—he taps him or her on the shoulder.

They bow together, and then the recipient bends to one side and *whack! whack! whack!* Other side: *whack! whack! whack!*

A *zendo* is not a place to space out. To take your seat and catch up on personal fantasies or zone out for a week. *Get out of your heads and into your* haras! the "encouragement stick" cries with every crack. *Activate your viscera with your breath. Gut sit!*

I got up. There was diarrhea running down my leg. It was terrible. I could smell it. I reeked of fresh human shit. I had the dubious good luck to be wearing Hot Chillys thermals, and all the excrement running down my legs puddled at the elastic at my ankles.

I stood there at the front of the *zendo,* holding the stick.

There's no rule saying the *jikijitsu* has to venture out among the meditators. I could just stand there for the whole twenty-five-minute sit if I chose, but Pema's words came back to me: "Opting for coziness, having that as your prime reason for existing, becomes a continual obstacle to taking a leap and doing something new, something unusual, like going as a stranger into a strange land."

Perhaps Suzuki Roshi put it best: "Zen is the path of no turning back."

When I first started practicing, there was one struggling student in particular who remained unconvinced by "boot-camp spirituality." He carried on every chance he got about how artificial the extreme discipline was, how "not me" the kanji chanting and the fierce meditation sessions and koan meetings were. He respected the practice, but he couldn't "get into it." It wasn't his thing.

That student was me, a million lifetimes ago, it seems.

What I failed to realize was that my resistance was in itself a pose, a stance—a result of my conditioning as a free-spirited, individualistic American prone to respecting all paths and choosing none. I'd never been stripped of myself, and so I mistook a cleverly embroidered outfit of attitudes for my deepest self, which

I had to "be true to." Through the path of negation of self, I began to get an inkling of just how thoroughly cloaked I was in attitudes and platitudes—in my own bullshit—and I also learned that despite this, I had to keep going.

Way down at the other end of the *zendo,* shivering, shaking, lost in himself, was Tico, our resident eccentric pseudo-shaman. My sphincter spasmed briefly in rage. He'd been a thorn in my authoritarian side all winter. Now, however, instead of a threat to be quelled, he merely looked as if his head were about to spin around in circles. I knew the feeling.

Standing there holding that stick, reeking like my nephew after he's filled his diaper, I realized that this is when true practice begins: when you are officially in way over your head. "To be fully alive, fully human, and completely awake," Pema tells us in *When Things Fall Apart,* "is to be continually thrown out of the nest. To live fully is to be always in no-man's-land, to experience each moment as completely new and fresh. To live is to be willing to die over and over again."

Zen is the practice of coming up out of yourself and into the situation, *any* situation, meeting it fully, with a complete heart—no holding back, no half measures, no room for doubt or selfishness. You run the razor of practice from ear to ear, decapitating the dualistic dictator within so that the blood of ego flows forth as the milk of self-sacrifice, nourishing the world.

Okay, maybe that's a little dramatic. I simply went among some Zen students with a load in my pants. This was my humble contribution to whatever they learned that day: how to move forward despite your imperfections, despite the fact that you're covered in your own shit.

5

Spring-Loaded

On the mountain where I live, the weather can be incredibly bi-polar, which is great fun. In the winter we get snowed in and in the summer the sun burns us all to hell. A big fan of the "middle way," though, my favorite time of year is . . . *today*, as it turns out: spring (which has arrived *painfully* behind schedule this snowy, soggy, foggy year).

Spring is when the mountain comes alive. If there's been a lot of snow and suddenly there's tons of sun, things start crawling out of the earth, stirred to life by the contrasts in their surroundings. The hills basically go nuts. You're walking down the gravel driveway under a canopy of chirping treetops and suddenly a pair of chipmunks falls on top of you. "Sorry, dude," their little scampering body language says, "but something's goin' *down* on this mountain and we're just part of it!"

It's always great fun to discover bugs fornicating, don't you think? They seem so composed and concentrated, their motionless ends connected in that weirdly dispassionate yet somehow touching configuration. They look like little kids focusing on some very adult task. Well, during the spring here you discover whole bug orgies, three or four thousand of them going at it in the rock field or on the dirt steps as you try to wend your way to the outhouse. There's nothing like a confluence of Japanese beetles in flagrante to remind you that the whole animal kingdom is having more fun than you. Poke them and they fly off, still connected, a technique that I much admire: airborne lovemaking, four-winged flight fucking.

Sometimes it's not just insects getting it on. Last spring, a cute new VW Beetle barrels up the driveway during one of our formal lunches. Said vehicle does not come back down. My suspicion meter tilts into the red. I march up to the other end of camp, where the car is parked at a weird angle by the fire circle and is shaking violently. *Murder! Murder! Someone's being murdered!* I think, stealth-stepping toward the vehicle, a technique I honed back when I was twelve and obsessed with Ninjas. . . . Baritone grunting; the passenger door half open . . . *What the?* Intense, powerful thrusting behind the tinted windows. It is brute animal sex, hard-core, for real, all-consuming, almost a little scary—and of course kind of hot.

I actually say this: "Guys, this is a monastery. Come *ooon*. I'm giving you twenty minutes to be out of here." Too bad I can't capture here just how pinched and priggish my tone was. "Sorry, man," comes a husky male voice from within. Just a couple kids, having fun, ruined by the monastic creeper. In my head, the young Mr. Baritone calls after me, "You let beetles screw their little shells off, but you begrudge your own species a place to mate? Hypocrite! Prude!" Nonetheless, I am happy for the opportunity to reaffirm the purpose of our grounds while simultaneously being reminded of how exciting and erotic—and ultimately, problematic—life gets once you exit them. (The couple visited me recently, believe it or not. She was pregnant. Neither of them was smiling.)

During spring, the fun doesn't stop at pornographic bugs (VW or otherwise): there's a surplus of purple and yellow wildflowers, teeming patches of color, as though a little bit of extra grace had fallen out of God's sack here and there; sap-sparkling sugar pine- cones the size of footballs, which hold tight to tree branches until you are directly below them and the invisible target appears on your bald head, at which point they let go; a species of squirrel whose chirp resembles a fire alarm that needs a new battery— *cheep! . . . cheep! . . . cheep! . . . ;* and finally, some damned mam- mal that keeps shitting directly on our walking meditation path: lengthy coiled turds, almost sculpted, like the inverse of a beauti- ful French pastry.

And let's not forget those more formidable beasts—ticks, black widows, and tarantulas that are hairier than the inner thigh of a Speedo-clad Greek tourist; scorpions, rattlesnakes, mountain li- ons, black bears; and perhaps the most difficult and dangerous animal of all: residents from nearby Los Angeles. Their voices waft in through the open windows of our *zendo* as we try to sit *zazen,* proffering poignant springtime observations such as:

"Oh, my God . . . I didn't know bugs *do it!*"

"Of course bugs do it, stupid. Everything does it."

"Bet those monks in that meditation hall there don't do it," and so on.

"It's so beautiful here . . . it's so beautiful here . . . it's so beau- tiful here. . . ." I hear this again and again and again from folks visiting the mountain at this time of year. I want to say, "You should stop by when there's six feet of snow or a blistering mid- summer heat wave. What you're witnessing is the rare and pre- cious fruit of the ongoing argument this mountain has with itself in the form of sun and snow." When neither party is win- ning, when the wet, chilly hills are warmed and the sunlight is cooled in the damp and thunderously quiet earth, the result is a perfect balance of natural opposites—the middle way incarnate. Then, instead of arguing with itself, the mountain seems to be . . . how to put it tactfully? . . . knocking itself up.

And it's knocking me up too. I'm full of life—*wild* inside. Not at all the staid and starchy monk I appear to be on the surface, especially when dealing with random visitors, who tend to regard me as just another natural curiosity on a mountain full of them. In fact, I kid you not, they often pat me on my bald head as though I were a friendly mountain goat, all but trying to feed me peanuts and get me to lick tin cans clean.

"What do you study here?" they invariably ask, sizing up our bleak and banal stone-and-wood cabins. *Perhaps you were expecting Shangri-la with* zafu *meditation cushions?* I want to ask.

"We call it the Middle Way," I tell them, for lack of a better answer.

They nod, totally bored. "So are you like, all peaceful inside?"

"Sure," I tell them, gesturing widely, putting on my best Saint Francis grin. "About as peaceful as this mountain." This they seem to get, nodding and snapping cell phone pics of flitting finches and swaying, majestic conifers. "It's *soooo* peaceful here," they concur.

"*Get the snake catcher!*" a nun cries just then from up by the compost pits.

I leap the stone steps two apiece and discover a six-foot western rattler coiled atop a mountain of moldering eggplants. Its almost semisentient tongue flickers like the frailest of confetti twitching in the wind. This slithering tube of poison and scales has presence. *Yeah, that's right,* the serpent seems to be saying, *I got Eve to eat the apple, and Mick Jagger wrote a song about me. What have you* done lately? Within minutes I've got the enraged blur of fangs and pink throat by its neck via our crude, metallic snake-catcher claw; I seal it off in a bucket and drive it down the sun-bleached mountain with a fellow monk to release it by the rocky creek. It is hissing wildly in the bucket in my lap—the sound of a hose with an enormous amount of water pressure built up that has suddenly sprung a massive leak. *Sssssssssssssss!*

Maybe it'll jump out, burst through the top of the bucket, pull an eyeball out of my skull as my monk peer squeals in terror and drives off the edge of the cliff.

I am terrified. I am thrilled. Anything can happen during this time of year. Spring is a free-for-all of life. Not one bit do I miss my former existence as a struggling screenwriter in West Hollywood, where the only wild things were method actresses and the somewhat bossy cockroaches that used to hold conferences under my sink. It was terrible crushing them (the cockroaches, not the actresses) in that dim little apartment, goopy vigor leaking from their broken shells into the dismal brown carpet, a carpet already soaked through with the life and vitality that had been steadily leaking from me during my decade's imprisonment in that soul-sucking city.

Later that evening I will kill two scorpions: one that has fallen from a pair of jeans I'm sliding into and one scrambling right over my electric toothbrush in the upper camp washroom. *The way I see it*, I will whisper inwardly to their dead scorpion souls, *if you come into this world with supersized pincers for hands and a monstrous stinger rising up over your armored fanny, expect to leave it as you lived in it—violently.* I imagine that in killing them I am teaching them a lesson, that they will be reincarnated as butterflies in their next life, trading their steel-belted torsos and poisonous pin tails for pink-veined wings as thin as thoughts, flickering dustily through the morning light. Then it occurs to me that perhaps the scorpion is a reincarnated butterfly, killed in a previous life because it lacked the means to defend itself, and I reconsider my stance on the death penalty for all of God's killers, great and small.

After my dual homicide I will return to my cabin, disrobe, open the windows, smell the night, and listen in the dark as the rumbling row of SUVs, Jettas, and Subaru Foresters beyond our tree line returns to civilization, signaling the end of the city folks' day trip to the mountaintop.

And if I listen really closely, I can hear their voices—or at least I imagine I do. . . .

Those monks were creepy.

How can they live there?

What do they do all day?

Is it just me, or was the weird one with the big ears and knobby knees like, staring *at my bra strap?*

No girl, I saw it.

God, even monks *are horny?*

I want to blast out the cabin door in my boxer shorts, a bald, pale thing, rail thin and feral. I want to jump between their cars shouting, screaming—a madman, a prophet: *Fling a Molotov cocktail into your Mercedes! Put a brick through your wide-screen TV! Stomp on your shrink's spectacles! Knife a hole in your memory-foam mattress! Join me on this mountain, friends! You'll live more here in five minutes than you'll live in twenty-five years down in that City of Angles (sic), with its cannonball boob jobs and Twittering tweens and acres of traffic and minimalls and celebrity-chef restaurants—and screenwriters with skin the color of congealed bologna—and tank-topped gay musclemen with those small yapping dogs and all the sad pretty actresses with their sad new pretty actress names, Rain and Sky and Hope. . . .*

But alas—beneath all of my Kerouac-meets-Hakuin hubris, I also hear my ex-girlfriend Killjoy's sobering voice, the words of family and friends, of those I left behind when I moved here . . . *You're just running away from life. . . . You're afraid of the real world. . . . How long are you going to stay up there?. . . What will you do when you return to "the marketplace," as you must, as all Rinzai Zen monks eventually must? . . . What will you put on your résumé when you apply for a job: "I can sit really still in one spot for long periods of time—oh, and I can chant sutras I don't understand in a language I can't speak"?*

These negative voices coalesce into a Symphony of Terror: *Condescend to us at your peril, mountain monk. We are the world, we are unavoidable, and we are waiting for you—with a name tag that says "Welcome to Taco Bell" and has your name printed on it (your ordained name, in kanji, of course).*

Finally, through an act of radiant will (or maybe I'm just tired), I crush all of these imaginary voices—these by-products of a brain bursting and teeming and straight-up mad with spring fever—and I just lie there in the dark and close my bleary eyes and let sing me to sleep the sonorous and melancholic chirp of jelly-bean-bellied crickets: trillions of them from the sounds of it, all looking to get laid. But first, before I sink into the ink of unconsciousness, I compose a prayer, the Spring Prayer, to see the day's visitors off as the soft surf of tire rubber and road laps backward, downhill, until the air is blank with silence.

Whether all at once
Or in fits and starts
May something small green and beautiful grow
In the emptiness
Of our hearts

6

Three Girlfriends, One Pregnancy Test

Abortion is one of those loaded terms, like "physician-assisted suicide" or "prop comic," that few people can remain neutral about. It seems that everyone has his or her Teflon-coated take on the topic, which brings me to Shade, an older black man I worked with on a box-factory assembly line one summer. After giving my unsolicited opinion on the issue, he shrugged and sucked the drool off the filter of his smoldering Winston and turned to me sideways, fixing me with his one good eye, which he nonetheless rolled, while offering, "Well, chump, thanks for the opinion, but like daddy useta say, opinions is like farts—everybody's stinks but'cha own."

That remains one of the wiser things I've heard with regard to the abortion debate.

My own journey into the heart of the "life versus choice" smackdown is analogous to that of the Zen practitioner who struggles seemingly against all hope to solve his koan, the paradoxical metaphysical riddle provided to him compliments of his maddeningly savvy and sagacious Zen master. Koan work is an attempt to sidestep certain difficulties inherent in transmitting spiritual wisdom. It stems from a critique of religion itself, which tends to go wrong again and again in the exact same way: the holy one has an Experience, from which he or she draws certain inferences, which his or her followers then turn into doctrine or law and use to make fixated, one-sided statements about the nature of reality. Tautologically enough, the followers work their way backward from the inferences the holy one drew from the initial experience to the experience itself, which they now claim to know by proxy, through the inferences. Really, all they know are the inferences, which is like smelling someone else's fast-food wrapper and claiming that you've eaten lunch.

Koan work eschews this game. It keeps you honest and humble by making you experience, over and over, what you claim to know already. Thus, instead of becoming dogma, this knowledge ripens into wisdom, a way of life, and is never merely a clever ruse for avoiding the difficulties of life via the creation of an alternate "spiritual" one, that is, an afterlife and those imaginary rules that govern your getting there. The searching, open-ended nature of koan work yields the kinds of answers that frustrate easy analysis, not to mention that most exquisite of all human pleasures: being "right." Ultimately, koan practice teaches that as long as a question is alive in the world around us, it should not—indeed, *cannot*—be settled once and for all within us. Koan practice does not put life's deepest issues "to bed." It wakes these issues up within us, waking us up in the process.

The abortion koan is on all of America's mind this morning, not just mine. The exotic menagerie of our cultural politics abounds with squalling, squabbling, and screeching. The Life Monkeys are flinging dung balls rearward at their accusers as they backpedal from certain uncomfortable implications in their position. Meanwhile, the Choice Donkeys are on the attack, snorting and hoof pointing, stomping in circles and kicking up dust. The online headlines—those fat, frantic carrier pigeons perpetually flying into glass windows—carry news about an abortion doctor murdered in Kansas yesterday as he stepped into church.

I bow out of line during walking meditation, hide my face in my hands, and weep for our fucked-up world, which is just too much to bear sometimes. Meanwhile, the morning's news has dislodged long-buried memories of an antiabortion activist I knew at my highly conservative (like, *Mel Gibson conservative*) Catholic college in Texas. How radically "pro-life" was this peer? She built her senior philosophy thesis around the question, Is it morally acceptable to kill an abortionist? Conflating abortion MDs with Nazi concentration camp doctors, her thought process went something like this: If you had Dr. Mengele in your cross-hairs, wouldn't you pull the trigger?

Frankly, I always had a hard time picturing little Tessa with a Colt .45, emptying a clip into the back of the miserable German doctor as he darned his lederhosen during a quiet moment. Teeming with spunky innocence, Tessa took cute right up to the doorstep of gorgeous. A true Texas sweetheart and an incurable optimist, she was the kind of charismatic rascal who would have baked Dr. Mengele a batch of snickerdoodles and tried to charm him out of his role in the holocaust. "Now, Dr. Mengele—may I call you Josef? How 'bout Joey? Now, Joey . . ." As far as pro-lifers go, T. had cred. This wildly popular, befreckled brunette (a childhood actress, she was the runner-up behind Soleil Moon Frye for the title role in the TV show *Punky Brewster*) made it safely out of the womb solely because an antiabortion activist just like her had once talked her birth mother out of the procedure. (She was then adopted by a loving family of professors and lawyers, the patriarch of which was the president of Texas Right to Life.)

Using her own life—the very fact of it—as the basis for her investigation, the answer she eventually arrived at to the question posed by her philosophy thesis was, emphatically, predictably, No: it is not morally justifiable to kill an abortionist. "What business do you have telling me not to get an abortion?!" a student peer—oddly enough, a man—once hollered at her in our bioethics class. She just sat there, calmly embodying herself. She was, in every sense, the living answer to this question. "Because someone told my mother not to, and guess what? Here I am today, healthy, wealthy, and wise." She grinned. (He quickly fell in love with her and changed his own position on the issue.)

Ah, Tessa! An hour after meeting her, I scribbled a poem on a paper towel in the campus rathskeller bathroom, limning my plans to one day wed her. (Like most of my poems of the era, it was inspired but widely off the mark.) She revolutionized my heart, and I made her laugh until milk spilled out her nose. We lasted all four years of college. People accused us of being twins, identical as we were in every way—matching big ears, narrow shoulders, brown hair and eyes, geekitude, scrapper build, astrological sign (Sagittarius), major (philosophy), and views on abortion. Lying in bed after doing "everything but," rubbing each other's back, we often engaged in pro-life pillow talk: "Hey, honeybuns, what do you think the karmic and cosmic consequences are of all of those tens of millions of medical waste bags in our landfills teeming with . . . a little to the left, between the shoulder blades . . . yeah, there . . . teeming with thwarted human lives?"

And yet, there I sat at my Ikea desk just a few short years later: a Hollywood screenwriter penning a musical satire of the pro-life movement. This brief animated-film script included a chorus line of fetuses kicking their blobbed legs in unison as a cute Silly Putty–like embryo stepped forward (think: Little Orphan Annie, but preborn) with all of its earthly possessions tied up in a bandana at the end of a broomstick. The chorus sang, "Take a goooood look now 'cos you'll probably never meet us." To which the little embryo added, "Evicted from the womb, I'm a hobo fetus."

By then I was fed up with young Christian America: all of those grinning, narrow-minded virgins in overlong denim skirts, and their stern-but-neutered, khaki-clad, dittohead/Limbaugh-quoting boyfriends who touched them "nowhere a soccer uniform covers." How heavy, how grim, how moralistic they were! Their manners and minds stilted, their blood running thick with religious lies! (Or so went my inner cant during that era.) After graduating from college and ditching Texas, my conservative Catholic faith, and eventually, Tessa, I relocated to—where else?—West Hollywood, where I got busy reinventing myself as a sophisticated left-coast liberal.

It didn't take long before I became intimate with the whole pro-choice side of the abortion debate. Among the interests that Jane, a Bronx-bred, Jewish-Italian OB-GYN, listed on her Internet dating profile were feminist literature, New York–style pizza ("You just can't get a good pie on the West Coast!"), and asphyxiation. Instead of "everything but," Dr. Jane and I did "everything *and.*" Dark and compact, like a Camus novel, sexually all over the map, her mouth slightly deformed into a cocksure sneer from a childhood Big Wheel accident, Dr. Jane specialized—she reveled—in providing abortions for East LA women, most of whom were crack- or meth-addled prostitutes.

How about the story she told me (she came home with stories like this Every. Single. Night.) about the bedraggled streetwalker who charged into the hospital with Charlie Sheen levels of drugs surging through her system while wailing "*Terminate it! Ter-minate it!*"? To this day Dr. Jane is still searching for adjectives to describe the smell that filled the room when this teenager, after sobering up per the law and then choosing once again to "*Terminate it, motherfuckers!*" parted her legs and Jane went to perform the procedure. The fetuses—there were two in her—had died long ago and were busy decomposing.

The births at this hospital of horrors were worse than the abortions. Nothing saddened the already-pretty-sad Jane—with her bottomless black eyes and sexual fetish for being choked—more than passing an infant she'd just delivered into the black-and-blue arms of its mother and then watching, a few weeks later, as the woman disappeared down the hall with the man who had beaten her senseless and initiated her premature labor the night that she came to the hospital. Jane was brilliant and cruel—a potent combination for me at the time, like single malt Scotch and Nat Sherman cigarettes. The darker her life became (it started off dark: "My dad made me give him a hand job when I was twelve," was the second or third thing that she told me about herself), the more inspired and warped and intricately beautiful was her sense of humor.

"Some people are just not quite ready to welcome a child into this world!" she would rant in my arms. "'What to expect when you're expecting' should not be a multiple choice question, you know, like: 'You're pregnant. That knock on the door is (a) your lovely mother-in-law with a gift basket of prenatal tinctures, (b) that obsessed john with the creepy collection of headless dolls, or (c) your drunken monster hubby warming up his knuckles?'"

She was thrilling to be around—her touch intoxicating. If Tessa was warm, wonderful, predictable, Jane was somewhere between hot to the touch and electrifying. She was also a cheater and a nasty piece of work, and she made me realize that sometimes you can dislike very much the person that you love. She transcended ethics and let the people in her life pay the price. Yet in the end, what drove us apart was that I could not keep up with her. This was not her flaw nor my own. It was the reality of being outmatched, whereas Tessa and I had been too perfectly matched (making me look at her and realize that I wanted to change myself).

For me, then, the abortion argument will forever be split down the middle and embodied equally in these two very different women. And so, at this point a quick glance at the scoreboard reveals that in the Ethical Wimbledon within, my Inner Tessa and my Inner Jane are still at love-love—not such a bad place to be, metaphorically speaking. On that note, I find myself wondering not *Am I pro- or anti- life or choice?* but rather, *Which of these captivating and commanding goddesses did I love more: the antichoice wingnut or the merciless fetus slaughterer?* Such a deep and poignant query can be answered only by applying that most timeless test of true love: Which one had your ATM pin number?

Neither. That honor belonged to a third girlfriend.

I met Mara at a cross-dressing party in Venice Beach, which is to say that when the sparks first began to fly, I was wearing an ebony satin sequined number, tight on the hips, loose in the chest, with matching jet-black pumps; meanwhile, Mara was in a suit, tie, and fedora, the whole outfit loud and yellow, à la Jim Carrey in *The Mask,* if Jim Carrey had cleavage and radiated the kind of maternal warmth that can quicken instantly into sexual dynamism. This set the tone for who would wear the pants in the relationship. Curvy, crazy, and irresistible, with shimmering cornflower-blue eyes that you all but needed welding goggles to gaze into directly, Mara was a strong, heady, bisexual blend of Tessa and Dr. Jane. She was innocent and plucky in spirit, envelope pushing and extemporaneous in deed. Which I guess is just a fancy way of saying that we had a lot of unprotected sex. Which led to the inevitable pregnancy scare. A test was taken. Negative. But when I fished that damnable "wand" out of the trash an hour later just to be sure, it had changed its mind—now it read positive!

Standing in line at Rite Aid to purchase test number two, amid the teeming midnight throng of cough-syrup and condom-buying humanity, I experienced a pregnancy-scare satori: "If she is preggers, I will finally be a card-carrying member of the human race—connected to all who came before me and all who will arrive after. . . ." There was peace and a sense of fulfillment in this insight that I had never known before. Angsty and lonerish, I'd always felt cut off from the natural order; now I was potentially its latest standard-bearer. I could die leaving behind something more than eight hundred pounds of unproduced screenplay drafts and a handful of masturbation socks.

But I also found myself simultaneously thinking *I can't have this child right now—no way José.* Both impulses were equally strong: my connection to the idea of life within Mara and my determination that I could not be responsible for it, not now. It just wasn't meant to be. When you know, you know.

If she gets an abortion, I wondered, what will we be nipping in the bud? A son or a daughter? Or a life of forced fatherhood I never wanted and would probably deeply resent, with all the ensuing complications—affairs, professional compromises, negligent parenting? Would it be evil of me to choose a destiny that did not include children or merely responsible and levelheaded? Something in me ached with longing and love at the thought of having a kid. I had recently seen a child asleep in a car seat—a child I knew to be a spoiled brat, in fact—and suddenly I had thought, despite myself and all I knew about the minimonster, *Ah, my little angel. I want one of you.*

Yet there was another part of me that groaned: Don't be a fool. She's not the one. If you have this kid out of guilt, you will pay the price—and so will the kid. You know Mara's heart and soul by now. She is not well in the head. She is a destroyer. She will annihilate you and take this kid down with her.

Things got raw and real: a love of words can be a curse, for I remember a string of terrifying ones unfolding through my head as though on a ticker tape: *Which will you flush down the toilet? Your own life—your future? Or this embryo?*

Choose.

On the one hand, I reasoned, you can't equate a glob of cells that has the potential to become, say, Einstein, with just any old glob of cells: a tapeworm, for example, or Michael Moore. On the other hand, a fetus is not really "human" in the same way the rest of us are, is it? For one thing, it can't vote on *American Idol.* So how, then, do we classify it? Depending on the situation, as a blessing or a burden, it would seem. It is an entity unto itself yet inextricably part of its mother.

It is a koan, a riddle of life.

Standing there in Rite Aid, struggling to make sense of the fetus, I had a vision of my older brother, Geoff. A preemie born the size of a field mouse, Geoff died moments later as my sobbing father cupped him in one palm. As a kid I imagined that the unborn souls of Geoff and I had once duked it out on some metaphysical plane for the right to be born the "big brother" in my family. I not only won, but in crushing him in our time- and dimensionless cage match, I inherited (or stole) all of his mojo, consuming his life force and essentially becoming two men in one. It's a ridiculous theory, of course, probably spawned from watching too many movies like *Highlander*. ("There can be only one!") But is it really that much more absurd than any of our theories about the prelife? None of us has a clue about what happened on the greatest journey any of us has ever taken: the journey from nothingness to somethingness. Part of what makes the abortion question so difficult is that on some level the fetus is still making that journey. On the one hand, it's easy to grant it saintly status; on the other, it's easy to dismiss it entirely: for in either case we just aren't sure *what exactly it is*. It is something like an inkblot upon which we project our fears and fantasies, our beliefs and worldviews, ourselves.

The foundation of life is a nut that neither science nor religion has cracked to either's satisfaction. It is a mystery, I'm afraid. There is a classical Zen koan that addresses this problem: What did your original face look like before your parents were born? Countless times I've failed to answer koans like this to my teacher's satisfaction, as signaled by his ringing his bell, an effect fortunate only in that it drowns out his laughter. Gradually, through this painstaking process of trial and failure, it's occurred to me that the stumbling-block nature of life's deepest questions is not necessarily an obstacle to understanding the human condition— rather, it speaks to the very heart of it.

Why are so many of the conflicts at the heart of life logically and ethically "unsolvable" one way or another? Could it be because they are the very conflicts that *generate* life? Think of the sun and the sea, which embody certain traits or "values" that when looked at separately contradict and negate each other but when brought together, in just the right measure, create a natural balance that sustains, nourishes, and produces life. If either the sun or the sea "won" the respective arguments they embody, we would have a very dry or a very wet—and an essentially unlivable—planet. Perhaps when we deanthropomorphize culture clashes like pro-life versus pro-choice, they operate on essentially the same principle: by endlessly renewing and replenishing each other with arguments, both sides of any debate energize and move a people forward—or into a kind of dizzying dance of life—this, by matching each other step for step in what appears to be the effort to stomp each other out.

Arguably, the emotional and intellectual ecosystems that are our inner lives need a similar balance of opposing energies to thrive. In my experience, hearts and minds loosen and bloom only through an active engagement with, rather than one-sided resolutions to, life's deepest, most meaningful inquiries. In Zen you learn to sit with "impossible" questions or koans, letting them work on you, transforming you from within, while you work on them. Instead of resolutions that narrow your focus, some of life's most jaw-dropping head scratchers—like, Where does the fetus end and the mother begin?—open the other way, toward an abundance of meanings. The more you consider them, the richer with contradictions they become. The result is wild, fertile, teeming: an inner climate activated and not crippled by opposites.

The middle way represented by Buddhism is not about "not choosing" one way or another. It's about embracing both sides, bringing them together within you, and letting the sparks fly. Yes, perhaps I've elevated the defining negative traits of my generation—political apathy, slacker indecisiveness, an allergic reaction to ultimatums—into spiritual virtues. Perhaps I've merely rationalized my own inability to commit to a cause or take a stand on the issues. So be it. I used to look for a definitive, set-in-cement answer to the abortion question. That was a mistake. Both sides of the debate are right and both sides are wrong. I say this because both sides of the debate are still alive within me, in my heart and the heart's memory, which is longer than an elephant's. This isn't to say that I don't vote a certain way on the issue. But ultimately my Zen practice is not political: my politics are beholden to and part of the bigger picture that is my practice. I try to embrace both sides of the issue, then, and search for a personal resolution not in a logical argument for either but in an unspoken and embodied synthesis of the two—

Yeah, yeah, yeah, you interrupt, *but what about those moments when life forces you to choose one way or another?* You are angling, of course, to find out whether or not I knocked up Mara.

When I arrived at Mara's sylvan Topanga Canyon cottage late that evening with pregnancy test redux, she was in bed with her sleeping mask on, her collie on one side of her, her overweight butterscotch tabby on the other. None of them were happy to see me.

"What the fuck," she said.

I explained the situation.

"You fished the pregnancy test—*out of the trash*?" The collie began to growl.

"Just pee on the new stick," I begged, holding it up like a lollipop. "What harm can come of it?"

Moments later I was standing beside Mara in the bathroom, the walls of which she had, inexplicably, painted blood red. Her blowtorch-blue eyes were too powerful to stare into straight on, and so I was regarding her reflection in the mirror. Her sleeping mask was pushed up on her forehead, half covering one eye. She looked like a pissed-off pirate. Suddenly she turned from the toilet and fixed me with her one visible eye. Never good with words, she had a real gift for finding the right ones when it came to what was wrong with me:

"Jack? You and I, we've had a lot of fun, okay."

I nodded, instantly terrified. I think I probably began to cry.

"But sometimes life forces you to choose. That means: fun's over. When life forces you to choose, you better be clear. And to be clear means to know both sides. And to know yourself. Then you can make the right decision—*either way.*"

The wand now peed upon, she encased it in its cap and set it on the sink, as though giving it some space to make up its mind.

"And buddy? You ain't clear. 'Cos if I am pregnant, there are only two options. And you're at peace with neither—much less *either.* You keep searching for 'the formula' to solve all of life's problems one way or another, this way or that way, but baby, life's like me—it goes both ways."

She'd recently shaved her head on a whim, a dare, or to make some kind of spiritual statement or as a passive-aggressive measure to ensure her chronic unemployability—I can't remember which. I often think back on her, sitting on the throne with her underpants at her ankles, ranting baldly, as being my very first Zen master, failing me at my very first koan: "the pregnancy test."

On the upside, I also had my very first deep and undeniable insight into my "true self" just then:

"I'm an idiot," I stated.

"You're a child," she sighed.

She became soft now, as she often did after she'd broken me. "What makes you think I'd want to have your little monster anyway?" she chided, sliding her hand into mine. "It'd probably come out with a tail, smelling of sulfur."

"Would you?" I asked her for the first time. "Would you have it?"

She looked at me. "How could I kill your baby, baby?" Then she kept looking, and her smile went slack. "But how could I do anything *but?*"

Our eyes drifted together to the EPT wand, busy tabulating our fate beneath its plastic hood. The moment was pregnant with possibility. Several futures could emerge. I imagined waving good-bye to Mara as she departed Union Station in an old-timey train, as there was no way our already-ailing relationship would survive an abortion. Then I pictured what it would be like to actually have a child with this headstrong woman. I saw myself in an apron, breastfeeding our infant as Mara left our cave to go club wildebeest for dinner. She was right: I was at peace with neither option. But most crucially, I was not at peace with myself.

Time slowed as the results of the pregnancy test became clear. Mara held the wand up to the light, and in that moment I came to know one thing with absolute certainty: *I will never, ever, ever have sex again,* I thought.

As always, the only thing I was really wrong about that evening was that of which I was most convinced.

7

Son of a Gun

The phone rang, I answered it, and it was my dad. This made it exactly once that he'd rung me since I'd moved to the monastery several years earlier. *Oh, no,* I thought, *who died?*

It was New Years Eve 2007, the Year of the Pig. I was in the electronics cabin, camped in front of the PC, perusing year-end Web site summaries of the Iraqi Horror Picture Show. Though intimately acquainted with personal failure (I'm something of a renaissance Willy Loman), I had never known dysfunction on a national level like the Iraq War. There was a palpable sense in the air that something terrible was happening, and we were responsible for it. There was blood on our hands. *Oops,* America was crying, like Lennie from *Of Mice and Men*, large, dumb, and dangerous, looking up at George from the crushed child in his arms, *we've really fucked up this time.*

"Yello, is Jack there? This is his old man," Dad began, recognizing neither my voice nor my ordained name when I answered the phone. He waited in silence, I suppose, for me to go find myself, which is pretty much how he'd approached my tenure at the monastery. Few American parents want this for their child. They never say, "God, I hope Zippy grows up and becomes a robed celibate without a paycheck. That's the ticket!" You give your son the greatest gift of all, the gift of life, and here he is running off to a mountaintop and questioning it, trying to figure out where he was before he was and where he'll be after he is no more. Some gratitude! I have no spouse, house, kids, car, or career, not to mention a single lock of hair on my head. I scrub dishes, meditate, try to stay out of the cold. It's a simple life—the value of which I have never, not once, been able to communicate to my father.

"Pops, it's me," I confessed.

"Mr. Magoo!" he cried, his nickname for me from my scrunchy-faced infant days. No one had died after all, which left us with little to talk about. Like the war in Iraq, our conversation started off strong and went quickly downhill from there—and I had no exit strategy.

"How's the machine shop?" I tried.

"Business is great!" he boomed, embarking upon the kind of work-related monologue that for me is on par with watching a houseplant photosynthesize.

"Uh-huh," I inserted at the appropriate cues, or "Hmm" when that seemed stale. I was still on the computer, stealth-typing so he wouldn't catch on. All of the leading Web sites were hot to find that one image or metaphor that would serve as the CliffsNote for 2007, which was all but a thing of the past, a beast stuffed and mounted, awaiting observation. I nosed down a trail of hyperlinks far off the mainstream Internet path until I stumbled upon a lonely little rant-filled home page that said it all.

Just then, I caught my Dad saying, ". . . but if the war ends we can expect a thirty-three percent drop in sales."

On my screen was a single snapshot of the blown-open head of an Iraqi infant. Somehow more of her dusty blue bonnet had managed to survive the IED blast than her face. Open on the desk, my journal received the first thought to steam into the mental void rent by this image.

I scribbled, "The Death of God Left a God-Sized Hole."

"Still," Dad continued through my silence, "two oh oh seven was our best year ever!"

This got me thinking—who does he mean by *our*?

Pops hadn't always been a winner. He came home successful for the first time in our lives when I was ten, and we were never the same again. Inheritor of a struggling machine shop from his "son-of-a-bitch old man," he labored for years retrofitting a bank of World War Two–era machines, rendering them accurate to within one five-thousandths of an inch, an eighth the diameter of a human hair. One night he walked through the front door with a completely different expression on his face: he was a man who had outpaced the demons of failure. He gripped in his hands the completed product. Glistening and stinking like a jarful of dirty pennies (also my father's smell), it was still slick with lubricant from the machining process. My two brothers and I took turns holding it—holding our futures: cars, clothes, college. We were like the Clampetts gathered on the front lawn as up from the ground came the bubblin' crude. It was the first of what would become hundreds of thousands of rifle barrels.

I often worked in the shop through high school and college, drilling bits of metal on some large machine or another and generally wishing that Dad owned a used-book store or a tanning salon near an all-girls' college. I graduated with a bachelor's in philosophy, which is right up there with a degree from clown school, and frequently found myself unemployed in my post-college skylarking years. It became a soft tradition, whenever I would visit home, to work in the shop for a day or two to earn some extra cabbage. The custom continued after I demolished Dad's remaining hopes that I might make something of myself and became "Magoo the Monk."

"So, you wanna come into work today?" Dad proposed one

morning when I was visiting home. Fine by me. I needed respite from the question I'd resolved to answer before my one-week family visit concluded: Would I ask for ordination when I returned to the monastery? Or, after three years, was it time to flee monastic life and pursue my spiritual journey elsewhere? (I was thinking along the lines of shorter hours and more hallucinogens.) As Dad would say, it was a "shit or get off the pot" moment.

"This is the first step in the life of a rifle barrel," Dad explained later that afternoon, guiding me through the thirteen-hundred-square-foot labyrinth of turning lathes, Pratt and Whitney spindle drills, and blipping computer-numerical-control fluters. I whiled away the workday at the sandblasting station, stripping rusty shells off chrome-moly steel barrel blanks, Frank Zappa pumping through my headphones. I was on my eighteenth piece of steel, thinking nothing of it, thinking nothing at all, lost in a Zappa coma, when a chill suddenly ran the length of my spine, slicing me right down the middle like a blade of ice. I racked the barrel I was working on beside its peers and scaled a ladder leading to a platform above a row of massive cryogenic freezing tanks. I squinted out across the shop. Silver Afro wigs of steel shavings burst festively from reamer gutters. Air hoses hissed—*phhhtt!* Breathing deeply, I took in that strong, heavy smell from my childhood, the smell of my father, of oil-wet steel and progress, the smell of things getting done.

"We make three hundred barrels for B-Rifles a month," Dad had told me earlier of his key client, "ninety-nine if not a hundred percent of which are being shipped overseas to Iraq."

I've seen deer shot in my lifetime. I've heard and smelled what guns do: the opened-up redness; the great, splattered shock; the gutted and blue-marbled spread of the dead, unique as a snowflake or a fingerprint. Something is always captured in the eyes of your kill, like a Polaroid snapshot in reverse—fading away instead of sharpening into focus by the time you reach it. It wasn't hard for me to imagine what it might be like to take a human life with one of my father's guns. What got me was the memory of my mother's wails at my grandmother's funeral. She broke down outside the church, and I had to catch her and take her into my arms. It wasn't hard for me to imagine these same wails coming from the mother of a dead Iraqi teen, and I was a very clear link in the chain of events leading to this death. I was tangibly part of the process by which this war was alive and real in our world. I had my hands on the gun barrel—I was shaping its destiny along with my father, my brothers, the U.S. government, the American people.

As I sat on that cryo tank with my back against the aluminum ladder, I kept saying to myself, *I don't want my hands on that barrel. I just don't want to hold it in my hands and do work on it, no matter how insignificant that work may be.* I felt unmoored from my own genes, as if I could no longer own the family name. In the forest-sage tradition of Indian mysticism from which Buddhism sprang, the first step on the spiritual path was to leave home. Perhaps this moment was the first step in my eventual ordination, for it was then that I realized, without any rancor or bitterness but a kind of lonely heartbreak, that I was no longer just my father's son. I was my own man now, and my true home was somewhere beyond the physical boundaries of my childhood address.

I thought of Indra's net, the metaphor Buddhism uses to explain our oneness. The universe is a web of interconnectedness, everything in it a diamond, each reflecting and reflected in all the others. Instead of gems, I imagined bombs, one going off, setting off the rest.

In the Buddhist view, I depend on you for my existence. All things depend on each other, equally. Welcome to the doctrine of dependent origination. It's teeter-totter metaphysics—I arise, you arise; you arise, I arise. Forget about our presumed Maker, the divine machinist in the sky. Take a look at this moment right now. You are you because you are not something else; therefore, what you are not—the chair beneath you, the air in your lungs, these words—births you through an infinity of opposites. It's like the ultimate Dr. Seuss riddle: Without all the things that are not you, who would you be you to? There's no Higher Power in this system to grab on to for support; we are all already supporting each other. Pull a person or people the wrong way and you immediately redefine yourself in light of what you've done to your neighbor.

As I camped out there on the leviathan cryo tanks and my dad and brothers began to call around for me down below, I did what I do best: I sat on my ass and thought about something—in this case, about how starkly the Buddhist paradigm of *interdependence* contrasted with the ideal of *independence* I was weaned on.

It is now, with a measure of discomfort—and, strangely, pride—that I admit to being raised a child of the religious right. Its trajectory was mine. The movement was conceived at the same time I was, by earnest and disgruntled parents, as the flower child era wilted and marijuana and free love began their eventual festering into crack and AIDS. Its voice changed along with mine in Reagan's eighties and came into power—with Ralph Reed and the Christian Coalition—as I came of age and rejected it in college. Now it is as though this thing from my childhood, a private and ugly disease I thought only I had, has infected the entire country. But I can't snub it outright, because I know its heart. I sucked its milk.

Back then, my parents were radical conservatives—ultraindividualists. They loved their Brady Bunch–sized family as deeply as they feared for us and the world they'd brought us into. As such, they begot an alternate world, a new world within the New World, more American than America itself. They had all three bases covered—mind: Mom home schooled us; body: we were on a special health food diet and were born at home (hospitals were not to be trusted); and soul: ours was a Vatican II–defying Latin mass held at Marchese's, an Italian dance hall that renegade old-school Catholics rented from what I was sure was a Milwaukee Mafioso.

(Saint Peter's it was not. A disco ball hung from the ceiling over the makeshift altar, and there was a large stocked bar lined with ashtrays back by our cherubic choir. Did I come to church one Sunday in my clip-on tie and polyester slacks and find a drunk on the lawn sleeping off a hangover? I did.)

Completing this circle of über-wingnut self-enclosure was the family business. H Barrels, Dad's company, enmeshed us in a subculture of John Birchers, urban warfare "survivalists," and perpetually frazzled housemoms prone to whipping a teat out in public to feed one of their several yammering "little angels." These were my people, and we took our cues from the very top. I remember thinking that God the Father was like the ultimate rugged individualist. He stood completely alone at the center of the universe, a deitific John Wayne, the commander in chief from whom the very stars and neutrinos took their marching orders. Like Frank Sinatra, he did it his way, from the ground up. He created something from nothing—talk about pulling yourself up by the bootstraps! This Supreme Being franchised the operation of existence to us inferior human beings, begot in his image and likeness, who were then expected to emulate his formula.

If extreme, our ethos of individuality was hardly unique: it's what made us American. In school we memorize the Declaration of Independence, not Interdependence, after all. Walt Whitman did not suggest: Fit in, harmonize! "*Sound your barbaric yawp!*" roared the poet laureate of the land that gave us professional wrestling, Ayn Rand's fiction, and an inexhaustible queue of helium-voiced, silicone-fatted reality-TV monsters.

If the bedrock of your upbringing was man's individuality—his right to make choices and bear arms and fend for himself—over his interconnectedness, his mind, body, and soul over his heart, then you could make peace with the idea of selling gun barrels. The burden of responsibility was on the person you were selling them *to*. What he eventually did with the guns was his business, not yours. Morally, you were in the clear. *Your responsibility ended where his free will began.* Not yet a Zen Buddhist monk but no longer a Catholic conservative, I had to ask myself that day at Dad's shop the question: *Where am I?* Where did I stand on making rifle barrels for grunts and jarheads in Iraq? Could I even finish out the workday, or was it time to yank Pops into his office for the Bloody and Rueful Confrontation?

To further complicate things, earlier that morning my brother Teddy had shown me a photo that a U.S. Marine had e-mailed my father. (Servicemen are always e-mailing my father—he's the Enzo Ferrari of the gun set.) "He's standing over a dead Iraqi, holding a fifty-caliber sniper rifle with one of our barrels on it," Teddy said. "He's grinning from ear to ear, and his boot's on the corpse like it's a trophy kill, like those pictures of Dad standing over the water buffalo he shot in Zimbabwe. It made me sick."

But then Teddy studied the photo closer. It turns out the dead Iraqi was wearing a shrapnel-and-C4-packed explosive vest. When he took the bullet from my father's barrel, a barrel built in this shop on these clacking, whirring machines, he was sprinting toward a U.S. checkpoint. Did my father aid in the taking of a life or in the saving of dozens—dozens like the soldier in the picture and that blue-bonneted Iraqi infant? The "Barrel Baron" makes a markedly superior product, and for better or worse our country is requesting it. If he takes the moral high ground and tells B-Rifles to stuff it, that he's donating his barrels to MoveOn.org to melt down and cast into antiwar buttons, our soldiers go into battle without the best possible equipment. Who does that serve?

"My first job is to protect my family," he once explained. "Then my country."

Back when I was a cuticle-chewing bundle of nerves and an incurable bed wetter, it fell upon my dad to wake me up every night at 3 A.M., when the only sound in our old farmhouse was the antique clock at the bottom of the stairs. He would lift me in his great arms and carry me to the cool, green-tiled bathroom he'd remodeled himself. There I remember him softly telling me, so as not to wake Mom down the hall, the story of how, on the night I was born, he dreamed I was a POW in Vietnam and he and his hunting buddies had to bust me out, "guns a-blazin'!"

"And I'd do it, too, if I had to," he whispered. "You know I would." And I did. All he ever wanted was to protect me and help me grow and become strong, capable, and self-sufficient. His love of guns, ironically, is an expression of his desire for peace and a safer, happier world—his desire to protect and empower the weak, the disenfranchised and lonely, of whose ranks he and his eldest son have always been card-carrying members.

"Magoo?" he now called, crunching down the concrete path strewn with steel curlicues. From my perch, I could see the bald spot atop his old familiar pate. The sudden storm of sobs precipitated by this image solved both nothing and everything for me and was lost forever under the cacophonous din of machinery.

"Ya know, one day you're gonna wake up and realize you missed your nieces and nephews growing up!" Dad growled as our New Year's Eve phone call—along with his patience—neared its end.

Once a creepy cast of right-wing outsiders, the Munsters in scapulars, we Haubners are in something of a golden era right now: the siblings are married and employed; the grandkids (all eleven) are charmingly prepubescent; the grandparents are still sharp and healthy enough to enjoy it all. Christmas is the one time of year when we all converge to celebrate four generations of survival together, and every year, because of the start of our formal winter training at the monastery, I miss it. In fact, I was the first child, in thirty-two Christmases straight, to miss it, and my father, who has perhaps worked the hardest and suffered the most to make this golden era possible, cannot wrap his head around this. The reason for his mysterious New Year's Eve phone call, I finally understood, was to get to the bottom of Magoo the Monk.

"Please tell me why you're up on that mountain scratchin' your nuts and smellin' your fingers, missing the Christmas ham with us every year" was how he put it. "'Cos I ain't getting any younger, ya know. I'm fallin' apart faster than a Chinese motorcycle."

It was a valid question. I could see it in the classic koan e-books centuries from now—Big Jack asked his knuckleheaded son: Knucklehead, why bother with a spiritual practice, especially if it takes you away from your beloved family?

Like many American dads', my father's religion was his career. It gave him thrust, purpose, kept him up at night and got him out of bed every morning. He put everything he had on the line to start H Barrels. Had he failed, I would have carried his failure into my adult life and would have been compelled to succeed at any cost. Instead, I watched him become extremely successful, and I watched success fail to fulfill him. From the ashes of his unhappiness rose the phoenix of my spiritual calling. I can't stand in judgment of him, because I am the result of him—any insights or developments on my path began their journeys through the barrel of a gun. I have inherited his spiritual discontent and have devoted myself to overcoming it—or at least exploring it—with the same single-minded passion with which he has pursued guns.

As I sat on the phone with him, reaching deep inside for the right words to explain all of this, how much he means to me and why I've set out on the course I have, the answer was right there in front of me all along. In my journal, instead of "The Death of God Left a God-Sized Hole," I'd accidentally scribbled "The Death of God Left a God-Sized Whole."

For years, I was convinced that the death of a spiritual father figure—the death of God—was cause for eternal mourning and head shaking and teeth gnashing. Now I'm beginning to see that it may be the very path to liberation. The first thing people want to know when they find out I'm a Buddhist monk is whether or not I still believe in God. If they're atheists I tell them no; Christians, yes (or the other way around if I'm feeling truculent). But the truth is more complex and personal, and it mirrors my feelings toward my father. I still believe in Dad's sincerity, integrity, and intentions, for instance, but long ago I stopped looking to him for answers or intervention, for him to rescue me—"guns a-blazin'!"—from whatever personal Vietnam I might be suffering through. As with God, my relationship with my father has been marked by disillusionment, reassessment, and, finally, a search for deeper understanding. While I agree with him that our first job is to protect our families and then our country, for example, I don't think our responsibility stops there, not anymore. In this day and age, it extends to the whole planet.

God's death creates a wide-open chasm of responsibility that we must fill. For me, the God-sized hole, through the prism of Buddhist thinking, has become a God-sized whole.

After hanging up the phone, having resolved nothing, I said a quiet prayer back in my cabin, the kind I learned as a kid—a true prayer, the type that releases itself from within and is a kind of call, a cry, a blind thrust in what always turns out to be the right, the only, direction. It did not begin with "Our Father," although I did have my forebears in mind. It went, simply, "Help," repeated over and over with increasing intensity, until suddenly I came out the other side of the request. Instead of begging for help from some unknown source of the universe, I was telling myself to *give* it. The plea was its own answer, its own solution—a vocation.

I stayed on my knees for quite a while, as the year's first snow-fall soundproofed the mountains outside. Then the distant snap of townie gunshots broke the silence and rang in the New Year.

8

Surrender the Tender

My second winter at the monastery, I was given the officer position of *tenzo,* or cook—at which point, strange as this may sound, my goal became to grow a much bigger ass.

I wanted to become fat and enlightened—jolly and jowly—like the plaster Buddhas that greet you from old-timey *ka-ching!* cash registers in Koreatown. Not rail thin and eternally maligned, like the bloody and bummed-out Savior that had hung in my childhood dining room, staring me down from his crucified perch every meal: the ultimate appetite suppressant.

Growing up, I felt that my mother's cooking and her religion were of a piece: bland, perfunctory. For her, health was found not in food itself but in supplements: pills and vitamins. It had to be imported from the outside, from beyond, or *trans*food. So, too, the key to human happiness and fulfillment had to be imported from beyond this veil of tears entirely, from something transcendent of this world: from God the Father (that great Archie Bunker in the sky, as I saw him). The narrative I told myself for many years was that my mom stuffed me with vitamins and Catholicism but neither took, because both were poor substitutes for what I truly craved: tangible expressions of maternal love. And so I remained scrawny and nihilistic, unhealthy in body and mind, right up to my thirty-third birthday, which I pseudocelebrated in my Zen kitchen, where a nun told me, after I ruined the baking of my own cake, "Never trust a skinny cook."

I knew then that it was time to man up and grow an ass. The math was simple here: I wanted to be trusted as a cook, and so I needed to put some junk in my trunk. Less frail-and-frowning Hamlet, more fat 'n' funny Falstaff. Good-bye Kate Moss, hello Kirstie Alley! When I passed gas, the bones of my emaciated posterior rattled together like a wood chime in a windstorm. This would not do. No, for the first time in my chronically underweight life, I would extend backward. During my winter in the kitchen I would resolve my mother issues by becoming the tender, sensual, fun-loving matriarch I'd never had.

"Operation Maletriarch: Man of Love" was just kicking into high gear when the *shika,* or head monk, told me I would be getting a kitchen helper. "This new guy really needs some guidance, a mentor, someone with a . . . firm hand but a light touch," he said, scratching one of his two chins thoughtfully. (He was enviably well padded!) "And for my money, you're the man for the job." Which was his way of saying: I need a contained environment into which I can stick this latest lunatic and not have to worry about him. "Crazies and lazies, that's who you get as kitchen help," a wise and wizened old nun had warned me, waggling her finger and rattling her oxygen tank: "People in camp who won't swing an ax and people *you don't want* swinging an ax."

But I didn't care. I was a den mother, a nurturer, a hero in an apron. In shepherding this disturbed young soul through his rite of passage and into manhood, I would achieve my own belated rite of passage retroactively, which had been denied to me the first time around, I felt, by a mother who had been too frigid and distant to help me mature properly. And by the first spring thaw my helper and I would emerge from our kitchen chrysalis as fully formed grown-ups! And me, with a fully formed ass!

In retrospect, if I wanted to see a great big ass, all I needed to do was look in the mirror: there one stood, looking back at me. I myself was the ass of the hour, as I would soon discover.

I was triaging a crate of gangrenous radish sprouts late that afternoon when suddenly I had an instinct to spin around: there in the slightly cracked doorway was a human head. Watching me. Saying nothing. Just a head. The pale pink face was buckshot with acne; the hair a high-piled raccoon pelt, thick, brown, brambly. Those eyes: seventy shades and four dimensions of pure ocean-and-sky blue. Amazing eyes. Gorgeous.

Limbs appeared, loose and wiry, followed by a trim torso, which was elongated in the style of a mannerist painting. He had the posture of a Western movie hero just shot, sort of stunned and beginning to slump. Midtwenties but agelessly adolescent. His mouth, scruff cobwebbed and vaguely pubic looking, gaped a nervous oval as he stepped in and inhaled his new surroundings.

"Can I put this somewhere?" he murmured, dropping his army surplus parka onto the floor.

He spoke with a faint speech impediment that I could not place, as though his voice box were a hair crooked and the words came out in kind. To compensate, as I would soon learn, he had down cold the verbal patterns of several different personas, including the mealy, pedantic cant of a Harvard-educated shrink and the rap-a-tat-tat rhyming pattern of a cold-blooded urban gangsta.

I rushed over to greet him. There ensued pleasantries, which were not very pleasant. Right out of the gates he was truculent, moody. A puppy before it sinks its teeth into your arm.

"Well, anyway, it's great having you in my kitchen," I lied, anxious to get back to work.

"What's that?!" he cried, pointing past the hand I was politely offering him to shake. "Looks like an ass with no crack!"

I thought it might be nice for him to learn how to make a yeasted bread, and I had a bulb of dough rising by the mixer. Matched with that wild hair and the shattered blue glass of his eyes, his untrimmed fingernails made him look eerily like a warlock. Largely ignoring my instructions, he plunged his chapped, scaly, unwashed finger fangs into the dough bowl. As he violently massaged the voluptuous, flesh-toned mass, it assumed the kinds of crevices and crinkles, flaps and folds and buxom bulging beiges that would even have made a vaginista like Georgia O'Keeffe blush. This greatly pleased my new kitchen colleague.

"You gotsta git up in there and work it, but'cha can't tear it," he explained. "You gotta apply the right amount of force and finesse, just like—" And here he spasmodically thrust his hips and released a horrible moaning parody of an orgasm. "Dat's what *I'm* talkin' 'bout." Far from erotic, his convulsions were those of a terminally ill patient who has just had his breathing tube yanked out.

When kneading became groping, then full-on fondling, I demoted him to cucumber chopping, figuring he'd be less enthused by phallic foodstuff. Sure enough, after mangling a few "green weenies," as he called them, he retired the knife completely and slumped in his chair, staring at the ceiling, lips parted, eyes searching, as though he'd thrown a peanut in the air to mouth catch and eat, only it'd never returned.

Those baby blues—they spangle brilliantly, like two dents on a silver bumper, I remember thinking, *but is there anybody home behind them?*

Coffee-bean grinding, lemon-peel zesting, compost-bucket hauling—all jobs, great and small? Kryptonite to his Superman. "How can I put this?" he said, tweaking his Fu Manchu face pubes thoughtfully. "The color of my rainbow ain't cucumber green, if you know what I mean. My therapist, Bernie, says someone like me with a genius-level IQ needs to search for fulfilling work." He paused, as though this were my cue to prime him with a question. "Hundred forty," he finally offered. "I have a hundred forty IQ." He looked me up and down. "I'm *smarter* than you *weigh*."

Hoping to draw some of this native intelligence out of hiding, I switched tacks completely and trusted him with the evening's pièce de résistance: an entire soup. I soon learned that he had a knack for failing in bafflingly creative new ways in the kitchen. Somehow he boiled the miso curds until they burned, killing the live, active cultures that give the fermented bean its nutrition and flavor—its life. I stared into the soup pot, the smell of rusty nails wafting up. Had a surveillance camera been mounted above the stove, tape of that moment would reveal me as a shiny-scalped young man in an apron and underrobes, crossing his slender arms and taking a deep breath, like a drag queen who'd forgotten to don her wig for a performance of *The Long-Suffering Mother*.

"Miso horny." He giggled, his towering coif jiggling out of sync with the rest of his body. "Get it? *Me-so* horny?"

He then proceeded to unburden himself of his sexual history. Alas, it was a history that had yet to be written, a tabula rasa. "I ain' never git none!" he explained. "So yo, I decided: I'mma learn how to dance!"

But all of his moves were self-taught and more martial art than mating call.

"Check it," he croaked. His arms at sharp Egyptian-art angles, he made duck faces out of both hands. Without warning he began whirling in dervishly swift circles, legs shooting out suddenly, as if designed to repel any partner foolish enough to drift within conjugal distance. His head spun to each of the hands/duck faces, which each in turn faced him and then turned away as he reversed his profile to address the other hand/duck face. It was as if an Edgar Allen Poe madman had been dropped into a poorly choreographed eighties Devo video.

"Engage the ducks!" he yowled, his hands yapping and he leaning close as if listening. "Engage them muthafuckin' ducks. This is how we do it—this is how we *da-yance!*"

My lips were pulled tight against my teeth, as though I meant to bite his head off. "All right, enough! Look . . ." Then I realized that I hadn't learned his name.

He spun on me, flashing his "million dolla' scowl" and finally taking and shaking my hand, which I was no longer offering: "Call me T-Bone, and I'm gonna call you—" He thought about it for a moment, sizing me up: "Slim."

"Well," I replied, "you're supposed to address me as *tenzo*."

"Okay, Slim," he returned.

The environment at a Zen monastery is analogous to a beautifully pristine and simple Japanese sand garden. You can feel this purity of purpose when you step through the gates. It's as though all the people on the grounds were making a tremendous effort to rake out their own invisible footprints: to remove any and all traces of their selves. We share this environment, and it works only if everyone's on the same (blank) page. Then the practice manifests as vast, naked, womb-like space that holds us together as a unified body of practitioners and not scattered individuals.

"It's simple but not easy," I always tell new students. "Zen is oneness practice."

But every once in a while someone gets in who not only isn't "raking out his footprints" but who looks around and says, *Oooh lookit! Everyone cleared this empty space just for me! Finally!*—and then proceeds to stomp through it, walking all over you and your peers.

"You aren't doing T-Brat any favors by covering for him," the *shika* piped up from an adjacent toilet stall one morning.

I knew he meant business. Bathrooms, showers, and kitchens are places of unequivocal silence at a Zen monastery. He wanted to give T-Bone the monastic equivalent of a pink slip and had wised up to the fact that I'd been telling little white lies to protect him. We represented two responses to the T-Bone problem: extend a lot of compassion to one troublemaker and keep him around or extend a little compassion to everyone and kick him out.

"This isn't the right place for him. The sooner he gets out of here, the sooner he can find his own people. Although," he sighed, "I have no idea who those people could possibly be."

T-Bone was a termite student: always there, in the background, quietly eating away at the foundation of everything you were trying to build. I began to obsess over the "Boner koan." How do you know when to keep taking care of the truly difficult people in your life, I wondered, and when to cut them loose? When do you fire someone from your heart? Are the impossible practitioners foils on your spiritual path or an integral part of it? Can people like T-Bone be helped, or are they hopeless cases?

"Even a dead tree adds to the forest," my teacher once told me (referring to a Zen student who, among other things, was in the habit of stepping into a running shower fully clothed). Fair enough. But some "dead trees" carry Dutch elm disease, which eventually spreads to the healthy members of the forest and wipes them out. Like a single sick tree, one truly terrible Zen student can slowly, over time, infect the harmony, sincerity, and work ethic of an entire population of healthy practitioners.

One brisk and wind-frisky morning, after T-Bone had abandoned the kitchen for a cigarette out in the rock field, the *shika* banged through the door belly first: "I'm pulling T-Boob from your kitchen. I think it'll be good for him to do our first winter retreat in the *zendo* full-time."

I was silent, but the tension between us practically spoke English. Nineteen hours a day, for seven days, sitting stock-still, buffered on either side by the meditation hall's stern commanders: Could T-Bone handle a retreat in the *zendo*? Of course not. Without the relative safety and freedom of the kitchen, he would become a *zendo* "red shirt" (that peripheral character you've never seen before who suddenly appears in a *Star Trek* episode and who you know will be dead before the hour's up). And that was the point. T-Bone was being pushed. Either deeper into himself and his practice—or out the door.

"The kitchen's loss is the *zendo's* gain," I said, as though my heart were broken by the news but, alas, I was being overruled. Truth is, this was exactly what I wanted: to remain the good guy while getting my kitchen "deboned."

My new crew for the next seven days consisted of a willowy, statuesque sculptress from Vienna and a freshly ordained, self-proclaimed lotus-eater with shock-white hair and elocution worthy of Shakespeare in the Park: "*Ha ha ha—mahvelous,* dear!" I called them "my girls." Together we fired out soups, salads, stews, stir-fries, cookies, and a carrot cake—and looked good doing it. By day five of the weeklong intensive, I was sure that I was having my very first menstrual cycle and that all three of us were on this cycle together, like women in an ancient tribe locked in the menstruation hut, surging with the same cocktail of hormones and barking femininely at the moon.

"*Wooo-hoooo!*" I cried, waving a cast-iron skillet over my head like the four-hundred-pound Nubian Matriarch of a Toni Morrison novel. "Now we're cookin' with gas, sistas!"

And that's when the *shika* charged through the kitchen door— "The Bonemeister's having a bit of a meltdown. He needs a timeout from the *zendo,*" he whispered, making a *T* with his hands.

T-Bone filled the doorway like the villain in a slasher film. His gaping maw was bent at a horrified angle, as though Picasso had done his makeup that morning. His face was blistered with splats of fresh acne, as if he'd been driving through a bug storm and stuck his head out the window. Horns of hair, wet with oil, hung over his blinking red eyes.

His limbs and torso ballooned and swished—he was wearing a snowmobile suit under his student's robes—as he waddled into the kitchen à la the Pillsbury Doughboy. He toddled a few more excruciating steps, like a moose hit in the flank with an arrow, and then collapsed into a chair, clutching at the offending organ and mewling, "My brain hurts. My braaaaain hurrrrrts."

I gazed deeply into his bloodshot eyes: they were twin black holes from which nothing light or lovely would ever escape.

"Get him on a miso soup," the *shika* proffered, running for the door. "Nobody can screw up miso soup."

Vitamixing zucchini, snaking the sink he clogged, sitting in a corner and shutting the hell up: there was no task too great or too small for T-Bone. He failed at all equally, instantly. He had no skill set, no niche, nothing whatsoever to bring to the table. My girls went silent. First they exchanged looks with me, then only with each other. I was losing my kitchen.

"Do you see these?" I exploded that afternoon, clutching at my bony chest. "No one is getting between my teat and the *zendo's* mouth!"

He was unmoved. "What can I say? I'm a rebel." He stepped between me and the stove, where my spaghetti noodles were boiling over.

"I'm not 'the man.' I'm not trying to 'keep you down.' I'm trying to serve food to hungry people, and I need your help."

"Yo, if I was white, you wouldn't be talkin' to me like this."

"You *are* white!"

"You really know how to wound a brother, man."

T-Bone's rebellion was not merely childish. It was pernicious. In hamstringing my progress in the kitchen, he was lowering the quality of everyone's food. I'm not a fighter. I'll do anything to avoid conflict. But if I backed down now, monks and nuns would begin to taste just how out of balance our kitchen was. They would taste the mood of our practice. The food would be too bitter, sweet, salty, or sour.

"You want to know who you're pushing against?" I cried, getting in his face. It was as though my heart had had a sex change while my body tripled its testosterone. I would pick clean the bones of anyone who sabotaged my quest for culinary compassion!

"Um, against a bitter old maid with a soup ladle up her bony butt?" he pleasantly replied.

"You're pushing against the people who are *holding this place up*."

11:49 A.M., day seven of the retreat. There I am, just about on my knees demanding that my growly, O-mouthed nemesis juice a brimming box of tangelos for lunch tea. So far, his primary contributions to the kitchen have been (a) lumbering to and fro, sans regulation robes, a mumbling Zen bag lady stripped to his homemade, silk-screened I'VE GOT A BONER FOR BUDDHISM T-shirt and borrowed periwinkle yoga sweats, tight on the hips, flared at the ankles, the word PRINCESS emblazoned on the butt; (b) flashing made-up gang signs (even though he hailed from the posh white suburbs of Scottsdale, Arizona) and trying to pick pseudogangster fights with me—"Whatchoo got?! You maddoggin' me?! You betta *recognize*!"; (c) blowing in my helpers' ears and then throwing up his hands while cackling "Personal Space Violation—two hundred dollar fine!"

On one occasion he varies this pattern by disappearing into the dusky, vacant dining hall and arguing furiously with himself in the gathering darkness for close to an hour, returning to announce: "No resolution."

I try again. "Please. Juice. This. Citrus."

"Fine, Slim!"

"*And don't call me Slim! I am 'tenzo' to you!*"

With each citrus half the crotchety old juicer groans and shrieks, which draws forth similar clamor from T-Bone, his signature wail of frustration, somewhere between the song of the humpback whale and microphone feedback—"*raaaaaaaahhhh-hhhhh!*"

Five tangelos in and he's done. I study him from across the kitchen table, my breath measured, my gaze lowered, askance: an alpha ape sizing up a nuisance recently reclassified as a threat.

He's tipping forward on his creaky folding chair, tense and alert. Nay, this is not one of his usual slacker comas. This is a deep, almost meditative silence. His furry mouth, though matted with the usual food flecks, is clamped tight for a change. His eyes, a kaleidoscope of blues, are lit from behind, from within his skull, and are floor fixed straight ahead. He's in the throes, at the crest of the wave.

"How's my little Sisyphus of citrus," I coo, anxiously tapping my watch.

Slowly he turns to me, as if startled, and instantly I am ashamed of my tone. His look, off guard and slightly wounded, penetrates to the bottom of my heart like a pebble dropped into a koi pond. I realize now that for the past two days T-Bone has been passing through something in my kitchen. His expression bears evidence of the gelling of some kind of conclusion, from which I have prematurely roused him. This whole time his hand has been poised with a citrus half à la Jimmy Cagney, the juicer quietly humming in anticipation.

When he finally speaks, I reply, "Huh?" setting down a steaming colander of carrot rounds and appearing at his side. I heard him, only I want to hear it again. Something has clicked: I can feel it in his voice. He knows what the Question is now.

So rarely in life do we finally figure out what the Question is.

"I saaaaaaid, *What if there's no place for me in this world?*"

That question: so astute in content, so funereal in tone! It resonated within me for weeks, like a pop song I couldn't get out of my head. "See, the practice works," I told myself. "T-Bone is questioning himself. He's ready to change!" I hoped that with a little introspection, this *puer aeternus* would die to his numbnut self and be reborn a true Zen student. It did not work out that way. And so I began to learn something key about Zen monastic life, why the training is so difficult, especially in the beginning, and why seasoned monks are such hard-asses, especially toward new students.

The key image in Zen Buddhism is the black ink circle from the careful yet spontaneous brush of a Japanese *enso* artist. The key practice in Zen is to follow the breath as the inhale and exhale continually loop back into each other. Meanwhile, the logic of koan practice with your teacher often feels entirely circular. In sum, Zen practice leads you in circles, over and over—but not the *same* circles. It leads you in circles, and you build velocity and then break through to a greater *circle of awareness*. Repetitious practice patterns and a lack of changing scenery force you to experience anew what's always there. Your eyes open, you see more, you include more—your eyes open, your mind opens, and your heart opens. You could call this "spherical" practice. The circular gains dimension, becomes spherical: all-encompassing. You have eyes in the back of your head. You are not limited to a single perspective.

The danger, however, is that you get into a rut. You cut a groove, get comfortable, go round and round and round, lulled into complacency. Your circle of awareness becomes a vicious circle. "There is no destination and no goal in Zen," you tell yourself, "so how can my head be up my own ass?"

T-Bone's practice, peers, and teacher had led him to a crossroads on his spiritual path. So far, so good, right? This is what a monastery is supposed to do. Force a crisis. Force you to look very deeply into your self and start asking really difficult—and ultimately liberating—questions about the source of your problems and suffering. Instead, faced with a life-altering question, which he had finally articulated, T-Bone collapsed within himself and essentially started the whole process all over again, repeating over the arc of the next few weeks the same pattern of negative behavior that had led him to the crisis point in the first place.

This is the human lot in a nutshell: We produce suffering by trying to run away from it. The problems within ourselves that we refuse to face today manifest as the catastrophes out in the world that we smack into face-first tomorrow. While considering

T-Bone's plight, I had an image of the bleakly vivid *bhavacakra* mandalas in Tibetan Buddhism, which depict lost human souls caught up in endless samsara, the torturous cycle of death, rebirth, and suffering. I even pencilled a self-portrait in my journal. I had the body of a pig, the tongue of a snake, and the head of a rooster: Buddhism's symbols of greed, hatred, and delusion, the three poisons. With my serpent's tongue flicking from my rooster's beak, I was licking my own piggy behind, the vicious circle of self-love and self-loathing complete.

T-Bone's selfishly circular behavior was that of someone who won't or can't grow up. "It all comes back to me," he told me. Working closely in the kitchen with postcrisis T-Bone, waiting for him to change, waiting and waiting and waiting . . . I began to feel that he was, ultimately, childhood incarnate. His life was one big cry to be understood rather than to understand, to be loved instead of learning how to love. I quickly learned that the more attention I gave him, the more he demanded. It was as if he were addicted to affection—and getting it meant needing it even more. Needing it even more meant creating conflict out of thin air so that he could extort deeper intimacies from me. He would intensify some slight, often needling me into truly insulting or hurting him. After I had embarrassed myself with a display of anger or frustration, I usually capitulated and gave him a compliment or a series of warm smiles and conversation starters—and now he had what he'd wanted in the first place: more of me. It was like a con game with love instead of cash at stake. T-Bone was an intimacy grifter.

Or at least that's the picture of him that my journals from that era paint. Lord knows I gave the guy enough thought. It often seems that the only people we think about more intensely than ourselves are our enemies. We know them more intimately than we know the people we love. With the passage of time, though, I've figured out what I disliked the most about T-Bone: I saw in him all of those undeveloped and puerile parts of me that I had yet to bring to light and deal with. I doubled up my efforts to change him instead of pausing and reflecting on what his behavior was bringing out in me. I employed that old oxymoron, tough love, and withheld every last scrap of affection and attention. His mood blackened, so to speak, and he transformed from his psychobabbling therapyspeak self into his gangsta rapper alter ego, chasing me around the kitchen while issuing ghetto raps 'n' snaps.

Hovering over me as I tried to scramble a dozen eggs: "Nigga with ya skillet, my belly's grumblin', ya gonna fill it?" He went on like this every morning, puffing out his wire-cage chest and getting, to use his parlance, all up in m'grill: "Muthafucka gonna feed us wit' dem fuckin' chicken fetuses?!"

His "snaps" revolved around the imagined sex habits and weight problems of my mother, often combining the two in an extradeft display of put-down prowess, as in his classic and oft-repeated: "Yo mama so fat, when we have sex I gotsta ask fo' directions." It cracked him up every time: "Directions fo' yo erections!"

I was able to remain passive for only so long. Then I became passive-aggressive. "Stevie Ray Vaughn was a great *technical* guitarist," I would muse aloud, as though to myself. "But he wasn't an artist. Oh, he could mimic or riff on existing themes," and I'd smirk, "but he couldn't *create*."

The only thing that T-Bone loved more than playing guitar was listening to art-guitar blues, his great passion in life aside from strippers. (At the time he was between music scholarships at two major American universities.)

"Although," I'd continue, "his version of 'Little Wing' is certainly better than the original by Mr. Technicolor Stretchpants, Jimi Hendrix!"

"You're just like every goddamn *American Idol*–watching shit-for-ears out there!" he would finally explode, his eyes whirling like cerulean pinwheels. "You 'hear' music, but you don't know how to *listen*!"

"What's that?" I'd say, putting a hand to my ear. "Come again?"

"You like simple raw tunes and don't have an appreciation for subtler sounds."

I would consider this. "Well, Boner, you're a guitar nerd." I'd shrug, and he'd collapse in his folding chair, blinking rapidly, his jaw loose and lips curled, his face frozen in a perpetual *duh*. . . .

Score one for the *tenzo*!

As I recall, to my shame, this was always where I wanted him. Stunned, perplexed, off his game. The secret to defeating T-Bone was that he couldn't let anything go. Days after I'd gotten in a particularly good insult (mind you, usually hurled only in defense), he'd still be trying to reengage me in the same argument so that he could finish it to his advantage. Once I figured this out, I simply refused his bait and watched him suffer the same wound over and over. At the time I thought it was great fun and quite economical. I got days of mileage out of one little insult.

It wasn't just to torture T-bone that I waged these trite and monstrous games, though that was certainly part of it. Oftentimes the only way I could get him to shut up was to strike him so hard and so repeatedly, to verbally beat him down so soundly that his fevered little brain went into stunned shock, which meant a moment's respite for me. Silence. . . . Yet he always found a way to get me back. He was cunning and brilliant. But most of all he was hypersensitive and, if crossed, vengeful.

And never was it more apparent how outclassed I was in the realm of no-holds-barred revenge than the day his mother visited. T-Bone led her into our kitchen with a long, slow grin that curled darkly at both edges, à la Jack Nicholson in *The Shining*. He introduced me to this inconspicuous gray-haired woman and then said the following. (Yes, I exaggerate a lot, but about this, there will be no dispute.)

"Know how you keep saying you want to knock the bottom out of my mom? Well, here she is."

It was true. In recent weeks I'd said this, and much worse, about that gentle, puzzled hippie mom shifting on both sandals before me now. I had been trying to match T-Bone's "Yo mama so fat'n slutty" snaps. I did not, however, think it would help my cause just now to explain this: "Oh, no, I don't *really* want to knock your bottom out, ma'am. I was just getting back at your son, who has expressed a consistent desire to sleep with *my* mom in creative and disgusting ways."

What followed were the singlemost excruciating twenty minutes of my already pretty embarrassing thirty-three-year career as a human being. The kitchen, five or six of us in total, tried to talk loudly about the water damage to the ceiling and how to properly clean cast-iron skillets, as T-Bone shouted over us and ticked off every vulgar thing I'd ever said about his mother, a vast and extensive list.

"Remember how you mentioned that they should raise the minimum wage so my mother would be properly compensated for the work she does in the Nevada brothels?" he began.

"She is big-breasted, which, as I recall, is important to you." And with a broad gesture to the specimen before him: "Well, do you find my mother's mammary glands pleasing?"

The most amazing thing was that during this whole nightmare, his mother did not utter a single word. Nor, for that matter, did his father, who was handing off dishes for me to dry. Had they spoken up, he would have snapped. He was spoiling for a fight. They knew him well. I could barely even comprehend this kind of parental patience, much less emulate it. As a mother figure, I was a failure.

I locked eyes with T-Bone, and I will never forget that grin he flashed back, his eyes a mad clash of stormy blues. We were like two countries that have called off all talks and are headed for war.

Late one evening, during the aptly monikered final breakdown, where the kitchen crew takes the kitchen apart (and tries not to fall apart themselves because of exhaustion), the reek of a dead animal descended over my head like a plastic bag, all but asphyxiating me.

At least he didn't say "Pull my finger" this time. T-Bone stood in the heat of the open oven, ruffling his lower *hakama* robes. I surmised from his little sniff sniffs that he was trying to release whatever was left of the putrid smell still trapped up there so that he might properly enjoy it. Truth be told, I'd just let one loose myself. Now I wasn't sure if what I was smelling belonged to me or to him.

Oh, damnable foe!

This invasion of my nostrils—this olfactory assault, this nasal rape, the fact that he'd crawled inside my breathing faculties, inside my lungs, inside *me,* when I'd worked tirelessly to erect strong clear boundaries to *keep him out*—was the last straw.

"T-Bone! Sweep up those piles. Now!" I roared, thrusting the broom handle at him.

And apparently this was the last straw for him: my interrupting his self-savoring. His face purpling, elbows bending, those bird-like hands balling into scaly fists, he quivered with spittle-dribbling rage and whispered, "This. Isn't. Working. For. Me."

I tossed my Comet cylinder into the sink and started for him, giving him the finger the whole way—my ring finger. "What is this, a marriage? It's not *supposed* to work for you! It's not *about you*! It's Zen practice! It's supposed to change you! But you don't change. No, you expect the whole world to change to fit you and your filthy, selfish needs!"

Tears doused the fire in his eyes, and his face dropped along with his fists: "We've been working in this kitchen for two months and I still don't know the first thing about you. You don't treat me like a person. You don't share your feelings with me."

"Who am I, Oprah?" I screamed. "Do you know who fucks up a miso soup? Nobody. Nobody fucks up a miso soup. Nobody—fucks up—a miso soup—*except for you*. I can't even trust you to make the simplest soup in the *Moosewood Cookbook*. Do you honestly think I'm going to trust you with my feelings? With my emotional life? Get real dude! You're a *child*!"

In a spasm of rage he swung the broom. The first compost

pail, stacked on the kitchen table, plowed into the second, which dominoed the third—and all three pails pitched to the floor in a window-pane-rattling boom. . . . How magically colorful the linoleum now looked! A mighty splat of coffee-ground black and cheese-casserole orange, eggshell and apple-core white; the mildewy tan of old quinoa, fried rice . . . . Read the colors. They said: one more hour of work tacked onto our already impossibly tight evening schedule.

All at once I had to lean against the Wolf range for support. Suddenly I was exhausted to the point of collapse. I tried to speak, but my voice squeaked prepubescently. My face broke open. Tears came out.

T-Bone moved in for the kill: "Wow, I can see your emotional needs are not being met in this kitchen either. It's okay to be angry. You should express yourself freely more often."

He inched closer, I inched back. "If I may say so: I'm not the only one in this kitchen who needs to have sexual intercourse," he said. "You're wound pretty tight! But you're not going to attract the opposite sex walking around here looking like you've been sucking on lemons. You need to lighten up, and open up. It is time . . . [dramatic pause] . . . to surrender the tender, m'friend!"

He was upon me. His arms swung wide, and he took me into them. He held me there, still reeking of the odor that had instigated this blowout in the first place. I'd like to report that I squeezed him back, but my arms hung at my sides like two dead catfish.

And there, in his clutches, my failure was complete. For it was almost spring. Speedo season was upon us. And the fanny fairy had yet to touch my twiggy tush with her fatty wand. I had failed to grow an ass—which is to say, a heart. I had not become warm and loving, fleshed out and fulsome. No, I had not become Big Mama Monk, the living embodiment of a Hallmark Mother's Day card with testicles, my goal for the training season.

What *had* I become? Uptight, anal, withdrawn. Frigid and

rigid. All business, no sugar. In other words, the person I had always accused my mother of being.

But really . . . could you blame me?

My mom used to look at me after our many fights, her eyes filled with so much love and sadness, eyes that scared the hell out of me for all the truth they held, and held back, and she would break out that old maternal chestnut: "Someday when you have kids of your own, you'll understand." *Understand what?* I wondered, pausing briefly before baring my fangs and tearing into her once more.

Now I understood, and I saw her in a whole new light. My mother gave me everything she had—her time, money, youth, care, car keys. Yet it all wound up being so much backdrop against which I held everything she did *not* give me against her. Quite simply, what I ultimately wanted from her was what she did not or could not provide. And this is what I went out into the world to seek. This is how nature intended it. I never would have left home otherwise.

I remembered the first time I left home. It was on a Huffy Thunder Trail bike. My mother's hand was on the banana seat behind me. Then she let go, and I went from learning how to ride a bike to *riding* a bike. I was on my own. Yet my eyes stayed fast to my mother behind me. I stared at her expression. She was beckoning me to turn around.

"Watch the road!"

The bun she always kept her black hair fastidiously pinned up in had come undone. She stood there with her knuckles against her hips looking wild and fresh. She was terrified, fascinated. This child that she had set in motion, first at birth and then on his bike here today, had suddenly broken free. Some part of herself, more herself *than* herself, was speeding away from her: *Where are you going? What are you doing?*

She was suspended in time during this moment. It is this suspension that parents live for: the stunned, joyous shock of their children coming to life before them beyond their wildest expectations.

"Watch the road!"

I remember taking one last look at my mother before cranking the handlebars and leaning hard into a sharp right turn. I sped across the threshold of our spindly, provincial driveway and out into the world beyond. In many ways I have never gone back. As a relatively liberal Zen Buddhist monk, I've traveled pretty far from my staunchly conservative Catholic roots. Yet it was my mother who laid the groundwork for my journey beyond her. Pilgrimages to distant places require a sturdy home base, a firm hand guiding you from behind until you can achieve balance and build momentum on your own.

On the surface, my mother had been plain hearted in her dealings with me. But good parents, especially good conservative ones, don't work on the surface. They are the ground beneath you, supporting you while you go out into the world to find your own way. It is always the most solid foundation that we take completely for granted. And the strongest foundation of any family is not political, religious, or even nearly identical DNA or shared blood. It is unconditional love, which my mother expressed not through effusive gestures or tasty but unhealthy comfort food but through a bottomless willingness and capacity to accommodate me, to carve out from herself even more space so that I might fit into her life in some new way: first as a fetus, then as a bratty child, then as a truculent teenager, then as a college liberal, then as a Hollywood hedonist, and now—horror of horrors—as a Zen Buddhist monk.

"She gots yo' back," is how T-Bone would put it.

Or, to put it another way, thanks to her, I had a strong behind. A solid seat, if you will. And every time I took that seat in the *zendo,* it grew more robust and supportive beneath me as I sent roots deep into the earth and branches far into the sky.

It seemed that the great big bedrock of a behind I had sought all winter was beneath me all along.

Zen has a bad reputation as an overly patriarchal tradition, an "old Buddhist boys' club." There is not much talk in the history of Zen of mothers, daughters, or wives. After all, the first Zen master, Shakyamuni Buddha, left his wife and their child in the middle of the night to pursue truth elsewhere, away from them. Yet any true spiritual path will ultimately, at its deeper levels, circle back around to "the mother" in some meaningful way. It was from her that we gained entry to this life. She is our ontological bedrock, the source of our physical person. There was a time when we were indistinguishable from her body in a way that provides deep clues as we now try to understand ourselves as indistinguishable from the body of the whole cosmos. Mystically minded men spend lifetimes trying to become "experts" in nonduality, but women actually manifest the complete fusing of self and other in their pregnant wombs, which are the physical embodiment of our "circle of awareness" expanding to encompass, ultimately, all things.

And the question now was: Could I expand my arms to encompass this troubled, smelly young man in front of me? Perhaps not. I tried to wriggle free. He gripped tighter. "I ain' feelin' it, bro, but it's cool that you're tryin'," he assured me, breathing heavily into my ear.

Like Zen practice, life is full of circles. Patterns. Small patterns giving way to larger ones, becoming designs—destinies. A son straying so far from home yet somehow, in the end, coming full circle, shocked and amazed that he is following in his mother's footsteps after all, which are right there underneath his feet, leading him along what he had thought was his own personal, private journey *away* from home. As we work our way through the problems of our past, those problems work their way through us, often turning us into their embodiment—into, in my case, my mother. As I was once inside her, now she was inside me, pulling the strings. The quest to escape her influence had led me back to the space deep within where I was still holding on to her, holding tight, gripping her like T-Bone was now gripping me.

And so I hugged the Boner back. As a way of embracing my past, a gesture of reconciliation to my own mother, whom I had become, and to the twelve-year-old boy I had once been, who was still buried somewhere deep inside me and who, like T-Bone, had never really grown up. I was carrying myself around like my mother had once carried me. It was a heavy burden, and it was time to let go. So I hugged T-Bone tight and true, in an attempt to let go.

Then I extracted myself from him, pulled up two chairs, and said, "We need to start over."

"Well," he said, crossing his hairy arms on the chair across from me, "I'm waiting for your apology, Slim."

I reddened. My pulse quickened. *This little shit is impossible!* I fumed. *My circle of awareness will never be largehearted enough to include him! And whose fault is this—mine? Or his?!* But I knew the answer. If you have enough awareness to ask the question, then the answer is clear. The very first crucial step in Zen practice is the step outside yourself—outside the vicious circle *of* self—where you look back, look *in*, and say, with aching release, *I am selfish. I am screwed up. Not the world, not my peers, not my family, not my enemies—me.* As long as you can admit this, there is hope for you.

I took a deep breath. "I'm sorry, dude," I said. "And you know what else?"

He leaned forward. His breath smelled vaguely fungal, but I leaned forward too. In an attempt to hold forth the ultimate verbal olive branch, I began: "Yo mama so fat, when we have sex, I gotsta ask dat big-assed girl fo' directions!"

A smile cricked his chapped and peeling lips. He nodded his approval. I had finally learned how to be terrible, and he loved it. "Directions for your erections!" he said. He held out his fist and I gave him a bump, we being homeboys and all.

"Yeah, well, yo mama so fat dat poor girl gots her own zip code!" he said, as we went back to sweeping and mopping and, later, over the course of that winter, cooking, baking, organizing meal after meal for our peers, and trying to finish the work that every mother begins and hopes to see her child fulfill: to become a truly mature human being.

9

A Zen Zealot Comes Home

A Zen Buddhist monk in my tradition gets exactly one week off a year. This time is specifically designated for a family visit. There's a reason for this, I am convinced. Far from being a respite from Zen practice, family visits are a crash course in patience and perseverance the likes of which you can't even fathom while safely ensconced in your hallowed monastic halls, supposedly mastering these very qualities. Every year I prove right that old Zen adage: Think you're getting closer to enlightenment? Try spending a week with your parents.

Here's how it goes:

My father picks me up from Mitchell International Airport in Milwaukee. I first lay eyes on him as he flanks a bank of arrival monitors, distinguished but weathered, in the same clothes he wore last year: a flannel button-down from Mills Fleet Farm (Dad's the kind of guy who buys his boxer shorts, power tools, and pretzels all in the same store) and washed-out denim Dad jeans, in the collapsed seat of which I see the future of my own behind: a deflated balloon, slowly hissing into backdoor oblivion.

"Mr. Magoo!" he cries, leading me once again to speculate as to the size and shape of my head at the time of my infancy, when I received this moniker.

Pushing seventy, Pop's eyes are Betty Boop–big behind ever-thickening glasses, and his upper body has bulbed into a soft parody of his bodybuilding boom years. But he's still six foot and solid, with the laconic, winning presence of a small-business owner who's punched adversity in the gut a few times and never cheated on his wife or his taxes.

We hug. I smell his rifle-barrel business all over him. If metal grew on trees, this is what it would smell like: rusty and wet, the living smell of industry. I've been smelling sweaty steel in our hugs my whole life. Instantly I am transported back to my scrawny, scowling youth. The chemicals released in my nervous system by the combination of my father's machine-shop musk and coffee breath retard any and all spiritual progress I have made over the past year, and I am, like the hero in some Hollywood time-traveling comedy, fourteen years old again.

We go home. I hug Mom—and spot the fridge behind her, at which point I morph into googly-eyed Gollum in the presence of his "precious": *Oh, you frost-foggy joy box of sweet rich fatty foods, the kind I never get at the monastery!* I dine. I dine again. I dine thrice. Then, pleasantly nauseated, I collapse on the leather La-Z-Boy and flick on a flat-screen TV the width of an RV windshield. Naturally, it is tuned to *Fox News*. My parents are the *Fox News* constituency. They voted for G. W. Bush, had four years to think about it, and then went ahead and voted for him again.

Just hearing the voices of the Fox telegogues makes my skin crawl. My father, not content with leaving work at the shop, has hung guns from every wall in the house—ancient guns, modern guns, guns for dropping rhinoceroses or a fleeing Navajo squaw at a hundred yards. I consider pulling one down and silencing forever this TV, which is as large and loud as a helipad, its sound waves rippling my cheeks like air blast from propeller blades.

My father enters the room. I am sitting in his chair, which fact I am reminded of by his shadow as he hovers over me silently. I repair to the couch as Dad navigates our TV watching from Fox to a dramatic medical reenactment and then roots for a seventeen-inch tapeworm as it makes its dramatically reenacted black-and-white exit from the tastefully blurred behind of the woman offscreen, who is shrieking *"Ain' no one tol' me mama's home cookin' gonna lead to this!"* her voice competing with the one ricocheting throughout my skull: *Why-in-the-HELL did I come back home again?!*

The smartest anti-intellectual I know, my father has a saying (he has many—my siblings and I call them Dad-isms): "We Germans think with our hands." Years ago he was roughing out a rifle stock on a table saw when he buzzed into the top half of his right index finger. (Yes, his trigger finger.) After several medical mishaps, that digit is now missing. In its place is a curiously malformed combination of flesh and scar tissue that bears a striking resemblance to another typically less visible part of the male anatomy.

"My pecker," he calls it, waving the stubby appendage up and down in a suggestive manner.

If Germans think with their hands, I ask my father, what does that truncated phallus finger imply about his thought process? Although we laugh about this—"Are you calling me a dickhand?"—my father's provocatively mangled finger has always struck me as symbolic of certain shortcomings (deformities?) in his worldview, which we could safely file under the heading Pretty Damn Conservative.

I once tried to tell him about *takuhatsu*—monastic begging rounds. Once a week a monk drives our Tacoma down to the produce market in Los Angeles and partakes in a Buddhist mendicancy ritual with a husky-voiced, quietly rich Brooklyn-Italian vendor, who then packs our pickup with produce. My father could not hide his horror.

"Phew," he groaned, studying me to see if I was for real, "I can't imagine anything worse than having to beg for my food." He really gave it some thought. "Maybe having to beg for a place to crap, but that's about it."

Dad does not like to rely on others. He's proficient in plumbing, electricity, machining, carpentry, tile work, flint knapping arrowheads, and just about anything else that requires intelligent hands. Not only would this ultraindividualistic, self-made man never beg for lunch: he keeps a large food stash in his pre-Y2K-built, fourteen-inch-thick, concrete-walled second basement/bomb shelter for when "the shit hits the fan," and as we've joked, he needs to survive in a postapocalyptic Wisconsin, with its roving bands of cheese marauders: "You betcha, it's a brave new world—now hand over the Gouda!"

"Begging is a lesson in humility, Dad," I tried to explain.

"Yeah," he said, a bit exasperated, as though this were the very problem. "I'll *bet* it is."

More than God, America, or the Green Bay Packers, the Barrel Baron (as he's known to industry friends) loves guns, and not just because, as per his mantra, "I like to make things go bang." The firearm is a key metaphysical prop in his eminently Ted Nugentian belief in the individual: a life worth defending, perhaps even shooting someone dead for, is a life that *means* something; it's a life that has heft, solidity, weight—that is singular, precious, real. It is in distinction from others that the individualist's existence gains value, but for the practicing Buddhist, it is in union with others that a human life finds true meaning. "Being Buddhist monk means you look at others, you see yourself," my Japanese Zen master explained in his broken English at my *tokudo-shiki* ordination ceremony. Hard to see yourself when you're looking at others through the crosshairs, in my opinion.

And so, whenever I come home, politics and religion become

the proxy arenas wherein my father and I—the individualist and the Buddhist—slug out all of our unresolved father-son issues, most of which can be traced back to a few key episodes from days gone by where my old man acted out the violence that I've come to see, fairly or not, as inherent in his gun-loving mind-set. My dad has argued before both me and a special subcommittee of the U.S. Congress that firearms are necessary to protect his family. Yet in my experience, when it comes to home protection, it's often each other that we need protection from. Violence mostly enters a home from within, where, like cancer, it eats its host behind closed doors and pulled curtains—under the skin of things.

Which brings us to the last time my father smacked me: I was twelve. It was subzero in the front yard, where I was busy flinging my younger sister into a snowbank. I disliked the fact that she was highly intelligent but spoke with a speech impediment. For example: "Wiwa Caffer, aufor of *O Pioneews!* is pouwnd fow pouwnd supewiow to any mascuwine aufor of the twentief centuwy—I'm tawking to you, Ewnest Hemingway!" It was this combination of weakness and intelligence in her that so frightened and infuriated me: the same combination of factors in me that had a similar effect on my father, he confessed not long ago.

I jammed sidewalk slush into her nostrils, ears, eye sockets—raked my frosty fists across her face. I was practiced in the art of inflicting just enough punishment on my siblings to fly under my parents' radar.

But not this time—

As if by magic I lifted off the ground. My vision went ice black, and I was suddenly gagging down fistfuls of snow myself. It was my father, taking me to task. It wasn't the first time. I have five distinct memories of receiving severe physical punishment from him. This is the last.

Our figures dotted the sloping sledding hill that unfolded from beneath our old farmhouse, which topped a butte overlooking cornfields of white and desolate patches of snow-bewigged treetops.

It was the setting for our big showdown—the last time I was going to let him touch me.

It wasn't much of a showdown, really. He was atop me, words snapping off his lips: *"How do you like it?"*—*"Teach you not to hit your sister!"* A congenital wimp, I wasn't really capable of fighting back per se. It's more like I spazzed out. I was an explosion of frizzled, maniac, little-kid energy—screaming, spitting, fuming, flailing: a kitten when you step on its tail. But I got my point across. He crawled off me, totally cured of his own temper tantrum, as though I'd inhaled it right out of him, like oxygen sucking under the door of a house afire.

I sprung to my feet and shot off into the wind-bitten woods surrounding our house, getting deeply lost in its spiny thickets. And in many ways I am still stumbling through the moonlit thickets of our estrangement today: furious with my father, in love with him, resembling him, and baffling him and he me; charging oppositely through cold and fog, pounding out a path through life with him firmly at my back . . . yet always running full circle, a wide loop, boomeranging back to him with each family visit; racing against the numbness spreading from my fingers and toes toward that most central of organs; determined to resolve the unresolved issues he has passed along to me from his legendarily glacial relationship with his own "hard-assed old man."

Not that I'm holding a grudge or anything.

I flew in on a Friday—straight from our balmy Southern California monastery back to a heart-stopping Midwestern ice storm. Six days later, by Thursday's Thanksgiving dinner, things were cordial between the Gun Guru and Magoo the Monk—no meltdowns over the Second Amendment or "flaky Eastern religions" yet. Hefty SUVs thundered into the driveway; eleven grandchildren flooded my childhood home; my father dropped a vintage early eighties Dad-ism: "There's more kids around here than *people!*" and all twenty-three of our immediate family members—parents, nieces, nephews, spouses, brothers, sisters, uncles, aunts, gun-barrel maker and Rinzai Zen monk—sat down at a pair of dinner tables to increase our collective body weight by several hundred pounds.

My mother, a pint-sized but commanding matriarch with olive skin and ebony hair tinseled silver, said grace with tears in her deep Hungarian eyes. *What could possibly go wrong tonight?* her complex smile cried.

Then I brought out the sake—the elixir of choice for naughty monks when they "jump the wall" (ditch the monastery for an impromptu night of R & R).

This seemingly innocuous gesture was actually a ploy in my ongoing mission to expose my parents to "new things" and so juxtapose my West Coast world-traveler sophistication with their Red State, hunkered-at-home hillbillyism. "Warm wine?! What in tarnation?!" I imagined my father shouting, scratching his head. Then he would take a sip and marvel. "Wine the temperature o' soup! Who'd a thunk?" "Made from *rice*, no less," Mama would cry, snapping her suspenders.

Holiday dinners in my family have a distinctive rhythm, and it doesn't involve inebriation. We're too busy very carefully loving on each other, Wisconsin style: with lots of head nods and *oh, ya, you betcha*'s, and the nearly messianic quest to get each other to consume as much sugar and fat as possible. (Everyone is always either eating or exercising or talking about one or the other in our house.) And so I, the Buddhist monk, introduced a new tradition this year. Drinking!

Ever allergic to direct conflict, like most Midwesterners, my dad communicates criticism in code: with snippy offhand comments that, like a timed-release poison pill, slowly leak into your bloodstream over the next few hours. Fully enraged by a comment he'd dropped at lunch—"Boy, free groceries, a roof over your head: sounds to me like you're on Zen welfare, *ha ha ha*!"—I guzzled and slugged my unappreciated sake.

My voice rose. In-laws carefully looked away from me. My

favorite little Kewpie doll–eyed niece, sensing a priceless opportunity to talk an adult into making an ass of himself, suggested I dust off the old "flatulent tarantula" routine from my long-retired stand-up comedy act. Video footage from the evening betrays me furiously jiggling my "hairy spider" behind, spraying imaginary web and flatulence and spilling my drink all over the green felt of Dad's prized pool table.

"Sake," my Zen master once noted: "sometimes medicine, sometimes poison." Tonight? Pure poison.

My father swung his toddler granddaughter Ella into his lap. Ah, Ella! One of those unbearably cute kids who aren't happy giving their love to one adult unless they're noticeably taking it away from another. My father studied me for a moment, then pointed me out to Ella. "See that? That's your uncle Jack. He's a monk. Know what *heeee* does all day?"

"What he does?" Ella sniggered, looking down her little button nose at me.

"He stares at his navel all day!"

They laughed and cooed and pointed at me.

I sobered up instantly. Rage will do that to you. Whether he truly meant to or not, my dad had finally tipped his hand. How many times had I calmly and patiently (condescendingly?) explained to him how intense and challenging and ultimately rewarding my life is on the misty mountaintop? Countless and vast were the verbal portraits I'd painted of the American Zen monastic experience, Rockwellian in earnest detail, Daliesque with surreal flourishes—I wanted him to grok in his very gut what it means to watch yourself grow old in robes.

He had nodded and he had smiled, but he had not understood.

Anger filled me—my skull cupped molten lead: *You think I'm just some saffron-swathed saintly cipher, perma-grinning his life away on a* zafu *cushion at a year-round Japanese-themed summer camp, with chanting and sitting and perhaps tofu-dog barbecues.* (It doesn't help that the monastery where I live is an ex–Boy Scout camp.)

J. Alfred Prufmonk, that's me! I cried inside—*measuring my meaningless life out in matcha spoons!*

As the Barrel Baron roared and tickled Ella with that ghastly penile finger, besotted insights broke free from far below and gushed to my consciousness with alarming clarity: *Years ago you knocked something loose those few times you hit me, and then Mom didn't love it all back together again like she was supposed to—and so the pain and brokenness inside me grew and grew until it reached epic, mythic proportions that only a new religion and my full dedication to it could resolve! You don't respect the lifestyle* that you drove me to *with those blows to my backside—and once to the side of my face (wherein I came to understand firsthand the term* glass jaw*)!*

None of my five brothers and sisters ever got it from him like I did. Why? I reminded him of himself. "Here's the last thing you wanna hear, but it's true: You and I? Are a loooooot alike!" he used to proclaim. And for someone who hated himself as much as my father hated himself, that was *the* unforgivable offense. And so, on five occasions, he tried to beat out of me all the parts of himself that he recognized. The weakness, the confusion, the fear. But he only beat them in deeper—and now, after seven years of intensely introspective Zen practice, that boyhood self was surfacing, black souled and mutilated from decades of subconscious lockdown, aided and abetted and inflamed in his unlikely resurrection by that most stygian of liberators: Sensei Sake.

I knew then, with the absolute certainty of the truly drunk, that I would never become my own man until I stood up to my old man and defended the sanctity and nobleness of bald, berobed Buddhists everywhere, preferably with four-letter words. I stumbled to my feet. And then had to sit down again. And then really stumbled back up, dedicated to making a statement this time. But . . . wait a minute . . . I was facing the wrong way. And plus maybe more sake was needed for this grand declaration of mine.

Miraculously, before I could do permanent damage to my liver or familial relations, I was struck by a booze-and-stress migraine so crippling that I thought I was having a brain hemorrhage. I belched my good nights and pointed myself upstairs.

A voice boomed behind me: "There he goes," Dad said, leveling a parting Dad-ism as I tried to choose which of the two blurry staircases before me was real: "he's off like last week's underwear."

A night's sleep salved no wounds. Rancor and sake had curdled, and I woke up foul to the bone and ready to spill blood.

My parents were already eating lunch. "Good mooooorning sunshine," my dad called out from behind his copy of *Shotgun News*.

I fell to the table and gripped my veiny bald skull, inside of which a small demon with a big drumstick was beating out a very fast song on both sides of my brain. I thought about locking myself in the only bathroom Dad hadn't stunk up that morning, where I would crank the radio Mom keeps tuned to AM 1130, tickle my tonsils, and embark on one of my strident and dramatic barfscapades while Rush Limbaugh railed in the background.

But then I remembered that I was flying out that afternoon. *You're not gonna see these two again for a whole year,* I realized. At which point Mom closed her *Journal-Sentinel,* groaning. Her lips fell open and two words flew out like a pair of killer bees, headed ass first straight for my jugular:

"Climate change!"

This is how it works during these family visits. Everyone can fake it for a while, but when you share living space and you don't have the opportunity to take leave of one another, your nastiest self wrangles to the fore, and what you're really thinking and who you really are outs. You just can't hide around your loved ones. That's what makes them so impossible to get along with.

Climate change is the euphemism hard-core conservatives whip out when trying to cast doubt on global warming, a phenomenon that they suspect exists largely within the perfervid imaginations of liberals as opposed to anywhere in the real world (unlike, say, guardian angels or archeological evidence of Noah's Ark). In fact, it didn't surprise her at all that environmental scientists in England had just been caught suppressing evidence that seemed to indicate that global warming was one big hoax.

"They're calling it Climategate on Fox," she enthused, and launched into an impersonation of Al Gore, who had spoken at the big state school nearby after losing the 2000 election. She did a marvelous job of painting him as a bloated, bearded whackjob flanked by a crew of black-suited ecoheavies who smothered any and all crowd dissent as Cy-Gore waxed robotically about environmental doomsday.

"Wel-come-to-the-*Al-pocalypse!*" she cried, doing her best stiff-armed Gorebot.

This was more than I could bear. Snarky political satire was the forte of *my* people—the creative liberal vanguard: Lenny Bruce! Jon Stewart!—not string-cheese-eating Wisconsin housewives! A short, fit-but-fleshy little munchkin, she was now on her Urban Rebounder, a miniexercise trampoline, bouncing up and down with a scrunched-up face, gesticulating wildly, clearly having a great time taking the former VP and "inventor of the Internet" down a few pegs.

"Damn liberals," my dad added, never looking up from his reading. "Useless as tits on a nun."

I'm never sure: Do they consciously know I more or less consider myself liberal? Are they insulting me to my face? Or are they so caught up in their own point of view that it doesn't even occur to them that in attacking people I may agree with, and beliefs I may hold, they are essentially attacking me? Am I, as their own flesh and blood, merely a kind of appendage around which they can behave as though they were for the most part alone, liberally excreting noxious opinions? Or are they deliberately going after me? Am I the enemy under their roof?

You have only three hours before you're on a 747 flying back to your people—your true *family—in their beautiful black robes with their glistening bald heads and sincere smiles and mutual mistrust of bat-faced female Republican senators,* I told myself. *Don't do it. . . . Don't Do It. . . . DON'T DO IT—*

"So . . ." I began, grinding my teeth, "you don't really—*honestly*—think global warming is a hoax . . . *do you?*"

It got ugly quickly.

When arguing with my parents, what I lack in facts and intelligence I like to make up for with arbitrary opinions delivered at an increasing volume. Like a boxer getting the shit kicked out of him, I lumbered around the rhetorical ring with my mother, that nimble little welterweight, taking bigger, sloppier, dizzier swings while she landed sharp stinging blow after blow. For every point I made up about melting ice caps and homeless polar bears, things I know nothing about, she requested facts, and when I made up facts she sought references, opening my brother's laptop and patiently waiting to Google them. She did these things jovially, without a trace of attitude, with the full and frightening certainty of a woman who was has suckled for decades at the woolly testosterone tits of talk radio tyrants.

My father put his magazine down and folded his hands over it and looked at it while not quite reading it as my mother tried to reason with me. He did not participate in the cage match. And so my mother became a stand-in for all of my pent-up rage against him. But wasn't she an adversary in her own right? After all, what kind of matriarch stands around and watches her husband knock their twelve-year-old boy around? Pickled overnight in a brine of sake, my thought process was cloudy and sour, and I concluded that long ago she had subjugated her own nature as a mother to the will of my father, a self-betrayal that she was now projecting globally onto the environment with her belief that Mother Nature was subservient to—and protected by—God the Father.

Sure carbon dioxide emissions were a problem: "Smog smells," she said, waving a hand past her face. But not a lethal one. "Nature will always bounce back. God made it that way."

A deep discontent with the monotheistic religious model had been brewing within me since my days as a college philosophy major, when I hated authority of any kind (especially the kind that refused to acknowledge my basic human right to underachieve and still make As). Fully nineteen again, only without the abs or hairline, I realized now that God was the Great Idea that had failed Western civilization, just as my parents had failed me. And for the same reasons! The primogenitor of Western religion—that great Rage Case in the Sky—also doubled as the template for the Classically Abusive Parent.

It was all coming together with brutal clarity. As my father, through his violence, had played a crucial role in my quest to answer, via Zen monastic life, the question of why we suffer, so, too, Western man was being driven in droves to Eastern forms of spiritual expression, Buddhism especially, by an intolerable deity whose all-too-human shortcomings—anger, jealousy, spite, a wild beard in need of some serious manscaping—were matched only by the implausibility that he existed at all.

How closely my personal problems mirrored our culture's deepest spiritual malaise! (A bit too closely, of course. As it is writ in the Gospel of Dad-isms: "Just 'cos your own ass aches doesn't mean the whole world's got hemorrhoids, Magoo!") This was shaping up to be one of those monumentally bad mornings where the ground under a relationship built over a single devastating fault finally shifts, opens, swallows, turning all edifices constructed on its surface into destitute, gobbled-up rubble.

"Lemme get this right," I began. "You think that this earth has some kind of eternally regenerative essence, that it'll just magically go on forever?"

"As long as we need it, yes," my mother quietly stated. She was stumbling around her kitchen with a dishrag, elbow greasing away invisible counter stains, pretending to be busy.

"And you think that *you* are gonna go on forever?"

"I believe in an eternal soul, yes."

"Because you believe in God, the super-über-duper '*I Am That I Am*'?"

She turned to me and stopped what she was doing. She said, "If I didn't, life would be unbearable."

A trap door opened within me, and the last of my patience disappeared through it: "I got news for you: for the most part, really, when you get down to it? Life *is* unbearable! It's called the First Noble Truth in Buddhism: *life is suffering*. And your religion only makes a basically bad world much, *much* worse!"

For decades our kitchen table has hosted a Virgin Mary plant holder, into the soil of which we kids used to hide the "daily dozen" (the numerous vitamins) our mother forced upon us. I gestured spastically, accidentally upending the botanical Virgin and her trailing vines, which I could hardly be bothered to then right.

Drunk on sake the night before . . . *stinking* drunk on rage today.

"This illusion of a Supreme Being, which leads to your illusion of an eternal human soul, which leads to your illusion of an indestructible planet, is *destroying* this very vulnerable planet and pretty much everything decent on it, Catholic, conservative, and otherwise!"

"I don't see the connection."

"*Exactly.* That's exactly the problem. You don't see how things are *connected.*"

"I don't understand," she said, wiping the spilled soil granules from my place mat.

"Well, let me spell it out for you then," I cried. "If we're all dependent on a miracle from God to save us and this planet, then we're conveniently excused from being responsible for each other, and life becomes every man for himself! Frankly, to me, that's the very definition of hell on earth!"

Here I turned my puny wrath on my father, who was studying his scuffed work boots, unable to meet my bloodshot gaze: "You people believe that this earth was just *given* to you by God and that it's yours to do whatever you want with. It's like you're on welfare and God is the nanny state and you just *take, take, take!*"

It came out in a spurt of inspired cruelty, and I took what can only be described as a nearly sexual pleasure in turning that old perennial conservative saw—the welfare argument—against a pair of lifelong Republicrats for a change. I closed my eyes and waited for my dear mother's tears. It was terrible to dynamite the very foundation of her religion like this, but it had to be done.

She sighed deeply and laid her cards on the table with an easy shrug. "Yeah, that *is* basically what I believe," she said. "God as a divine parent, watching over us, taking care of us and this planet."

And so she copped to it. Was there no stopping this woman?!

I was standing now, my face hard and denting all over, like sheet metal during a cyclone. "It's not enough that you take your 'self'—your ego—completely for granted! You externalize this mistake, give it some divine characteristics and call it God, and then you build a whole religion around this deified projection of your own self-importance." I proceeded to explain how my parents and their Christian cohorts from time immemorial had used this "God invention" as a weapon to pollute the planet, bomb Arabs, and burn books and witches; to dehumanize gays and women and outlaw condoms, premarital sex, and abortion; and as an excuse to lock Galileo in a bell tower and then turn around and harbor pedophile priests from the law.

If memory serves, I closed with something like, "And every single solitary Sunday you play that god-awful guitar and organ music at your soul-crushing masses—keyword: *masses,* as in 'Religion is the opiate of *the . . .* '" It was as though I'd stuck my finger down my throat and up splashed every steaming, blood-marbled complaint I'd ever had against the Western religio-political tradition in which they'd raised me.

"Take a good look at the world around you. Religious wars are going to destroy this planet," I spat. "They are going to *destroy this planet.*"

My father looked up from the table, and our eyes skidded into each other like a pair of bullets meeting in the sky. Time froze in his square-on gaze, and he finally spoke: "Yes, they are—starting with our family."

My ears rang. I couldn't pull air into my lungs fast enough. My throat was pinprick thick, like the Hungry Ghosts of Buddhist lore. I was asphyxiating myself with rage. It felt as if all the color had drained from my face—anger had made me an albino.

The apparatus of my apoplexy ground to a halt. My mind caught up with my mouth—always an awkward moment for those of us with tempers. By that divine alchemy wherein one internal energy becomes its better, my fury lost its redness, going clear, transforming into awareness, and for the first time that trip I really took them in: Dad's once-chiseled face, collapsing with age. Mom's hair, pinned up in a bun, one more step from dashing and distinguished gray to hoary and desolate white.

How old you have both become, I suddenly realized. *How many more home visits will I even be blessed with before I'm coming home to visit not you, but your graves?*

Wasn't their religion violent and insane—yet wasn't I manifesting these very qualities in an attempt to prove this and to offer Buddhism as an alternative? Here I was, the Zen zealot, screaming at my parents to think of the planet as their close relation while shattering the precious harmony of our own family to make my point.

All the fight went out of me. The "religious right" is an entity that's so much easier to abhor in the abstract. I slid into my seat at the table, dizzyingly nauseated with shame. We sat in silence together. Snow was falling outside, I remember that much, light flakes of it seemingly divinely spaced to fill out the air like visible grace. The marriage of frigidity and softness soothed me, and I dared to look up. . . .

These were not the same people who had failed me when I was young, and vice versa. Those people existed in my head alone— caged and rotting behind my tight, unhappy grin for decades while my actual parents got older, gentler, wiser; while their bodies fell apart and their souls grew deep and their hearts broke open. *Forgive them,* some part of me cried. Forgiveness removes blocks between you and the people before you—and so is a form of catching up to the present moment and living in the now; and so is a form of meditation, and so is a deep and necessary spiritual practice. *But it ain't easy.*

Why has he never apologized for beating me? I wondered. A fair question—and here was another: *Why haven't I apologized to my five siblings for all the beat downs, mind fucks, noogies, nipple twists, and occasional drubbings with a pair of foam-padded nunchucks that I once subjected them to?*

The sins for which you cannot forgive yourself are the sins for which you will never be able to apologize. Such is the catch-22 of extreme guilt: I can't come to terms with the violence I've committed until I can admit that I did it, but I can't admit that I did it until I can come to terms with the violence I've committed.

Suddenly I felt a twinge of kinship with my father. We were both at war with ourselves, not each other.

So much passed through me just then, with the ticking of the grandfather clock, my breath ragged and heavy, but all I can remember is this, which came to me as I watched the falling snow become one with the snow that had already fallen: familial love is our planet's most precious, limited resource, a delicate system of checks and balances, of giving and receiving, that must be protected from the toxic human ego and its pillaging and pollutants just like the oceans and sky.

Tears filled my heart and kept filling and filling it, never spilling down my face, just welling up underneath it all. I sat across from my father in silence, and in that silence I envisioned his heart overflowing into mine, with the tears spilled into him from his own "son-of-a-bitch old man," who in turn was once the vessel for *his* father's tears . . . and on and on, stretching all the way back to the first single-celled organism from which all sentient life evolved—which split itself into two, turned around and looked at itself in the form of another, found it didn't like what it saw, and the first family argument ensued.

I was about to rend the long clean linen of silence with a soulfelt apology when my father, a master of misreading social situations, piped up: "Welp!" he said, "we'd better get you to the airport, Magoo." Then he took a deep breath, turned to his wife of forty-five years, raised his mangled finger phallus, and declared: "We're off—like a turd of hurdles, I mean a herd of turtles."

Family visits always end suddenly, and they always end on the wrong note. They are a reminder in every way of why I went to the monastery in the first place—of what I was trying to escape from my past and what I went to face within myself, whether I knew it at the time or not. The seemingly light conversation on the way from my parents' house to the airport is always freighted with my desperate desire to take back every single infantile, heart-dead inanity I blathered over the past week.

"Gosh, do they have a Hummer dealership off the I-ninety-four now?"

"Yeah, it's the biggest Hummer dealership in the Midwest."

"Wow."

"Yeah, huh . . ."

It's impossible not to feel a lump rise in my throat as my best intentions for the week dissolve in wisps of forced small talk at its conclusion. *How'd I manage to be such a blithering überdouche yet again?* I wonder, futzing with the air-conditioning vent in silence. *I'm more enlightened than this!* But, of course, I'm not. And that's what my parents are there to remind me of, for one week every year.

As this last family trip ended and I stepped through the airport metal detector, I spun around and stole one last look at my father, again flanking the arrival monitors. In roughly one year he would be standing in roughly the same spot to pick me up, wearing roughly the same flannel-and-denim Dad duds and, ultimately, posing roughly the same challenges as always to my inflated opinion of my spiritual progress. I felt like a frightened and frail twelve-year-old heading off to church camp all over again. I was homesick: sick and tired of the conservative Catholic home I had been born into and couldn't seem ever to quite leave behind, and sick with fear over the home ahead of me, within the Zen Buddhist community that had helped sew the *koromo* robes in which I would one day be cremated.

With my heart airborne between these two worlds, my stomach bottomed out: suddenly I was terrified to fly, terrified to land, and terrified to invest another year of my life in that wintry patriarchal "manastery," where the principle pleasures were lukewarm showers, the occasional cheese condiment at a formal meal, and masturbation, and not in that order.

Lacking any other option, I tried to do my Zen practice right there while getting over-X-rayed—to be in my body, my senses, in the actual real-time situation itself instead of in my head/ideas about it. . . . But it was no use. My heart was a raw wound. Absolutely nothing could stop the pain pouring out of it.

Then it hit me: maybe I *was* in the "actual real-time situation" after all, and pain was just a part of it. I was in the moment—the moment just sucked. Just because you hurt doesn't mean you're doing something wrong, that you're weak, dumb, selfish, or hopelessly screwed up. If life is suffering, then pain simply means that you're alive. The excruciating ache in my heart was proof that there was blood beating in there. Zen practice, like life itself, is not about floating above your problems but passing through them, like the proverbial lotus flower rising from the murky depths of its own source, coming up for air, for light, for beauty, for all of those reasons that things keep living, growing, and returning home, no matter how miserable or painful or downright embarrassing the journey gets.

I'd been numb to my parents for decades, completely denying my rage and resentment. Now I was finally feeling something. I was feeling like shit, actually, but feeling like shit never felt so good. It was a start.

I gathered my shoes, my wallet, and myself on the other side of the metal detector and took what I knew would be my last watery glance at my father for a whole year. He was still there, still waving. I waved back; we waved in unison. Two Germans, thinking with their hands. That mangled minifinger he was waving at me could be read many ways: before, I saw it as a symbol of his shortcomings and deformities in his point of view. But now I saw it as a testament to all that he'd sacrificed for our family. For if Germans think with their hands, then Dad had raised me with his and had even lost part of his trigger finger while building the business that fed, clothed, and educated me to the point where I could think well enough to question the principles he lived by.

I made for the plane with tears in my eyes, feeling thawed inside for the first time since back before I outgrew Underoos. I could almost see my pops standing just beyond the icy woods of our estrangement, smiling broadly, sincerely; waving me forward, as he was now waving good-bye behind me; beckoning me into full adult- and monkhood with that wounded symbol of all that he'd sacrificed to help get me there.

10

Glorious Openings in the Windy City

A MONK'S MANIFESTO!

Part One

GLORY HOLES OF CHICAGO: A LOVE STORY

One Sunday afternoon about a decade ago, as I was slumped on my love seat in West Hollywood, generally suicidal but more specifically hungover, my mentor called. I was overjoyed and performed some elementary speed math: *It's been three long months since we last talked, Papi-san!*

"What up girl?" I asked, desperate to seem casual.

This was our standard greeting for each other, though we were not girls. We were what passes in our day and age for grown men. I was newly thirty at the time, and anonymous. Thirty and anonymous is not a good combination for a Hollywood screenwriter. I remember that I had on a loud button-down shirt with a large, shoulder-spanning turtle sewn on the back, which I had acquired at an expensive thrift store and which was supposed to say something about my personality, such as: *I'm over-it-all and worldly-wise, yet I'm also young at heart.* You know, the standard hipster fashion statement.

I was living the kind of life common to many young creative types struggling to make it in a big city. Deep down, I felt that my life had not quite started yet, because I hadn't figured out how to live it. I had not "found myself." When you don't know who you are, you don't generally hold yourself accountable for the you that is squatting in your skin until the real you shows up with an eviction notice. I had left my hometown years ago, and there was no one within a thousand-mile radius who genuinely loved me or whom I genuinely loved. I had an apartment but no home, acquaintances but no real friends, hookups but no significant other, coworkers but no family, dreams but no goals, credit but no money. I could get away with this kind of shit in my twenties. It was bohemian. In my thirties, however, it made me something closer to a bum.

In my twenties? "Hey, that guy's a free spirit." By thirty? "That guy's kind of a loser."

I had made the mistake of thinking of my life as though it were something like a car up on blocks with the gas pedal floored: I'm not going anywhere, I figured, so I can't be racking up any miles. Then I hit thirty, broke, single, and beginning to bald, and I realized no, the odometer had been going this whole time. In lieu of any real purpose or plan, I had embraced ambiguity as a lifestyle. Nowhere was this more apparent than in my attitude toward sex. Just about everyone I knew had at one time or another thought I was gay or at least bi. And I let them think it. I thought it was funny, yes, but avoiding the issue of my sexuality also meant that I didn't have to ask myself some difficult questions, starting with: If you're not gay, then why are you totally alone and without the company of a woman, especially at your age?

It was into this confused life that my mentor's call came that Sunday. His voice was even and unironic, like a sniper talking quietly from a great distance to a target he is sighting in on. I sat in half-lotus on my love seat and tried to give him my full attention. A bewildering conversation ensued. There were vague statements delivered with shimmering, steely intensity followed by long pauses, which I gathered I was supposed to fill with a confession of some kind. We hadn't spoken all summer, per his firm request, and now he'd called me out of the blue to accuse me of something quite dire while refusing to name the charge. It was all very weird.

"You want to just tell me what this is all about?" Silence . . . "Bless me father for I have sinned," I said. More silence.

"Meet me in Plummer Park in half an hour," he said.

"Shall I bring my lawyer?"

He hung up.

I spotted my mentor's tall, muscular frame on a park bench under a blossoming bough of magnolias just as the cloying floral fragrance struck my nervous gut like a fist. The muscles in his forehead were clenched so tightly you could've cracked a walnut between his eyebrows. He was not wearing anything interesting. Not the huge silver watch affixed to its thick leather wristband. No funny/cool T-shirt, nor a selection from his vast assortment of stylish hats. This more than anything scared the hell out of me. The vain bastard really meant business. He'd forgotten to accessorize!

He offered no greeting as I thudded down on the bench beside him. His chiseled face lapsed into the stillness of stone: craggy and adamantine. Again with the third degree. Was there anything I wanted to tell him? Was I sure of this? *Nothing at all?* . . .

"Dude, I have no idea what you're talking about," I said. This made him smile but in the wrong kind of way.

The park was an oasis of botany, dog poop, and gay men dressed for a warm day. I remember it was overcast and smelled of rain that would never come. The nearby rec room was being used for an audition. A crowd of beautiful, half-naked actors was split in two and facing each other, screaming, their lips moving silently behind large glass windows.

Through provocative silences and charged hints, it was as though he were setting before me a blank canvas upon which I was to scrawl my confession. I gladly would have, but I didn't know what the hell to say. I quickly ran out of words trying to defend myself against this horrifying crime I had evidently committed, the nature of which I remained wildly ignorant and he refused to make clear. Still, I got that feeling you get when someone you trust and love with all the blood and muscle in your heart thinks you've done something terribly wrong, and you begin to wonder if you haven't. The way you've been living, you know you're guilty of *something*: maybe this is it. . . .

After several minutes of gasping denials, I lapsed into silence, and we watched in immense psychological discomfort as a burly bearded man in a Mariah Carey–*Glitter* tank top followed the beckoning red anus of his Chihuahua with a plastic bag, swiping little brown nuggets before they could plunk to the ground.

Finally, my mentor broke the silence. His tone dipped with the opposite of reverence.

"*Glory Holes of Chicago*," he said.

Each word flew out of him like a pigeon released from some dark cage within. Freedom, disease, and chaos were suddenly in the air.

I looked at him blankly, point-blank.

"I saw your movie, Daniel Reed," he cried.

I tried to laugh. "I really do not know what you're talking about."

"You!" he said. "I'm talking about *you*. You're Daniel Reed. I saw your movie *Glory Holes of Chicago*!"

"You've gotta be kidding me," I said. My voice was shaking. "I've never been in a movie. You know that. You know everything about me."

He refused to meet my gaze. I always took my cues from him, and so we both stared straight ahead. He slowly crossed his arms, then his legs, all six-plus feet of him now looking very cross.

"I swear to God I have no idea what you're talking about," I said. "You apparently know something about me that *I don't know*. Please tell me what it is that you know." This seemed to be the most honest way to put it. I was suspended between breaths, like the instant after I got T-boned in my parents' Chrysler in college, when I was not yet sure what all was damaged and whether it included me.

"You were in a gay-porn film called *Glory Holes of Chicago*," he began. "You have a career in gay porn. You fuck men on camera. No, that's not right," he said, after a moment. "Men fuck you."

He studied my expression for a century or two. Whatever he was looking for, it was not there.

"Well then," he said, like a man who had prepared for every possible contingency: "Why don't we just go to Circus of Books and *rent it!*"

NOTES FROM THE UNDERGROUND *ZENDO*

I had met my mentor two years earlier. At the time, I was several years' worth of classes into another lineage of Buddhism. One day I walked into the meditation hall in that tradition and was suddenly put off by the busy altar, with its thick plumes of incense and multilimbed deity statues, and the colored prayer streamers draped loudly across the rafters. This had been my sophomore effort in the dharma. The first Buddhist group I'd encountered in LA consisted of a handful of Germans led by "Lama Schnitzel" of the "Ruby Way," who instructed me to "visualize ze chakras as ze colors of ze rainbow." I'd left that group after Lama Schnitzel launched into a tirade against religious fundamentalism, specifically Islamic (this was pre-9/11, and every single solitary word of his outburst, which at the time I thought was bilious gibberish, wound up coming true). Now I was on the move again, though I felt deeply grateful for both of these legs of a spiritual journey that I intuitively knew would hit its stride in a third phase.

Three weeks and several spiritual red herrings later, I followed the directions to a Zen temple off the back of a postcard I'd found in a stack at a nearby Buzz Coffee. *("Zen—it's not what you think,"* it had read.) I'd come with a question. A silly one, a clichéd one, compliments of an old Alan Watts lecture I'd just downloaded. *Zen Master Hakuin asked, "What is the sound of one hand clapping?"* ... With this chestnut roasting freshly in my fevered skull, I locked my bike to a wave rack and descended deep into the bowels of the parking garage in a famous shopping complex off Sunset Boulevard. On labyrinthine P-3, I finally stumbled upon a dank concrete "public room" that reeked of homeless persons' urine.

I will never forget that first image of my mentor, the spiritual love of my life.

There are two kinds of handsome: the kind that alienates you by suggesting your own deficiencies in contrast, and the kind that draws you in by making you a part of its glow. He was the latter: oven warm yet classically masculine, as though chiseled from marble in an ancient Greek studio; broad shouldered, long limbed, and thin lipped; freshly bald and fully accoutered in his slim *osho* (priest) belt and a *rakusu* monk's bib so sweat-and-grime infused it was as slick and shiny as fruit leather. My previous sitting group was led by nice, bland people surrounded by religious ostentation and adoring devotees. My mentor presented the opposite image. He was a five-star Zen general presiding over a few symmetrically lined-up and empty *zafu* cushions, in what amounted to a shitty little concrete cave that groaned under the weight of vehicles arriving and departing above and below us.

He was elegant and commanding, a cross-legged mountain of monkness gathered on a cushion before a single blond rose.

I paused in the doorway, and time, like an old friend, paused beside me. All around us the City of Angels raged ephemerally, being transformed by earthquakes, mud slides, riots, and dreams of fame, money, power, and sex, while my mentor sat there underneath it all, in his parking garage *zendo,* like a cloud-topped mountain, settling deeper and deeper into himself.

Then he looked up. Or at least I imagine he did. I walked up to the open doorway—and then walked past, caught my breath, and asked myself, *Who the hell is that? And where do I sign up?*

We became fast friends. The initial stages of my journey into the heart of formal Zen practice consisted not of strict meditation sits nor baffling koan encounters with the master but two-for-one margaritas at the "butt hut," as my mentor referred to our tropical-themed gay bar of choice. He was just coming off a ten-year tour of duty as a full-time monk at Mount Alcatraz Monastery and another five years as vice abbot of a city temple affiliate. Now he was transitioning back into society as a part-time hospital janitor and a lay Zen priest with a remarkably sparse sitting group. ("Bare Bones" was my suggestion for his temple name.)

At first I wasn't sure what the exact nature of our relationship was, but he clarified it. "I've done a decade and a half of nonstop formal Zen training," he said, the tunnel-and-bridge coming out in his Jersey lilt. "Now I just wanna be a regular Joe, and I'd really like to find a friend or two."

But there was nothing regular about him. His father died right in front of him of a sudden heart attack when my mentor was ten, and two of his three brothers committed suicide, the second just five years after the first. But it was being born a homosexual, and the self-hatred and loneliness catalyzed by this sexual orientation ("Half the world wants us fucking dead!" he told me. "And the other half just wants fashion advice."), that drove my mentor to a life of spiritual questing.

"I'm in a used bookstore in Brooklyn and I see this paperback with a really cool psychedelic cover. I thought it was science fiction, so I snatched it up. Turned out it was a book on Zen by Alan Watts. I was twenty when I found this practice," he told me. "And I'll tell you what—if I hadn't? I'd have hung myself from the rafters. Zen is like chemotherapy for me. It's brutal medicine that makes you go bald, but it beats the alternative."

As a Zen teacher, he was more of a kindhearted big brother than a charismatic player in the LA spiritual scene, with its celebriswamis and yogaristocrats and yuppiesattvas. He was the Zen equivalent of a country doctor, making house calls when needed to help those who are ill but otherwise living a quiet, humble life.

Well, not so quiet, as it turned out.

My mentor had his first sexual encounter with a member of the same sex when he was thirty-five, in the parking lot of the Manhole in San Diego. He was on a weekend's leave from the monastery and wound up in the backseat of his Camry with a tall, buff Oklahoman. "Boy, you sure do git right down to it," the Okie said, as my mentor helped his new friend out of his Wranglers.

"I finally figured, if I'm not attracted to women by now, it's just never gonna happen," my mentor explained to me one evening. "I really tried, God I tried, but boobies just aren't my thing."

"Yes." I winced. "Anyone who uses the term *boobies* probably does not have a thing for them."

"I'm sorry," he said. "Teats?"

As a closeted youth, he had developed a convincingly smooth and macho veneer, which persisted into his middle years. When men introduced themselves to us at bars, they assumed I was gay, not him. "It's that turtle shirt, dude," he said. "You gotta lose that turtle shirt." For more than two decades my mentor misled everyone about his sexuality, including himself. "I tried to be straight, I failed, and now that I'm slightly past my sexual prime, I'm makin' up for lost time," he said.

And how.

His stories from the Hollywood sex spa, a club where gay men went to couple (and oftentimes triple and quadruple, in one bed), were lurid and fascinating. "You walk down a corridor of open doors, and each room is like its own little hell realm. There's this beautiful blond kid, maybe nineteen or twenty, sitting on the edge of a bed. He looks like an angel, with downy skin and glowing features and this fine mist surrounding him, only he's totally emaciated and sucking on a glass pipe. You walk to the next open door, peek in, and there's an old fat guy wearing nothin' but Elton John sunglasses peeking back at you, just waiting and hoping and masturbating—the bed shaking, these big rolls of fat moving. You think 'maybe not' and walk on to door number three, where there's a guy in a leather hood with metal electroclamps on his nipples that are hooked up to a car battery . . . but that's not really what you notice."

"What do you notice?"

"What you notice is that his penis is wrapped in these leather strips with steel studs sticking out. Actually, I didn't even really notice that."

"And you noticed what?"

"His feet. He had smokin' hot feet." His eyes dropped downward. Suddenly I regretted putting on sandals that morning. "Gosh, you've got cute kickers too, lookit those guys . . . not bad, though your nails need a trimming"

"Please," I blushed, pretending to gag.

I should mention that he was also at the height of a five-month crystal meth "experiment" when we met. At the time, the drug was everywhere in gay LA and apparently he began with a naive puff offered by a handsome Internet hookup and then progressed from there. His usage was slightly more than casual but not quite self-destructive, and thankfully short-lived.

"I like to practice the middle way when I use hard drugs," he explained.

I imagine that right about now the record has scratched, the music has stopped, and everyone is staring my way. Monastic figures, after all, are not supposed to be gay-bathhouse-frequenting foot fetishists with meth pipes crooked in the corners of their mouths. They're supposed to be like Saint Francis of Assisi. If popular iconography serves, this most famous Western monk was so innocuous, such a mellow nonentity that the birds and creatures of the forest regularly mistook him for lawn furniture and perched atop his ring o' hair. As a folk legend, Saint Frank trades on the popular stereotype of the monk as someone who undergoes a spiritual lobotomy/castration and becomes peaceful and content at the expense of an interesting and juicy life. Contrast this image of monk as perma-grinning eunuch with the infamous Zen priest-poet Ikkyu. A totally rambunctious, off-the-charts "spiritual" maniac, this fifteenth-century Japanese iconoclast once remarked (no doubt in the throes of sacred ecstasy): "Her mouth plays with my cock like a cloud plays with the sky." Can you imagine Saint Francis coming up with a line like that? The pope? How about one of our contemporary megachurch preachers, with their rock-stadium-size masses for the masses, high-wattage smiles, and trophy wives?

Right out of the gates, my mentor's most important lesson was that Buddhist luminaries like Ikkyu or Bodhidharma, the gruff and pissy, tell-it-like-it-is founder of the Zen sect, have shown us that you can be spiritual without being moralistic—without being, or even wanting to be, perfect. They've shown us that Buddhist bigwigs can—they *should*—be different kinds of spiritual leaders than popes and preachers, rabbis and imams.

When I met my mentor, two seemingly irreconcilable notions of the spiritual life were battling toward a climax within me. Let's call them Friday-night spirituality and Sunday-morning spirituality. Friday-night spirituality, with its Blakean overtones and debt to Nietzsche, consisted of blurring the line between ecstasy and debauchery. I craved bad company, dangerous unions, consultation with demons—hearing *their* side of things. I would take illegal substances; wander into the loudest, darkest, most out-of-the-way gathering; and find silence within the unholy blast of an all-night music-and-mayhem marathon—throw my head back and get ravaged by the forces of the night. Transcendence through transgression. More than once I awoke in my own vomit or blood, or in someone else's. The point was to forget, so that something new was created. I wished to be carnally born again—and again and again—and isn't birth always, as it's happening, a searing, gushing, wild goddamned thing?

Sunday-morning spirituality took place in the fresh, crisp light of day. Though no longer Catholic, I would spend hours on my knees in an empty church on a weekday, just me and a few homeless guys, trying to strike up a conversation with God. And sometimes (mostly, actually), I *didn't* do drugs. And I didn't go out. I went to bed early, got up at daybreak, and gamboled through the Hollywood Hills, listening to birds imitate car alarms. At the time, I was both indulging in and deeply cynical about the excess-paved path to the grave taken by my various counterculture idols. Conservative at heart, I ached for a wholesome and sane approach to life—self-emptiness, not self-destruction.

After many hours of guzzling both green tea and whiskey with my mentor, I began to see how the two opposing spiritual armies within could be marshaled under one banner. My whole consciousness shifted the day I realized that the spiritual specimen that was my mentor needed his Zen practice—which was like a, clean, clear map dot proclaiming YOU ARE HERE!—so that he wouldn't get stranded in the sewers and sierras of a personal life gone totally off the grid in terms of conventional morality. And he needed his rich, steaming, red-blooded personal life so that he wouldn't get sucked into the arid and hypocritical death trap that the spiritual life, with all of its perfunctory practices, can become. The impersonal intensity of his formal Zen training pushed him to experiment more deeply with sexual intimacy, and the sheer rawness of his sexual encounters propelled him further down the perspective-providing spiritual path. He was Mary Magdalene and the Virgin Mary all rolled up in one buff, boyish, Irish-American package. Given my character, which is also prone to extremes and exploration and impiety, I could not have asked for a better introduction to what in the Buddhist tradition is referred to, and constantly misinterpreted, as the Middle Way.

Once a successful architect with a passion for photography, now a kind of renaissance ne'er-do-well, my mentor had a talent for both science and art and liked to put things in a clear, straightforward, and vivid way. He taught me that without the human world, "heaven" or the spiritual life is just a dream. And without heaven or spirituality, the human world is a nightmare. The two hold each other in balance. This is the middle way. Not getting stuck in a dream, not getting stuck in a nightmare, but fully and completely waking up right at the zero point where the two meet—dream and nightmare, pray and play, pleasure and worship, Friday-night fucking and Sunday-morning sacraments.

One evening, as we slugged a bottle of Jack Daniel's in my junky Ford Festiva (the Losermobile, he called it) outside of Rage, a gay dance club, my mentor leaned over to kiss me. Looking back, I think I handled the situation pretty well.

"Raaaaaaaaaaaaaaaaaaaaaaaape!" I cried, pushing him away.

"Look," I said, thereby inaugurating my long-standing tradition of expressing affection for him by insulting his looks, "if I was going to cross over it'd be for a man much less ravaged by age and far less barrel-chested. Think: a young Brad Pitt, not a latter-year Marlon Brando."

I watched him with unswerving intensity after this episode. Bone weary of Hollywood—where you don't grow up, you just grow old—I was in the market for a whole new way of life, and this was the test. What emerged was a portrait of someone who, while filled with desire, could take it or leave it when it came to seeing this desire through. He struck me as being alive and vital, not desperate and exploitive. My sense was that depending on the circumstances, he could head in either direction—affirming or denying a given desire—with equal commitment, putting his ass on the line one way or another and then experiencing completely whatever outcome fate handed him. He harbored zero regrets about anything. Life was its own reward, its own end, its own religion. He did not manipulate life for religious ends or manipulate religion to get what he wanted out of life.

In other words, he wasn't hung up on the idea of jumping my bones. And you know what? Thank God for that. If I had seen, beneath his insistence that egoism is the root of all suffering, a perverted little self-serving homunculus aiming its greedy mitts for my crotch, the whole house of cards that was my precious, tenuous foundation in Zen practice would have collapsed. I would have gone back to alternately sleeping with strangers and embarking on bouts of pseudospiritual celibacy—in other words, stagnating in indulgence or abstinence. But instead of treating me differently because he didn't get the relationship that he desired, he responded with genuine sincerity to the relationship that we had. He had done so much work on himself during his decade at the monastery that it was less as if he'd "built up" some special spiritual practice than simply removed layers of ego. He could get out of the way and let our relationship be what it was: mentor/mentee instead of lovers.

This is when he became the spiritual love of my life: when through him I rediscovered the innocent hope that "love" as an experience might actually be more vast than just our private human desires and designs. I desperately wanted to learn more about Zen practice and this egoless love, and I knew that he could help me, if his intentions were pure. And the purity of his intentions depended somewhat on mine. Was I clear about what I wanted from him? Clear about who I was? About my sexuality? Because if there was room to play . . . he wanted to play.

"I'm just not wired that way."

This was the last sentence of a long explanation I gave him after refusing his second and final pass at me. I was able to look into his eyes with great clarity that morning, for I had just passed through the most eye-openingly intense three days of my life, which had climaxed with my questioning my commitment to living itself.

We'd just shared a breakfast of waffles at Joey's Café. It was drizzling rain, and the crepe paper streamers from yesterday's Gay Pride parade were crying colorfully down telephone poles all around us. "I respect your wiring," he explained, "but I'm crushing on you. And when I crush, I crush hard." He thought it would be better if we stopped seeing each other for a while. That was the last I'd seen of him, walking oppositely down the misty Santa Monica Boulevard . . . disappearing behind a crowd of gay men wearing only Scottish kilts and top hats.

We'd spent the whole summer apart. Then he'd called that fateful Sunday morning with the four one one on my gay-porn career.

THE PUMPED-UP, RIPPED, SHAVED, AND HUNG HOTTIE-GAY VERSION OF . . . *WHO?*

My mentor and I left Plummer Park and marched in silence down Santa Monica Boulevard toward the Circus of Books to rent my alleged flesh flick. Ironically, I had wandered into this same establishment a few years earlier with Tessa, my sweet-as-apple-pie college girlfriend. "Oh, look, a bookstore! How charming!" we'd said, our conservative Catholic smiles dimming as we took in the display of Tom of Finland coffee table art books, with those handlebar-mustachioed caricatures, their preposterously beefy upper halves clad in studded leather jackets and sailor's caps, their naked ass cheeks bulbous and gleaming like matching fishbowls.

So much had changed since then! Living in WeHo, LA's gay district, for several years now, I'd become more than just queer friendly. I was like Kevin Costner in *Dances with Wolves*. I'd been adopted into the tribe. I'd gone native. (Marginalized outsiders both, my gays and Costner's braves had much in common, and not just that they both liked to wear buttless leather chaps and run around shirtless.) I had learned their customs, manners, and ways, their special language. ("Oh, my *gwad*, you are *not* wearing that shirt out! It has an *armadillo* on it." "It's a *turtle*!") I felt more at home around them than I did with my own people. Yes, I was basically gay, except for one minor detail: I did not like men sexually. Now even that was being called into question—and in a big way.

Cut to: the previous evening—Saturday night—twelve hours before my mentor called and got all *j'accuse* about *Glory Holes*. He was recouping in the Hollywood sex spa lounge, twiddling his thumbs while ogling his next prey, when suddenly something caught his eye. It was the big screen TV. He got up and walked over, his towel dropping, and with every step he took his jaw dropped wider . . . and wider . . . until he was standing inches from the TV, his penis practically poking it. There I was, on-screen, the guy who twice rejected his sexual advances on the grounds of irreversible heterosexuality: boxed in by a gang of supersized African-American studs. We were not discussing the Obama presidency.

"How could you not tell me about this part of your life?" His tone was an icy quiver.

"*Why?* Because today is the first I've ever heard of it!"

"Listen," he said, yanking open the bell-jingly door to Circus of Books: "It. Was. You."

Half an hour later we were side by side on the tatty burgundy love seat in my bachelor pad. "Two," he said, as the movie title came up on my TV screen. "It's *Glory Holes of Chicago Two*. Apparently there was a first one. This is the sequel. But you already know all of this, I'm sure." He shot me a withering glance as the synth-and-bass chords of the opening sound track announced themselves over the subtitle, *The Wind Isn't the Only Thing Blowing in Chicago*.

"I trust you," I said.

Here I was, entertaining the potential veracity of an accusation that I knew beyond a shadow of a doubt to be utterly ludicrous. I was taking the classic Kierkegaardian "leap of faith" in my spiritual teacher. Why, then, did I suddenly grow queasy, convinced that this was all a complex seduction ruse with the aim of getting me to watch gay porn, something he'd dreamed up with Mitch, his redheaded, steroid-inflated, gay-lothario friend? Much of their relationship consisted of the two of them sitting around trying to convince themselves that half of the planet was gay. I could just hear Mitch crudely holding forth: "Ha! Jack acts like he's Mr. Red-White-and-Blue, but he's pinker than a baboon's butt in heat. Get 'im to watch a little *Glory Holes of 'Chi Town'* and his ankles'll be behind his ears before you can say *The Crying Game*."

The American Buddhist landscape was littered with the whitened bones of spiritual lives slaughtered at the altar of the teacher's sexual ego. Would my nascent practice be the next casualty?

My mentor grabbed the remote. What passed were several uncomfortable moments of naked muscled men performing conjugal calisthenics at ridiculously fast speeds, their every imaginable positions changing every three seconds to form a kind of leaping, flailing, high-fiving, cartwheeling, multilimbed man-beast, a fucktopus, born from and collapsing into bedsheets.

How can a guy I adore more than any girlfriend or lover I've ever had be this *wrong about me?* I wondered. *Hell, he knows me better than I know myself!*

Then again, that wasn't saying much. My behavior over the past year had become increasingly bizarre, even volatile. It was as though something were trying to crawl out from the inside, a new life of some kind, and if it had to tear me apart to make its entrance, so be it. I had reached a crucial turning point in my adulthood, which felt decades in the making. ("Saturn returning, my friend," my mentor, the amateur astrologer, assured me. "You hit your late twenties and some serious shit starts going on in your charts.") Whoever I'd been running away from all of these years was finally catching up with me. And I was capable, it seemed, of doing just about anything to avoid facing him, facing *myself*—including, unfathomably enough, the near galactic self-deception it would take to remain unconscious of my own starring role in the *Glory Holes* franchise.

But I'm totally not *gay*, I reassured myself.

And my reply: *Then what are you? Who are you?*

I had no answer. *Then how can you say what or who you are* not?

My mentor's index finger rose from the fast-forward button as he turned to me, his expression so very "the butler in the den with a candlestick." The characters on-screen resumed their aerobic erotica at a regular pace. This was apparently my scene.

And so we both turned to the TV to have a look.

When I saw him, the first words out of my mouth were: "If my family ever saw this, I'd be dead."

On-screen, on his knees, wearing the same perky sailor's hat I often donned in gay clubs as a joke, was my mother's firstborn son—the guy on my driver's license—the angular chin and aquiline nose of the very same profile I used to study with two mirrors back in high school while gauging the growth of my mullet. He had my high-cheekboned, wide-eyed, slightly terrified grin, a cross between a young Matthew Broderick and Pee-wee Herman, I'm sorry to say.

But the strangest thing to me was watching him move. He was alive, this me that was not me—this Bizarro Jack—my doppel-gängbanger—alive and out there somewhere, identical to me in every possible way, doing all the usual stuff: perambulating with pals down some waterfront boardwalk on the weekends, buying milk from Trader Joe's, thanking our creator for gifting him with fabulously photogenic genitals, and so on.

I was beginning to feel dizzy. I didn't even know where to start. "No way those thighs are mine," I stammered.

"Three sets of squats three days a week for six months and them thighs are yours, partner," my mentor shot back.

Daniel Reed had my sinewy limbs, dimples, auburn eyes, protruding collarbone, carefully tousled brown hair—he thrust his hips like me, moaned in my voice. I would probably even have engaged in telefellatio like this guy: sort of sarcastic about it, but he wasn't stopping either. No doubt he needed the paycheck, an exact description of me at all of my day jobs.

My jaw was on the lime-green carpet. "He's the pumped-up, ripped, shaved, and hung hottie-gay version of *me,*" I blurted.

"Dude, he *is* you."

And who am I? I wondered, studying the TV. I'd been asking myself this question for years. *Is* this *who I am?*

Daniel Reed was my Rome. All paths led to him. (Led *inside* him, from the looks of it.)

Like a man on his sexual deathbed, my whole eccentric fornicatory history flashed before my eyes just then, as the probable culmination of that history jiggled and hammered and *yee-haw*ed on the TV before me. I took insta-stock of myself, for to understand how I'd gotten here—on-screen, lathered in baby oil, the eye of the pornado, my orifices the vanishing point to which the viewer's vision was drawn—I needed to look unflinchingly at who I had been: to follow the trail of used condoms, to retrace every single step that had led me to the brink of this yawning abyss that was *Glory Holes.*

Part Two

THE NERVOUS BREAKTHROUGH

Alas, I wish I'd met my mentor at an earlier age, long before I fell in love for the first time. His corrupting influence would have been good for me. I spent my sheltered Midwestern adolescence in relative Catholic purity, save one or two quixotic episodes wherein I tried to bury my face in my own crotch. (I was unsuccessful, as evidenced by the fact that I am not still hidden away in my childhood bedroom today.) *No sex till marriage!* was my mantra. *Hold out for that one true love.*

Then I met my one true love in college—and I had a nervous breakdown. (It involved a very dark night of the soul and then a lot of nudity in a lot of public places; it was a time of much streaking and many dick tricks.) The problem was, I knew how to withhold love but not how to give it. Mine was a negative morality.

Constantly hedging my bets against sin, it had never occurred to me that I would one day have to take a chance on love. I did not know that there are consequences for denying your desires just as there are consequences for indulging them.

Here I had done the "right thing" all eighteen of my cherry-cheeked, psalm-soaked years. I had said no to my high school sweetie's cone-shaped breasts; no to marijuana, alcohol, cigarettes, swearing; no to that violent, sexually aggressive, totally awesome N.W.A. album—*no* to every temptation that came along. "No" was all my heart knew. It turned on the word. Now that I'd fled Wisconsin for the University of Dallas and met Tessa, a Southern charmer who, upon second or third viewing (I can't remember which), caused me to walk into a plate glass door and crack it down the middle, I had no idea how to say "Yes!"

The moon and stars canopied above us as we stole through the dorm attic hatch, my first true love turned to me with those Irish freckles and soft brown eyes. And I sat on the gravel roof beside her—this pint-sized Texas spitfire, radiating heat waves and grinning pinkly—like a complete moron: paralyzed, terrified, a flopping fish in the net of overthinking. The count mounted: one day . . . two . . . a week . . . a month. And still I hadn't worked up the chutzpah to kiss her. It was ridiculous. Her vicious little cabal of dorm gossips were all taking bets on when it would finally happen.

I dropped to my knees in the Saint Aquinas chapel every single night for two weeks straight and dialed the divine Dr. Phil for guidance, implicitly blaming him for my woes: *You created my pitiful self-consciousness and nerve-wracked sexuality with your religious rules and prohibitions—do something about it!* The Almighty, however, had become this crushing, Godnormous version of my fucked-up, inescapable self. Where he picked up and I left off inside my tortured head, I hadn't a clue, and it seemed not to matter. Sunday mass had become an exercise in emptiness, little more than crisp-collared, frosty-haired socializing and clock-punching mob prayer. Silence and ritual? Try hullabaloo and habit. I studied the pews bitterly: *packed to the gills and empty as hell.*

Here I had lived a "good" life, and yet it had not assured me of a *better* one. I was not coming out ahead. In fact, I was handicapped in the realm of love. Guard the soul too closely, I realized, and the heart shuts down and the loins freeze up. Hawkeye your natural instincts for too long, and they burrow deep within and hibernate. After a while you can't coax them out of hiding.

But for now, I was merely uptight. Poor Father Rick, that cool, prethirty priest with his neatly trimmed beard and handsome glasses. "Tell me honestly, friend, what are you feeling?" he asked in the confessional one Sunday. "I kept my dick in my pants and wound up with a stick up my ass?" I snarled, tired of his theological runaround. "That was the trade-off?"

The problem and its manifestations were not merely sexual or romantic, not for a philosophy major like me. They were metaphysical and persisted long after I finally planted one hell of a kiss on Tessa. The breaking point came on Christmas Eve my sophomore year as I struggled to keep awake during a midnight mass held at Saint Peter's Basilica in Rome, where my Catholic college boasted a campus. Suddenly, right in the heart of Christendom, where I was supposed to be fortifying my faith, I had the eerie insight that church was actually a kind of "spiritual contraceptive" masquerading as fertile ground for the religious experience. As the birth control pill tricks the woman's body into thinking it's pregnant so that it never actually gets pregnant, our heavily ornamented and razzle-dazzle religious ceremonies were duping us into believing that we had a burgeoning spiritual life within, when in reality they were the very "piety prophylactics" keeping us as barren as Michelangelo's lifelike, yet lifeless, marble Madonna a few hundred feet away.

"*My morality is actually a kind of selfishness,*" I scribbled in my journal on Rome's Spanish Steps, the ink still tear blotched, last

I checked. "'*Saving myself* a way of hoarding myself, of keeping myself to myself. Trying to do the right thing*," I concluded, "*can be a subtle form of egomania based on fear.*"

It took a long time, however, for my actual life to catch up with these antireligious revelations. I talked pretty tough about the need to jettison the God ideal wholesale and to be free from the tendentious Abrahamic religious legacy, but when it came right down to it, I still wasn't nailing my girlfriend. TRUE LOVE WAITS, the campaign for teen chastity goes. Well, if you wait too long it'll pass you right by. First love has a shelf life: Tessa and I never consummated ours. Instead, after four collegiate years of doing "everything but," we moved to Los Angeles together and then suffered one of those endless, agonizing Breakups on the Installment Plan: a little more weeping, quarreling, and mutual exhaustion every month. And when we kissed and touched again, it was like missing the due date for a break-up bill, making us pay doubly from the humble purses of our broken hearts the next month, when we choked down a quiet cup of our favorite peppermint tea together with absolutely nothing left to say.

Suddenly one Sunday morning, as I rolled over in bed and remembered all over again that my Southern sweetie was nowhere near and never would be, I realized that we were more broken up than together, and that last flicker of hope and love went dark.

In its place, an insight sparked hotly: *I am so damn tired of being good.*

Was I celebrating or mourning the end of our relationship that evening when I stole through the iron door of the Tokyo Goodtime Massage Parlor in the Valley for a hand job? And weeks later, when a visiting high school friend whispered "Fuck me" as we fooled around drunkenly on my futon, I decided *You know what? I'm gonna do just that.* The instant I entered her I felt the quantum difference between doing "everything but" and doing *it.* It was all downhill from there.

From the very first stirrings of my sexual conscience, I knew that my bedroom ethics and my religious beliefs were inextricably linked. To give up the ideal of waiting until marriage to have sex was tantamount to losing my entire Catholic faith. And that's what happened: I got laid at age twenty-four and went from being a bad Catholic to being an ex-Catholic.

I began to look for models for a new way of life.

Driving the streets of LA alone at night for hours, I listened to a local college radio station, which replayed 1960s lectures on Zen by the silvery-voiced English-American icon Alan Watts. His accent was a tonic: *"The difficulty for most of us in the modern world is that the old-fashioned idea of God has become incredible or implausible. . . . What you are basically, deep, deep down, far, far in, is simply the fabric and structure of existence itself. . . . Ego is a social institution with no physical reality. The ego is simply your symbol of yourself. . . . Saints need sinners."* This eventually precipitated a weekend trip to the downtown LA library, with its movie-set-worthy book stacks and vaulted ceilings, where I sat mesmerized by Buddhist volumes in the Eastern Traditions section. As a historical-spiritual figure, the Buddha rivaled any I'd run across while studying the great books of the Western tradition. I researched his life meticulously, the idea being that I would scribble out a movie script inspired by his spiritual adventures. But I couldn't get a handle on the Buddha as a character. Instead of drawing conclusions about him, my investigation inspired ever more questions. And the primary question I asked of this mercurial mythical figure was the same question I was asking myself at that time: *Who are you?*

Here's what I found.

Twenty-six-hundred years prior to my lackluster deflowering, a spoiled young trust-funder, Prince Shakyamuni Gautama—the eventual Buddha, or "awakened one"—tried something like sex, drugs, and rock 'n' roll at his childhood palace, the ancient Indian version of the Playboy Mansion. Then he scrapped all of that for the life of a devout ascetic, fleeing the city for the forest, where he tacked 180 degrees and began praying feverishly, starving himself, wrenching his frame into tortured yoga positions, and perhaps worst of all, forgoing the company of women. What he ultimately discovered was that a life of pure denial or negation, the strictly "religious" life, was no more the answer to our suffering than a life of unrestrained indulgence or affirmation. Prudery and debauchery were both extremes, dead ends born from the illusion of an ego consciousness or "self" that exists in and of itself, apart from everything else, a soul or supernatural thumbprint to identify us as the same wearisome individuals for all eternity.

In other words, Shakyamuni Buddha went to the very end of human thinking and experience. What he found when he got there was that he himself was missing. That is, the definitive, fixed "This is *me*" that he thought he was seeking was nowhere to be found. What he discovered instead is that the entity that arises and in due course winds up on one's driver's license is a kind of composite relationship or dynamic intersection between a trillion shifting boundaries, inner and outer (time, space, hair color, memory, neural impulses, sunbeams, beefsteak, and on and on), with a little provisional flag sticking up out of it called *I Am*. For the Buddha, any attempt to pin yourself down as anything whatsoever, a hedonist or a moralist, for example, is sure to fail. By the time you've calculated the boundaries that define you, they've been rezoned by the worlds around and within you.

I came of age in a Christian culture, where all spiritual teachings were eternally anthropomorphized in the form of God, the Supreme Being, and saints and angels, the subsupremes. Right on up to the top—it was all "selves" the whole way, like the stack of infinite turtles upon the backs of which the earth was once presumed to rest. It never even occurred to me to take, as Dogen Zenji put it, the "backward step" and question what "the self" actually was. I just knew that I had to get mine right. I spent my teens and college years trying to find myself through religious morality and philosophy. That failed, and so I packed off to Southern California and attempted to lose myself via various Bacchanalian adventures while simultaneously trying to invent myself, to become famous and successful, as though getting others to believe I was "somebody" would make up for the fact that I had no idea who I was myself. Oh, those lost LA years! I variously tried to solve myself through psychology, perfect myself through learning, conjure myself through creativity, forge myself through ambition, transcend myself through mysticism. . . . Yet the part of me that happened to be pushing the rest of me into alignment at any given time was always pushing itself out of alignment in the process, so that I was never balanced as a human being.

What the hell was I missing here? What was I getting wrong? It seemed that the more attention I gave to getting myself and my life right, the more savagely I sabotaged that very project. Yet every time I swore off the search altogether, the call to find myself and my life purpose swelled in aching, unbearable proportion to the strength of my refusal to heed it.

Jean-Paul Sartre had it exactly wrong. Hell is not other people. Hell is when you both cannot find and cannot escape yourself.

My head was hell.

So there I sat, on the filthy carpet in my WeHo apartment, one 3 A.M., alone as usual, high on weed, trying to release tension by furiously massaging my own shoulders, kneading my own knots, a venture by definition as equally toilsome as pleasurable—that is, another perfect dead end—and me thinking, yet unable to stop, *You can never hit your own spot, baby! Never, never, never!* I was losing my mind—yet this was preferable to being crushed within the teeth of its viciously circular machinations.

Around this time I wrote a short Kafkaesque film about a tarantula who is enchanted by his own best asset and winds up spraying web right into his own face, blinding and suffocating himself. So like the spider myself, I couldn't see that its demise was the perfect metaphor for where I was in my life: spun up in and stuck on the productions of my self. As such, I had no clue how to enter into a genuine, fulfilling relationship with, say, a Match.com date or, for that matter, the slew of goldfish that went water moldy and belly-up under my watch. Rather, I could be found, on any given weekend, cruising for "queen bees" (female friends of gay men) at strobe-lit LA circuit parties while dropping several hits of Ecstasy and then waking up sobbing in my closet, having used up my entire weekly quota of serotonin in one night.

As I buried myself in research on the Buddha's life, I was suffering most acutely from the soul sickness he diagnosed as egoism, or an unconditional acceptance of one's self as the center of the universe. To wit, my single most pellucid memory from this period is also the most symbolic: I am snorting something that has no business being up my nose in such quantities and then pressing up against a stranger within the reflective silver surfaces of a fancy club toilet stall. I remember feeling something wet and warm creeping between our interlocked faces, pulling away, and seeing rivulets of blood cascading down the face before me. And this person across from me, now a human being, no longer just a hookup, looking back at me and seeing the exact same thing—and me seeing my horrifying self in this person's widening eyes, black blood pumping out of my nostrils like oil from a well (I was so fucking high).

And so, my story is the reverse of Shakyamuni Buddha's: I started off pure and *then* went to hell in a manbag.

But really, the saddest thing was I couldn't even go down the toilet properly. I was being outcrazied by a Zen Buddhist monk. For every one-night-stand story that I greedily shared with my mentor, he'd come back at me with a gay-pool-orgy saga that went down at some film producer's postmodern steel-and-stone SuperVilla in the Hills. ("By 3 A.M. the hot tub looked like egg drop soup!") Compared with my spiritual mentor, I was Mother Teresa.

"I'm twice the mess you are and only half as naughty. What's your secret?" I asked, shoving an imaginary microphone in his face.

At first his insistence on the core Buddhist doctrine of *anatta*, "not self," had the air of new age bullshit. I gripped my skull. What did he mean "*Where are you?*" I was right there, in front of him, with the Corona bottle and purple lei. "Where?" he would demand, touching his head and heart. "Your noodle? Which thought? Your ticker? Which feeling? Which part of which feeling? Beginning, middle, end? Point to the place—*touch* it—where the world ends and you begin. Prove to me that the boundary separating you from the entire universe is anything but totally arbitrary and ephemeral."

"I am my mind," I declared proudly, gesturing in the direction of my face with the beer bottle.

"Then don't you think you'd have more control over it? Your eyes have shot to the door three times in the last minute to see if any hotties have walked in. Okay? Don't tell me that was conscious. You can't *catch* yourself in the act of *being* yourself," he explained. "The more you apply the instrument of discovery, the more the object of inquiry evaporates. It's like trying to learn the true nature of water using fire as your tool, or vice versa."

This has the ring of truth, I thought, and listened to him patiently explain it again and again, in coffee shops, bars, and dance clubs (anywhere but his Bare Bones *zendo,* as I was more interested in hearing about Zen than practicing it). Then one morning, as I absently brushed my teeth while studying my nose hairs in the mirror, his mumbo jumbo clicked into place, like the tumblers on a lock. *A-ha!* I thought, speeding to a breakfast joint in Echo Park. *I get it!*

I carefully unveiled my fresh insight into *anatta*/not self over poached eggs. My mentor slowly rubbed his temples with all ten fingers.

"If there's six routes to wrong, you'll find a seventh. As usual, you misconstrue everything I say. Miss Construe!" He had alighted upon one of his many forgettable puns. "That's what we're going to start calling you. You've made a *self* out of *not self,* knucklehead!"

His eyelids clasped, remained dead for an instant, then sprang open. Like a man descending from a very great interior height, so that he might level his eyes at the spiritual dwarf sitting across from him, he laid it on me, whispering over the din of utensils, mood music, and laughter: "You know what you need to figure out, Jack?"

"What do I need to figure out?" I was no longer listening. I wanted to already know. I didn't want to *learn.* My trio of fatal flaws was classically American: I cared more about success than growth, more about being first than being right, and more about being right right away than discovering something new.

"Before I figured this out, I was just like you, Miss Construe," he said.

"What am I, anyway? That's the million-dollar question these days. If you've got the answer, breakfast is on me."

"Selfish. That's what you are."

I moved my mouth quickly: "Yes, but I forgive myself for this, and that's the important thing." I glanced away, but he could probably see from my deflating profile that he'd struck the mark.

"And you're going to remain selfish and miserable and alone until you figure something out," he persisted. "In Zen, the answer and the problem are always one. So what you need to figure out is how to make the cause of your separation *from* the world around you the means for your connection *to* the world around you."

"I'll get right on that."

But I was off and running—in the wrong direction, as usual. "Not self." That was my new shtick. At the time, aside from being a failed screenwriter, a failed novelist, a failed poet, a failed short story writer, and a failed playwright, I was also trying my hand and failing at stand-up comedy. I was supposedly using art to try to find myself, but it was more like I was trying to find myself so that I could use it in my art. Anything that happened in my life, great or small, I tried to whore it onto the page or stage. Inspired by my self-confirmed insight into not self, my stand-up routine centered on negating or making fun of myself. It was pitiful. After a particularly gruesome showing on open mike Sunday at Peterson's Coffee, a smartly dressed Jewish man in wire-rim glasses and a yarmulke approached. The crowd of comics parted. I was ecstatic. A Hollywood agent, and he chose me! He took out his card.

"Call me, we'll talk."

My comic peers circled, and we read the card together (I still have it somewhere): DR. JACOB COHEN, LICENSED THERAPIST/ MENTAL HEALTH PROFESSIONAL.

Here was my creative process: I've failed to do a stand-up comedy routine making fun of myself, so I'll do a stand-up comedy routine about how I've failed to do a stand-up comedy routine making fun of myself. After all, you should create art based on what you know, and what I knew best was being a failure. That failed, however, and so I took it one step further and did a routine making fun of how I failed to do a routine making fun of the routine where I made fun of myself. I even held up the card of one Dr. Jacob Cohen, licensed therapist/mental health professional. See? I'm a failure.

How far can you go with this?

If by far you mean how far down, the answer is pretty far.

I couldn't stop the free fall. I was trying to get to the bottom of myself, and I thought that one did this by hitting rock bottom. À la the avant-garde, envelope-pushing hijinks of the comic Andy Kaufman, minus the wit or courage, I developed a stupefyingly insensitive onstage persona called the me-tard. "I'm stoooopid with myself," it began, as I crossed my eyes and repeatedly slapped my cheeks with both hands. Yes, you are, read the sagging faces in the audience. I was in the Belly Room at the Comedy Store, where all the edgy comics try out new material. They were drumming their Doc Marten boots on the floor impatiently. Several famous faces gleamed out at me from the crowd. Mitzy Shore, the owner of the club, was on deck and watching. Somehow I'd gotten five minutes on a great night, my big shot, and I was bombing more brutally than the Luftwaffe. The dreaded red penlight dot appeared from the back row, indicating that my time was up. But I did not return the mike to its stand. I scanned the front row and singled out a local fixture in the LA open mike night comedy scene. I do not recall what I said. I just remember assaulting him with a comical fury totally unlike anything anyone in that club has seen before or since. Some of it was very funny. It was almost as though I had found my voice. I took all of that rage and hatred I had been directing toward myself for the last year and verbally beat this slightly crazy and probably homeless man to within an inch of his life.

He had a small wire cart on wheels that he used to carry around his few belongings. I remember his face—he was a black man, older than most of us comics by decades, with wild, springy hair and big white glasses with no lenses—as he stared at me with a kind of confused anguish. Then he got up and smiled and bowed a little to the crowd, who cheered for him a little, and slowly dragged that squeaky cart behind him as he left the room.

No one was really very impressed by my act, which ran about seven minutes longer than the allotted five, but I had this strange feeling come over me, to where I didn't care anymore. I just didn't care about anything or anyone. I wasn't a fool. I had made a fool of someone else instead. That was all that mattered. I left the club to scattered applause, went out back behind the parking lot Dumpster, and threw up the pair of Jack and Sevens I'd purchased earlier per the club's two-drink minimum for open mikers. (Yes, you must pay for this privilege of sucking ass publicly.)

You just get to that point where you don't want to be the fool anymore. You'll do anything to succeed. This, I thought, is how true assholes are born. And I don't want to be an asshole. I don't want to live like this anymore. And then it hit me: *I don't know if I want to live* at all *anymore.*

There comes a point when you cross the line from merely *thinking* about killing yourself, which I'd done a lot of, to actually *considering* killing yourself. And you know that you've crossed this line the moment you realize that this line exists to be crossed. This insight came to me around midnight, after I'd made a mess of a snack in bed and was suddenly too exhausted to go get a rag and clean up after myself. I felt a quickening, the satanic fetus of suicide forming fingernails and eyelids, seizing control from within. Potential suicide abortifacients: my mom and pops. I just couldn't get their imagined faces out of my head the moment they would receive the phone news of my abrupt halt on this planet, they who had embodied my arising on it. They would go to their graves with the lead of my self-slaughter running thick through their veins, their hearts a pair of matching stones. This was one very strong reason not to kill myself. But did I have a reason *to live*?

I remembered a recent conversation with my mentor. We were sitting in the plump, red-vinyl-covered booths at a slick retro diner eating fifteen-dollar buffalo burgers. Vintage rock boomed brightly from the Wurlitzer. The waitresses wore poodle skirts and the waiters were rocking checkered button-down shirts. *God they look like idiots,* I thought. The wretchedness I felt about spending so much money on a cheeseburger made the meat taste like shit in my mouth, and I hated myself for this. I was tired of eating canned food from the Dollar Store because I was too broke to be healthy; tired of being rejected by women who couldn't hold a candle to the college girlfriend I'd dumped but couldn't get over; tired of looking around and seeing that in every category that mattered—money, love, power, you name it—the brain-dead, soulless pricks were winning by a wide margin. Amid all of this fifties finery, I turned to my mentor and confessed that so much of what people consider to be "classically American" just made me want to put one of my father's high-caliber handguns to my head and squeeze the trigger. I said this casually, but I meant it. I remember being amazed that he picked up on this. In fact, I didn't know how serious I actually was *until* he picked up on it.

He put down his sandwich and fixed me from far behind the bottomless waters of those alternately icy and warm eyes and paused carefully. "Do it," he said, "and somehow, somewhere, in *some way,* you will have to face it all over again, whatever you were running away from in this life."

He blew through his straw and shot the wrapper at me. "There is just no way to escape this world except by goin' through it, my friend."

I laughed at this memory in my darkened bedroom, and somehow this loosened me up enough just to lie very quietly in my crumb-riddled bed, in a state halfway between total fatigue and incurable insomnia, which gradually transmogrified into supine *zazen* meditation. This was the first time I had really "sat"—even though I was lying down. And so I stayed, for hours and hours, following my breath as it entered and left what felt like that little funeral plot of my chest, the eternal LA traffic murmuring neurotically just beyond my window.

There are moments of levity in our lives, so that no matter how big a failure we are, no matter how rotten things have gotten, we can still laugh or experience joy or great love. These moments eventually come around, no matter how goddamned miserable our lives are in the meantime. This is the human spirit. I felt it, lying in bed that evening, something transcending all of my problems and all of my sins and all of my failings as a man. I felt my birthright as a human being. Regardless of what society thought about me, or even what I thought about myself, I felt the human spirit alive within me. This, I realized, is what I truly wanted to be—infused with this spirit. A conduit for it. Not a famous writer or stand-up comedian. Not "somebody." Not a soul. Not a saint. Not a sinner. Not even a god. Just open to the unfixed and inexhaustible wellspring of the human spirit.

My last thought on that longest day of my life was that I didn't want to have to be funny anymore. I just wanted to laugh freely again.

In my next memory from this strange week, I am cross-legged on a moist and grassy hillside. My mentor is beside me. We are outside the gorgeous Getty Museum in the Santa Monica foothills. The sun is bright and balmy, as though burning strictly for our leisure, the air freshly scrubbed from the previous night's rare rainfall. Throngs of the racially and culturally diverse promenade past us. After seventy-two hours of intense introspective lockdown in my apartment, I am in desperate need of the kind of vivifying visual tonic that the Los Angeles population so famously affords.

"She's hot," I said, as a tatted punk rock girl sauntered by in ragged fishnet stockings.

"So is he," my mentor said, pointing to her tank-topped rockabilly boyfriend.

So it is with us. A good-looking couple strolls past, and our attentions are momentarily split per our preferences. We sat there for the better half of a day as he taught me Zen ogling.

"Sit up . . . no, like this: straight but not rigid. Don't lean in with your head. That means you're thinking too much. No, no, don't puff out your chest: don't force it. Nope, don't slouch forward either, like you've got a divining rod in your shorts and it's just found a watering hole. Expand *out*, at your diaphragm. Lead with your *hara*, your breathing center—your gut."

I puffed out my belly and made my concentration face. "You look like you're trying to move your bowels," he said. "Straight guys always have trouble with this. You have to 'bottom' for the world around you. Let it in baby! Get knocked up! Use your body and mind as a vessel to express what's outside you. Throw your self away and *become* somebody else—striding along there in his skinny jeans, like a little runway model," he said, nodding to a young man in black eyeliner gliding by as though on a cloud of fabulousness. "Or sweating religiously inside her burka," he whispered, as a Muslim woman humped along with all the weight of her culture packed inside her heavy black shoes.

In bleak contrast to, say, a monastery, everyone in Los Angeles either is beautiful or dresses really cool—one or the other or both. Mahatma Gandhi himself would have had a hard time keeping his eyes down on a typical crowded LA street corner. And so, as the impossibly attractive and the homely-but-intriguing streamed by our park bench, it occurred to me that for all of my struggles all of these years to "find myself," the world around me was delivered free of charge right to my senses every instant of every day. Thinking, not to mention seeking, took work. But perception was effortless. Sound entered my ears and light slipped into my eyes and wind kissed my skin wholly without my will or permission. How could I have taken this miracle—and what other word was there for what was so eminently natural as to miss detection   for granted all of these years?

"On some fundamental level I'm designed to be open and receptive," it dawned on me, "to let the world in."

"You're built to love, my friend," my mentor said, "but you get in your own way."

About forty minutes later, after my mentor and I hugged our good-byes outside the Getty, I pulled the Losermobile over to the shoulder of Fairfax and San Vicente and just started sobbing. I was sobbing so hard I could barely keep my head above the steering wheel.

"It's so beautiful."

I said it over and over, a hundred times. *"It's so beautiful, so beautiful, so beautiful. . . ."*

Moments earlier this goofy disco song had come on 104.3, even though it was 5:30-ish and not at all noontime disco hour. There were no lyrics near this forgotten classic's nonsensical climax save a chorus of Alice in Wonderlandian incantations. At one time a large number of professional singers had gathered in some shag-carpeted seventies studio to tap their seven-inch platforms and finger the chest fur blasting out from their open-collared leisure suits while wailing in unison *"Funky*

wunky wonky woo, chubba lubba babba loo, nocka wonka wonka,
wonka wonka wunka wooooo!"

"I was crying and laughing at the exact same time as this crazy song just went right into me," I debriefed my mentor that evening, at the site of our most profound *dialogue interactifs*: le butt hut. "It was just so funny and so beautiful that this wacky music could get inside me and tickle me from the inside out. That things from the outside could travel to the inside of me, disappear somewhere in there, and then come back out again through my body, completely transformed into tears or humming or a little dance of my limbs to the *babalaboooo*s, I said, doing a little seated jig."

"Well, I would have put it differently," he said, rolling his eyes. "But anyway, it sounds like you finally got out of your own way and let the world in a little bit. Touché," he said, raising his margarita.

With the chink of our glasses came the perfect moment to debut a line I'd thought of earlier and saved for him: "It was like the wall of ego that's always separated me from the world suddenly disolved and became the very bridge uniting me to it."

"What do I always tell you?" He had that look in his eye.

"That I'll never truly know if I'm gay until I try it?"

"Besides that. The cause of separation is the means for connection," he said. "The answer and the problem are always one."

I upended my drink. "Okay, so where do we go from here? What's the final take-home, pops?"

He paused for a moment. Not because the answer wasn't there but to get it right, for me.

"Just *give*," he said.

"Give what?"

"Your self. Away."

"To what?"

"To whatever it is you're doing. Doesn't matter. Give yourself completely, every instant, every day; and every act is a holy one, no matter what you're doing. Whether you're on your knees in mass or in the Hollywood sex spa, as long as you're not trying to affirm yourself while you're doing it.

"It's not a practice for children," he stated very carefully. "But it's so damn simple anyone can understand it, including and especially children, and the childlike. Okay," he said, sliding our margaritas aside so that there was a clear path of communication between us, "I'm gonna hit ya with one of my überinsights. Pull down your blast shield, young Skywalker, 'cos this one's bright. You ready?"

I nodded.

"*Don't be selfish.* That's the meaning of life. It's the only real lesson we have to learn here, and the only one that matters. You can officially stop searching now and start putting the principle into practice," he said, handing me the bill.

Shouting there in the grass-hut booth at a tropical-themed bar, high on tequila, on a raucous and rowdy Gay Pride weekend, I experienced my own humble version of what they call in the Zen tradition mind-to-mind transmission. A fancy phrase that simply means that a truth jumps from the teacher's heart to yours, like one candle lighting another. It can be the most benign and seemingly offhanded comment, but if there is a real connection between you two and the groundwork has been laid, that single spark can burn to the ground the vast forest of illusions you've been wandering through your whole life.

Ah, Satori Night Fever! And so, did gamma rays of supernal insight blaze out of my eye sockets just then? Well, no, not exactly. "Hercules," our shirtless waiter in ball-hugger shorts, sidled up and served us another round of drinks with little umbrellas sticking out. Behind him, a table of sweaty falsettos shrieked in unison to Madonna's "Like a Prayer" as he bade me to rub his freshly waxed chest for luck.

"Nipple ripple, nipple ripple!" he cried, flexing his pecs rapid-fire.

"Like an angel flapping her wings," my mentor said.

I watched Hercules's beefy bro boobs jiggle like two molds of

Jell-O in an earthquake, but I did not touch. To the best of my knowledge, this pretty much summed up my gay life: observation, even admiration, but never participation. The following morning, after waffles at Joey's Café, when my mentor would lean in on a street corner and try to kiss me for the second and last time, I would put it thus: "Papi-san, after all I've been through this past week, there's very little I can say with certainty about myself, okay, but I will say this: When it comes to men, sexually? I'm just not wired that way."

A very long, hot, lonesome summer would follow my mentor's ensuing good-bye. I would look into myself repeatedly and be found wanting every time. I would become like the burrito I left on its plate for those three months. First I would rot a little and then grow very hard and very stuck. I would shrivel, discolor, lose any semblance of my former freshness and vitality. I would become something altogether different from what was originally intended. I would become trash, a disposable product of contemporary culture. I would work very little, masturbate a lot, sit on the futon with the shades drawn hoping vainly for something like Stockholm syndrome to set in so that I might finally come to crave the company of my captor, myself. I would attempt to preserve myself through alcohol. I would fail. Further rotting would take out those parts of me, of my heart and soul, the hope organs, which I had, in healthier moments, briefly resuscitated. Finally I would more or less give up on life. This would help a little, but not enough. Further death would be needed. And then somehow, hopefully a full resurrection.

Apparently it wasn't enough just to have a few insights, and a few experiences, and then expect to be able to go back to living my life as I had lived it before. My life, in light of those experiences and insights, was a grotesque joke. It was painful to stay the same—just too damn painful. But it's not like there was some new life ready-made and waiting for me to slip into as I shuffled the old one off like a tattered housecoat. Life-changing insights and experiences do not accessorize the existing life. They alter it for good. That's why they are so rare: not because they are so precious or obscure but because we are so rarely ready for them. "Don't be selfish." A bomb that banal, dropped at just the right moment, completely takes out all existing structures of thought and deed, so that if we wish to stick around and inhabit our same old mind-set and circumstances, we will be doing so atop a pile of scorched rubbish.

I was a ghost, a shape-shifter, *bakemono* in Japanese. I was in between worlds. It was a time of tremendous possibility. But I did not see it that way. I was terrified. I prayed a great deal. I had on my wall a Bass beer–ad poster featuring the black-and-white visage of Friedrich Nietzsche in full-bore contemplation mode. I had a vast, spangling, nearly psychedelic cloth mural dedicated to Our Lady of Guadalupe, crushing the brute animal skull of pig-nosed evil. I had a *thangka* poster of the Bodhisattva of Compassion, Avalokiteshvara, he of the slitted eyes and half smile (like someone, I always thought, secretly releasing a fart in a crowd). My holy trinity. I went before them daily, sometimes hourly, on my knees, my arms open, eyes shut, repeating the help prayer—*Help, help, help . . .* —over and over. Perhaps I said that word ten thousand times that summer. It was cheesy, but I didn't know what else to do. I hated religion as a matter of pride, but you don't go to your knees because you're proud. You go to your knees because you are brought to your knees.

It's not a choice. You go to your knees because you are desperate.

CLINGING TO THE TRUTH BY A SINGLE TOE

I guess knee-based activities were part of my karmic game plan, for at the end of that long, dry summer, as I sat reunited with my mentor in my apartment, my alleged alter ego, Daniel Reed, was on his on the TV before me. Mr. Reed was not praying, though I imagined it was one form of desperation or another that had brought him to his knees, as I had been brought to mine.

But were they *the same knees*?

Were we *the same person*?

I had two competing forms of evidence to work from: one, on the TV before me, which made a pretty compelling case that I needed to change the occupation box on my tax forms to big gay stud. And one haunting my skin from within, an inner certainty about what made my dick tick. Which of these reliable yet opposing witnesses did I believe: my eyes or my heart?

Every few moments during this ordeal I would pause to consider the absolute absurdity of the whole situation. *Are you kidding me? Are you actually unclear as to whether or not you've been moonlighting as a homosexual pornography icon?* I would focus my attention on my sphincter muscles and flex, attempting to "feel around" down there. Any signs of activity? Swelling? Pain? Increased circumference? These are the things you do when not only your sexuality but your actual sex life has suddenly been called into serious question.

And how seriously did I take this question? I can't truly recall. The afternoon is a blur of comic insanity and air so bone-dry and charged you could produce static electricity just by waving your hand through it. What I do recall is that I caught myself wondering how much a thespian in this genre earns and did I perhaps have a stash of hard-earned gay-porn cash stuffed away in a mattress somewhere? I was already practically spending it in my head. *(Certainly I'll need to set some aside for therapy. . . .)* And I remember that I very seriously suspended my belief in my own innocence in light of the evidence; and that I saw the situation entirely through my mentor's eyes, as I no longer trusted my own; and that unless proven otherwise, to his heart's satisfaction, Daniel Reed was . . .

. "*You*," he kept hollering, over and over, jabbing his finger at the TV screen and then back at me. *"He's you, he's you!"* All that was missing was talk show host Jerry Springer mediating between us while the crowd chanted *"Gay-porn-whore! Gay-porn-whore!"* (Or, perhaps just: *"He-ho, he-ho!"*)

And who was I, aside from being a dead ringer for a chap who made his living on all fours with his waxed fanny in the air? I went to a quiet place within, where a review of the grim facts was awaiting me. I was a touch fey, chronically single, and best friends going back to Jason Bennett, at age nine, with a long line of gay guys with whom I behaved like the bitchy, sex-withholding half of a grouchy old married couple. Not surprisingly, everyone from exes to my five siblings openly questioned my sexuality. And I'd been doing just enough drugs at that time to fuzz my grasp on reality even when I wasn't high (it doesn't take much—I have a sensitive constitution). Plus, I was a screenwriter with an over-active imagination—and furthermore, I was not, admittedly, the sanest or most stable person I knew. It was at least *possible* that I had multiple personalities (or at least two: I've never been a good multitasker) leading different lives, one of which was sexual piñata for a melting pot of linebacker-sized dandies. I was having one of those years wherein if I discovered that I was completely and totally insane I would probably have just shrugged and said, "That explains *so much.*"

A potent cocktail of fortuitous but frightening factors in my life—mainly Zen, drugs, and desperation—had led to a gradual blurring of the boundaries between what I'd traditionally consid-ered *I-me-mine* and *you-yours-its*. Until quite recently, I had out-fitted my ontological headquarters—a vast manor built of total self-absorption—with every manner of mirror, wherein I could look at and into myself and see myself reflected back, trillionfold. It was dazzling and distracting. Now I wasn't quite sure who or what this "self" even was. As it turned out, I had built the founda-tion of my identity over a fault line. I discovered this the hard way that Sunday afternoon, as the very pillars and walls of my sexual identity and personal history began to tremble and crack, all of those mirrors crashing down in shards around me.

After several minutes of futilely searching Daniel Reed's muscled torso for a birthmark, a mole, a third nipple, *any*thing, I gave up trying to prove my innocence and slumped on the love seat, letting the gaggle of gays have their way with me on-screen. The TV was like a sacred oracle upon which my soul was laid bare (as the soul usually is when the body sheds clothes). It's one thing to get your philosophical rocks off while half drunk in a cool LA gay bar, mocking your childhood Catholicism now that you've discovered the progressive Buddhist concept of *anatta*/not self. It's quite another to finally realize, with your eyes, mind, and heart, that your most cherished opinions about yourself are ultimately flaccid and worthless, like Daniel Reed at the end of a day's shoot. There was absolutely no idea of myself, great or small, that couldn't be toppled with enough raw evidence: I discovered this bit of truth as raw evidence of my career in celluloid sodomy groaned on the TV before me.

And what did this fact say about my ongoing journey to find, lose, create, invent—to dissect, reject, and protect—myself? Where could this "self" possibly be if it didn't even reside safely somewhere in my own head, heart, and loins, free from outside influence?

My psychological state was beginning to warp and buckle from the sheer intensity of the situation, like the *Millennium Falcon* blasting through the cosmos at warp speed for too long. I was heating up and falling apart inside. I had a vision of my mentor's penis as an umbilical cord, plugged right into me. I was connected to him this way. It's not just that I trusted him more than I trusted myself. Screw *him*. I trusted what *he* trusted. Dammit, I was ready to give myself over to what *he* had given himself to. Which was? It is finally not the who, what, how, where, when, or why that matters, I told myself. If you're fully dissolved, there's no questioner. There's no I. Nothing to be straight, gay, bi.

Deliver me unto and from myself, I thought, turning to my hero. We occupied a moment in time together on the love seat, just a kiss away. He was aimed fully at me, waiting for me to explain myself. Blood faced and furious. A demon-god waving ten billion arms, all of them curling an accusing finger at me.

"Fuck it, man," I finally admitted. "He's me."

But my mentor was not listening.

"Those feet," he exclaimed, "are not yours."

My porn double was on his back now. His feet were in the air, inviting closer examination.

"You've got cute kickers," he said. "Lookit the toes on that guy, yikes."

Mine are geisha feet, slight and delicate, with toes like ten little closed tulips. My on-screen twin, however, looked like he could pick up a tennis racket and play three sets with those ankle claws. I doffed my socks and kicked up my feet, such that I looked like I was taking an air poop.

"His second toe is longer than his big toe, whereas the opposite is true for you," my mentor intoned, a gay Columbo with a foot fetish cracking the case in the final five minutes of the show.

An intense conversation ensued. We both agreed that as opposed to my being a gay-porn star, which was merely unlikely but not impossible, it was just too far-fetched to assume that I was a gay-porn star who also wore prosthetic toes at the time of the shooting—to throw people off if they ever claimed to have seen my body of work.

This was, ultimately, what convinced him: and so too, me. What can I say, the dude knows feet.

Just like that, the air began to cool, oxygen filling the room again. I could hear things. Birds and traffic outside. The blood beating in my temples. My own breath returning to my lungs. I took it in. I hadn't breathed in an hour and a half. The nightmare was over. I had crawled into—through—and out the other end of the Great Asshole of Ultimate Doubt and Confusion. I needed a drink.

"I feel like the universe is trying to tell me something today," I said, burying my warm, wet face in my hands.

"Yeah," my mentor said. "If you worked out you could be really hot."

What were the chances that three months post that abortive second kiss on my hypothetically hetero lips, my mentor's many capricious adventures and appetites would deposit him in the Hollywood sex spa lounge at the exact same moment that they were playing the one gay-porn movie with an extended sequence starring someone identical to me in every possible way save our second toes? What would Dr. Carl Jung say about synchronicity like this? Outside of a gay-friendly God with a sublime sense of humor, how do you account for such events, and are you ever the same after they go down (or after you go down on a man on-screen)? Finally, why was my moment of great providence and spiritual significance so utterly from the gutter, so creepy and cheeky and ludicrous? So many unlikely circumstances had coincided just so that I would wind up in front of a TV that for my benefit alone was broadcasting one of life's most basic and crucial lessons: you think you know who you are, and then one day you wake up and see yourself in a sailor's hat servicing a row of multicultural mesomorphs. It was as though that great stand-up comedian Shakyamuni Buddha were personally delivering me a message from across the ages.

"What a great world," my mentor said. "I mean, how can *any* of us take our selves seriously if we live in a universe where a fully straight . . . ish dude like you can spend an entire afternoon doubting whether or not he was the lead boy toy in *Glory Holes of Chicago*?"

"*Two*," I reminded him. "*Glory Holes of Chicago Two.*"

"*Glorious Openings in the Windy City!*" he cried, in a *Masterpiece Theatre* accent. "Starring Jack Haubner as Daniel Reed, an innocent and naive sailor who just wanted to go the bathroom, when he found a curious hole in the stall wall—"

"—and decided to stick his wiener in it," I finished.

Coda

SHAKYAMUNI BUDDHA AND THE MILKMAID: AN XXX LOVE STORY

In offering clues on where to find "him," that is, his true self (not self), the randy and rambunctious Zen genius Ikkyu once wrote,

"If you need me look in the fish house, brothel, or tavern." Similarly, if I had stayed in the religious comfort zone of my youth and steered clear of hard living, homosexuals, and Hollywood, I would never have met my mentor, been pushed to the brink, and had this breakthrough experience of not self, or self-as-gay-porn-star. Spiritually speaking, I'd still be dragging my knuckles on the ground, labeling various portions of reality as good or bad and having no clue about the bigger picture from which "good and bad" draw their context. And if I'd ever come upon a gay-porn star in that alternate universe, I would surely have regarded him as the height of evil, or at least perversion. Whereas now, after having gone down the "Glory Hole," I could say, "Brother, I too once found myself on the giving end of a fellatio assembly line while the cameras rolled—*sort of.*" Whose shoes couldn't I walk in if a pair of gnarly feet was all that kept me from accepting my identity as the Clark Gable of surround-sound BJs?

On the other hand, for close to a decade I'd been trying to escape my prudish background—not to mention all sexual responsibility—by doing more and more. The result was I'd come to feel less and less. I'd glimpsed the end of that road that Sunday afternoon, that is, my mirror image, at the bottom of a sexual scrum in *Glory Holes*, faking life's most profound pleasure. Going numb with excess was no more the answer than being sexually frigid from restraint. Both were extremes, and either, taken as the final destination, was a dead end—as the Buddha discovered two and a half millennia ago.

I have it on good authority that before Shakyamuni Buddha had his enlightenment experience, he abruptly abandoned the forest where he'd been torturing himself in the name of the greater spiritual good. "Oh, screw it," he is reported to have said, stepping down from his religious pedestal and turning his back on all the dark and dazzling visions visited upon him there. According to my sources, while searching for a really good bed-and-breakfast, the Buddha happened upon a comely maid, who spotted him some rice milk. There are a number of ways to interpret this. Frankly, I think they made love. Whether they did or not, suffice it to say he took sustenance from her: on the verge of death—physical and spiritual—the Buddha was brought back to life by this maid through an act of love.

Perhaps we all have within ourselves a struggling saint and a slutty milkmaid. I know I do: throw all of my allegiance behind one and I become a prude: the other, a he-ho. But every once in a while they collide and a perfect balance is reached. *What is the sound of one hand clapping?* So goes Zen Master Hakuin's classic koan, the one I first sought to answer when I went to meet my mentor in his underground *zendo*. Perhaps it is the sound of the *sadhu*—the holy man—and the slut coming together. The sound of two hands—two halves—becoming one. Though he was celibate on the surface, "making love" every instant of every day of our difficult and amazing lives was ultimately the Buddha's greatest challenge to us. Buddhism is not a refuge from life. It is life stripped bare and known most intimately. Zen doesn't make you a "better person." It helps you become fully human. My mentor was no model for how to behave perfectly but for how to experience completely. He never told me how to live my life. He just helped me become alive. . . .

My mentor interrupted my musings, hit play, and the grunting and growling of *Glory Holes* resumed as my clone bit his lip and threw back his head and quivered like a man possessed, bringing the film to the only conclusion afforded per its genre.

"Why don't you get comfortable; I'll whip us up some appletinis," my mentor said, a faux gay Tony Curtis seducing my male Marilyn Monroe à la *Some Like it Flaming*. He paused on his way into the kitchen: "Hey, a lightbulb just went off. We could put you in a movie with your twin."

"It's a narcissist's wet dream," I admitted, "consummating my relationship with myself."

He lit one of my cigarettes, coughed, remembered that he

doesn't smoke, put it out—and suddenly I realized that I loved this man as deeply as I had ever loved Tessa, my Texas spitfire girlfriend. And once again I was not having sex with the person I loved. But if not our bodies, then our lives were entwined. Within the year I would be living around the clock at the monastery where he cut his teeth as a Zen monk for a decade. Meanwhile, he would go on to legally register as my domestic partner and assume the lease on my rent-controlled apartment, moving away from either a mountain monastery or a city temple for the first time in fifteen years.

"We've switched lives," I would marvel more than once as I transitioned into full-time formal practice and he reentered the world as a lay Zen priest with a tiny sitting group (but a huge foot fetish, which he continued to explore).

My God, was that really ten years ago? *Yes, yes!* I nod, and tears come to my eyes. Suddenly here I am pushing forty, and I feel the weight of my robes and the significance of people's judgments and expectations about them, and I look forward with trembling awe to a life spent trying to make sense of and fit into these robes and this role. And I try to trace this wild and nearly accidental calling back to a single point, a source moment—a task as futile to the Buddhist as trying to pinpoint the exact location of the self, which, like your shadow, moves with the very act of trying to touch it. And so I arbitrarily choose a moment, and it's always the same and can be summed up with a few spiritual keywords that I'm sure were never on the tip of the Buddha's tongue, though I bet the old sage would have approved of this new sacred mantra.

Come on, say it with me: *Glory Holes . . . Glory Holes of Chi Town . . . Glorious Openings in the Windy City!*

11

Mad Monk

A lot of pissed-off people wind up at our monastery. This place has a tractor beam like the Death Star's in *Star Wars* that pulls in anyone within a thousand-mile radius with a four-letter word on the tip of his or her tongue. Her marriage tanked; he's got an itch in his brain he just can't scratch; she's forty-five and smells of cabbage and lives in a small studio apartment and nobody ever calls her back. . . . They all wind up here, sold on the promise that Buddhism can alleviate suffering.

I said "they" all wind up here, but I guess I mean we. I had one of those moments recently where, upon the much-anticipated departure of an enemy that, as a Buddhist, I could never quite admit was an enemy, I found myself peering around the *zendo* and thinking, "Wow, there are no assholes living here anymore." Whereupon came a sinking feeling, "Wait a minute, there's always at least *one*. So if I'm looking around the *zendo* and I can't find him . . . guess who the asshole is!"

Zen practice is good for angry people. The form is tight. It squeezes that deep red heart pulp, pushing up emotions from way down inside you. A lot of "stuff" comes up when you do this practice. Zen gets your juices flowing. And with these juices come seeds—the seeds of your behavior, your character, your anger, all flushed out into the open for you to see.

In Zen we learn that human consciousness is an eminently natural operation. You plant a seed, it grows. Similarly, when something happens to you on the outside, in "the world," the seeds of this experience take root within you, becoming sensations, thoughts, memories—your inner life. Conversely, when something arises within you, some inner experience, a notion, emotion, or dream, then the seeds of this inner event are disseminated on the outside, in the world, through your words and actions. Buddhists call this codependent origination: all things arise together in a mutually interconnected and interpenetrating web of being. "To see the world in a grain of sand," William Blake wrote. Or as that great metaphysician Tom "Jerry Maguire" Cruise put it: "You complete me."

Sounds romantic. But what if the seeds at the root of your behavior are the seeds of hate and anger?

A year ago, freshly escaped from the monastery for a day, I was slaloming through bustling foot traffic on Santa Monica Boulevard with my mentor, whom I love and adore. We got into a fight about something and I smacked him. It came out of nowhere and was meant to be light. Only it clearly did not come out of nowhere, and it was not light. I can still hear the thwack of my open palm against his belly: the hollow thud of a red rubber ball hitting pavement. There was a long stretch of silence, wherein I should have begged for his forgiveness. But I couldn't catch up to the moment. I couldn't admit to the violence that had just erupted from within me. I couldn't tell whether I meant it, whether it was real, where it came from, or how it got there.

I have violence in me, unfortunately. The seeds were planted long ago by my father, the poor man. How about all the times he didn't whack me? The time he sighed and let it go when I stole one of his antique firearms and ran around the house with it or sat on a sibling and released a cloud of flatulence? No, I remember only the five moments when his anger broke through.

All it takes is one seed. I've apologized, and even sent my mentor a cute homemade card with two stick figures sitting *zazen* side by side. But my blow planted a hate seed in my mentor, and something irreconcilable has grown between us. I can't seem to reclaim the friendship. I feel as if I'm losing him.

Zen practice can be a tricky thing because, done right, sooner or later all the issues and energies you've been repressing your whole life will ooze, trickle, and burst to the surface through your tight little smile. And I'm afraid that the practice itself doesn't necessarily equip you to deal skillfully with these issues and energies. This is one of the great misconceptions about spiritual work: that if applied correctly, it will make us "better people" (whatever that means). Zen is not a psychiatric or therapeutic discipline; it's a spiritual one. It's supposed to get energy moving on a deep, fundamental, life-changing level. Its purpose is to orient you toward the truth, toward reality, whatever this takes. It's not supposed to boss you around with behavioral or self-help dictates or to shoehorn you into the slipper of well-adjusted citizenhood.

In other words, spiritual work isn't always just "instructive"—it's also transformative, and this kind of transformation can get messy. The Sanskrit term for this is *clusterfuck*.

Some people, for example, seem to be born angry. Not me. I was born a coward. So when the energy gets moving through Zen practice and I suddenly become angry rather than a quivering eunuch, this can feel like an improvement—or at least a new way to be screwed up rather than the same old patterns of screwed-up-ness. A sharp word suddenly tastes good in my mouth. Anger takes on the illusion of upward spiritual mobility in comparison with my habitual cravenness. In reality, however, it's a lateral move—to an adjacent room in the same hell.

None of this happens in a vacuum. Zen is a group practice, but the thing about groups is that they're made up of people, and we all know what people are like. So not only does Zen practice flush your issues out into the open, it does so within a certain context; it flushes them into the "container" of your relationships with fellow monks and nuns. Energies and issues that had no discernible dimension within you are externalized and embodied with the "help" of your peers, one of whom, say, unwittingly takes on the form of your stepmother, who once bullied and humiliated you. Meanwhile, to this peer you represent the weakness and stupidity within himself that for more than thirty years he has felt the compulsive need to stamp out, as his father once tried to stamp it out of him. (In beating ourselves up, we usually pick up where our parents left off.) Only neither of you realizes (at least initially) that the other represents something within yourself that needs to be dealt with, for it is only in the dramatic playing out of your interactions that these powerful patterns and deep psychological dysfunctions are brought to light.

I defer to Carl Jung, who spent a lot of time either in a nuthouse or in a monastery: "The psychological rule says that when an inner situation is not made conscious, it happens outside, as fate. That is to say, when the individual remains undivided and does not become conscious of his inner contradictions, the world must perforce act out the conflict and be torn in two opposite halves."

It's amazing to watch sometimes. These monastery battles royal can be downright epic. Forget about what happens when an immovable object meets an irresistible force. What happens when a weenie who's sworn off his cowardice meets a monster who can't help himself from bullying?

"First law of thermodynamics: Energy can be neither created nor destroyed. It simply changes forms!" So went the mantra of an erstwhile Zen peer, one of those quasi-scientific mystic types forever trying to link quantum physics with whacked-out spiritual mumbo jumbo. If you ever disagreed with him, he trembled, his jowls purpling: "That's . . . just . . . your . . . *ego!*" A regular fury farmer, this sower of hate seeds was one of those unfortunate American Zen *sangha* fixtures whose respect and admiration for the teacher is in inverse proportion to his resentment and suspicion of his peers. Once, a fed-up old nun, ornery and pugnacious in her own right, shot back: "Listen you! In a universe that wastes nothing, where does the butthead energy go when you lose your temper? What form does it change into?"

In about a week she got her answer. One morning this troubled monk we'll call "Tirade-san"—towering over six feet, girthy, garbed in his turquoise stretch pants and a T-shirt with a picture of the cosmos and an arrow indicating YOU ARE HERE—exploded at the *densu,* the monastery greeter, when she forgot to fetch a student from the airport. She in turn barfed a curdled remark on the *tenzo* after he misplaced her laminated chant sheets. The *tenzo* then went Vesuvius on the *shoji,* the *zendo* mother, when she innocently swung through the kitchen door to brew some green tea.

"Knock before entering!" the normally mild-mannered Pisces roared.

"Have a fucking cow!" the grandmother of three and part-time caregiver blasted back.

As *shika,* the head monk, I felt like Bill Paxton in *Twister,* chasing the tornado of devastating emotion as it touched down from one end of camp to the other.

Later, when I pushed through the sutra hall's great double doors for the monks' nightly meeting, I could feel T-san's glare frying the hairs on the back of my neck. Turns out I had forgotten to give the *densu* the flight details in the first place, which oversight had set off the whole Great Hissy Fit chain reaction that day. T-san bent his body language my way, trying to get my eye, like a boxer intimidating an opponent before the opening bell. Unable to meet his gaze, I studied my toenails—which, to top off the shameful matter, were badly in need of trimming.

Per meeting protocol we circled up, bowed, and took turns voicing the various petty and passive-aggressive concerns that arise when a group of people with anger issues decides to engage in a practice that deprives them of sleep, comfort, personal space, protein, Internet access, and even their hair. I nodded with great interest and jotted these concerns in my head-monk notebook, where they languish unaddressed to this day. Meanwhile, Evil Monk would soon have the floor, and I imagined him with a little toothbrush mustache, howling in German. I would get a chance to rebut him because the head monk speaks last, and believe me, I had every word—every last syllable—planned. *You can only take so much shit for so long!* I trembled inside, my sphincter clenched about as tight as the hydraulics in those machines that forge artificial diamonds.

Finally, it was the man-ape's turn to speak. I turned and bowed to him, and for the first time that day I looked him dead in the eyes—half expecting to see two hollow black holes brimming with the souls of dead children. And wouldn't you know it, he was smiling. He laughed lightly and bowed that mammoth wrecking ball atop his shoulders, indicating that he had nothing to say.

In that moment the hate seed fell out of me, dead like a stone— petrified in its own uselessness like an insect fossilized in amber. He put his great meaty hand on my back on the way out of the room. That's all it took for me to break down sobbing in my cabin about twenty minutes later, alone but warmhearted. Desperate, gushing, cleansing sobs. It was the kind of moment that buys you another five years of patience with, and passion for, monastic life. It's one of those breakthroughs of the heart.

People ask what is the hardest thing about living at a monastery. Is it no sex, cardboardy food, zero sleep, sandals gone rancid from perpetual socklessness, the measly fifty bucks a month "monk's allowance"? Is it the isolation from society, the heinous robes, those bone-crushing nineteen-hour days spent in the *zendo* or in the blistering sun or piercing cold? The hardest thing about living at a monastery, I tell them, is working with people with whom you have nothing in common save spiritual desperation. We monks shave our heads, I continue, because if we didn't we would surely tear out all of our hair in despair from having to live and work with one another. Anyone who's ever been married or had kids, or coworkers for that matter (work and family—those *other* group practices), probably knows what I'm talking about. It gets real when the illusions drop away, doesn't it?

Yet nine times out of ten the reason we get so irritated with the people who are closest to us is that they show us that we do not in fact correspond with the ideas we have of ourselves: we are meaner, weaker, dumber, and less interesting, tolerant, and sexy. In short, we are human, which typically comes as extremely disappointing news. You just cannot keep telling yourself how spiritually with-it you are when every time you sit down to read that Eckhart Tolle book the monastery cat jumps on your shoulders and claws your bald head and you fling it halfway across the room and scream, "Goddammit, I'm trying to read about patience and equanimity here. Can you at least wait till I've gotten past the 'Pain Body' chapter?!" Not that I, of course, have ever done that.

I used to imagine that spiritual work was undertaken alone in a cave somewhere with prayer beads and a leather-bound religious tome, the holy one enwrapped in a mist of grace, mystique, and body odor. Nowadays, that sounds to me more like a vacation from spiritual work. Group monastic living has taught me that the people in your life don't get in the way of your spiritual practice; these people *are* your spiritual practice.

Through each other we discover that if we have the heart—the willingness, the strength, the courage—we have the capacity to plant the seeds of kindness, compassion, forgiveness, seeds of a laid-back humor, a sense of letting go. But your heart must be quicker than your mind. Trust me, that organ between your ears is *always* spoiling for a fight. Its job is to divide and conquer. But the real fight is taking place inside you, within the "dharma organ," the heart, where the challenge is to unify and understand, where the seeds of love and compassion are struggling to lay roots, to gain ground.

Lend this struggle an ear. Just pause for three seconds. One banana . . . two banana . . . three banana . . . Pause and listen. Pause and breathe. Pause and gather your scattered, wild energies, your shattered soul . . . before you fling that seed of hate into the wind.

Mark my words, times are tough and the ground is fertile. That seed *will* grow.

12

Flinty McGee and Me

When being introduced to some slick new technology like an iPad, I always feel as if I were back in Hollywood and I've been seated next to a frigid, dazzling young actress at a dinner party. I resent her air of inevitability, yet I can't turn away. She glitters with the promise of ultimate connection. *I have no need for you,* both the actress and the iPad communicate, through their sleek lines and flashy features, *but we both know that* you *can't live without* me.

In retrospect, then, I wonder if I didn't lose the iPad accidentally on purpose. I wanted it not to exist in the first place so that I wouldn't have to need it, and so perhaps I simply nullified its existence by "forgetting" that it was ever there.

The tricky part was, it wasn't even mine.

It was a donation to my elderly Zen master and his attendant, or *inji*. To our teacher, the iPad was something like his Zen is to us students—very cool and somewhat incomprehensible. The *inji,* however, took to the iPad immediately, using it to organize all of our teacher's contacts and medical records, recording his daily diet and activities in detail, showing him photos of old students from eras past that he could no longer remember. When an earthquake ravaged Japan's north coast, where our teacher was first instituted as head of a temple more than six decades ago, the *inji* showed him footage. I still remember the two of them huddled before, with their faces lit by, the thin, elegant tablet, overwhelmed by images taken by helicopter: a pickup truck being swept away by the typhoon tidal wave, smashed and torn to pieces, the inhabitants surely drowning, dying before our eyes. It was a horrible thing to watch, and so sanctified the device upon which it was watched.

"*Yahhh*," our teacher said, turning to the *inji*, both of them Japanese, "our born country, now much trouble."

Something on-screen caught his eye. Squinting through bifocals, he slowly lowered his one-hundred-five-year-old hand to the iPad and, with his thumb and index finger, gently increased the image on the touch screen. An ancient man learning new technology: it was something like the inverse of watching a baby take its first steps—and just as touching and neat.

The iPad, in other words, had quickly become indispensable to the two of them. And who lost the damn thing? Yours truly.

There we were, the *inji* and I, ferrying our teacher through the byzantine wheelchair-check-in process at LAX airport. Then— somewhere between loading his carry-ons onto the X-ray conveyor belt and that octogenarian TSA employee, looking like Betty White in a souped-up mail carrier uniform, growling at me, "Yer gonna hafta take off that big belt of yers with that metal buckle, sugar; this ain't the ro-de-o!"—the iPad had a Phillip K. Dick moment, plunged down a wormhole into an alternate universe, and I completely lost track of it.

"*Moshi moshi!*" I shouted, waving to my teacher and the *inji*, saying hello in Japanese when I should have been saying goodbye. Frankly, I was thrilled to be free of them for a week, though

I was certain that in their absence "we" would begin to have all kinds of scintillating conversations. It is the strange curse of a loner who hates to be lonely that I spend much of my time bantering in my head with the people that I care about when they are not around, but when they are in my presence, I am often trying to get away from them to be alone . . . so that I can talk freely to them.

A few hours later, I was alone in the monastery office, and caffeinated. My eyes were wide, my bowels were twitching: I felt on the edge of some great discovery, but perhaps I just needed to use the toilet. Solitude and caffeine are two of my favorite things, and both are typically in short supply at the monastery. It felt good to be wired and even better to be alone. I have an antisocial streak that belies all of my interactions in Zen, that group practice, and on planet Earth in general, that group project. I can be a real prick, in other words. To avoid this tendency, I overcompensate and try to put out a "nice guy" vibe. I am nonconfrontational. I hold everything in. But my repressed anxieties and issues always come out in weird, passive-aggressive, even faux macho ways.

The monastery staff had joined our teacher and the *inji* for a retreat in Northern California, and with the grounds all to myself, I was engaged in that most pitiful of a monk's guilty pleasures: YouTubing spiritual teachers from various traditions and haughtily disagreeing with them, mostly because they didn't say something exactly the way I would, had I the courage and compassion necessary for someone to want to make a video of me sharing spiritual teachings in the first place.

"*Idiot!* That's the stupidest thing I've ever heard!" I cried at some perfectly respectable teacher holding forth on my Mac. "Where'd you get your teaching credentials, from a new age crystal healer?" I crossed my eyes and wagged my finger: "Hey, Shirley MacLaine called, she wants her craaazy pills back!"

Outside, the wind was blowing hard and a fog was setting in. A brutal snowstorm was gathering like the fingers of a fist in the gray haze above. But interesting weather patterns are always wasted on the self-absorbed. Even still, I moved to the window and studied the fir trees bucking in the wind like Hindu gods waving their many spindly arms in warning. I felt the presence of someone out there; there was a vague uneasiness in my gut. Who was looking in at me? Only myself, I realized, and turned from my perplexed reflection in the window pane.

Suddenly the phone blasted forth from oblivion. I jumped three feet into the air. The real world was calling.

"Bad news," said the *inji* on the other end. She and our teacher had just touched down in Oakland. I could make out flight announcements in the background.

"*Dame da,*" she cried.

"Huh?"

"Not good, not good, not good."

"What's up?" I asked, taking a hit from my coffee mug.

She let out a long, slow moan. "*Yokunai . . .*"

"Stop speaking Japanese and tell me what's going on."

There was stillness on the other end. I waited. . . . "The iPad's gone," she announced.

"What do you mean it's gone?" I cried, spitting coffee onto the paused teacher on my computer screen.

"I cannot find it. It didn't make it onto the plane, Shozan."

There was an edge in her tone: true terror. It was as though she had left me in charge of our infant at an alligator ranch, and now the child was no longer in his stroller.

She hung up with: "You must find it."

"I—"

"*You must find it.*" Click.

My breath, like the wind through the trees outside, grew heavy. Everything went very still, and I felt my scrotum tighten. I repeated the orthodox Buddhist mantra that Zen monks have invoked for centuries during moments of crisis: "Damn, damn, damn, *stupid,* shit, damn!"

I pictured the uppity electronic device imprisoned in LAX's lost and found, huddled in the dank chiaroscuro of a single swinging lightbulb, slim and vulnerable beside a menacing Cold War–era rotary phone, its precious little cursor quickening like a terrified heartbeat.

A cold dead fear came over me: *And if it's not at LAX's lost and found?*

Failure to locate and liberate the iPad meant I would have to face the nun who donated it. Though in her midfifties, "Angela-san" is spry, fit, and wrinkleless and has that lithe, compact, ageless look common to many Asian women. With her buzzed nun cut she even resembles a little Japanese boy from behind. To fail her, then, would mean the worst of both worlds. She would look at me both with the eyes of a let-down little lad and the disgust and disappointment of an older woman. My life is complicated enough without having to navigate all the complex emotional signals given off by a prepubescent yet grandmotherly gaze.

And so I shed my robes for civvies, abandoned my propane-heated office, and pioneered our battered old Tacoma down the icy driveway. A few snowboarders had begun to gather at the slick curve that dumps steeply into our parking lot. During winter our Zen center quite literally exists in tension with the outside world, which ascends the mountain like an overbearing, slobbering dog and stomps right up to our gates. Snow play is ubiquitous on our grounds and consists of hordes from nearby Upland sledding down our driveway until it is the consistency of a bobsled run, singing "Freebird" or "La Bamba" loudly and badly to an acoustic guitar, grilling sausages in our parking lot, and, inevitably, leaving a long, ugly human turd in some creative place on the property.

The only thing keeping these "invaders" off the Zen Center proper is a flimsy chain (mobsters carry gold bullets around their necks on links bigger than this thing) attached to a pair of two-foot poles that stretches across the driveway around the halfway mark. Over the years this chain has, for me, come to symbolize the precious and privileged isolation that genuine monasticism requires.

My how I've changed, I thought, recalling those early "Shawshank" years, when I saw the monastery as a kind of penitentiary. *I used to think of that chain as a barrier keeping* me in, *not* others out.

I honked the horn and the snow thrashers scattered as I threw the truck into park, jumped out, unlocked the chain, laid it down, drove forward a little, got back out, dragged the chain across the driveway, and repadlocked it behind me.

I paused while climbing back through the truck doorway; my nostrils flared like a vice cop's. "Guys," I sighed heavily, "can you not smoke that here? This is a Buddhist monastery."

I fixed the small neon-jacketed mob with a stern gaze while inhaling deeply, quietly, savoring the smell of weed, of my erstwhile, gloriously unhinged premonastery life, where I used to smoke a ton of dope and then wander around West Hollywood looking for trouble, usually of the sexual kind, invariably finding none (the evening always ending with a proposition from the same drag queen, with her cheap pink pumps and eyes as menacing as they were fabulously long lashed: it was my old life, you see, that *truly* resembled life inside a prison). That life was gone now, and I resented being reminded of it, mostly because it made me feel old to think of who I had once been and who I had become.

"Sorry, man. Thanks for letting us board here," said a college kid. She shook out a head of orange curls as frazzled and lively as bolts of electricity. As her hand flashed, followed by the sizzle of a joint in the snowbank behind her, I felt my hackles rise again. I looked over my shoulder; perhaps some prankster sneaking up from behind? No, no one. I turned back to the kids.

"Just don't go on that end of camp, please," I grumbled, pointing to our dismal and vaguely haunted-looking cabins.

"Hadn't even crossed our minds," the electric redhead assured me.

My mood pitched black as I merged west onto the I-10 freeway toward LAX, the heart of air-travel darkness. *"Relax!"* I screamed at myself, *"go into the breath! You and the traffic? You're one, my man. Dissolve your egoic self and* become *the situation."*

I appreciated my insights, and paused to admire my phrasing, until—*"Fricking city Metro bus! What is it with you guys? Just 'cos you HONK first doesn't mean it's okay to cut right in front of me! Announcing your intention to be an asshole doesn't negate your being one!"*

I caught my reflection in the rearview mirror. I had that petulant middle-aged-man look, like a giant horrifying baby who needs his diaper changed. (See YouTube, keyword: "Tea Party rally.") My lungs lunged at breath like a man seizing the steering wheel as his car skids off an icy bridge. I forced a confrontation between my face and the one in the rearview mirror. I fought with myself, the only enemy I've ever truly known. . . . I really drank in the reflection of my eyes, with my eyes. Then I recognized who was staring back at me: the same sinister presence I'd felt creeping up on me earlier.

Oh, dear God, I gulped, *not you!*

A voice within replied: *"Yes, it's me, Flinty McGee!"*

Flinty McGee is my mentor's nickname for me. It refers to that part of me that is hard-hearted and full of hate. Flinty McGee is my alter ego. (Or maybe I am his. Sometimes it's hard to tell.)

There he was, staring back at me from behind my own eyes. At least ninety-nine years old, with the maturity level of a fetus. Scrawny and pinched, his face veiny, blotchy, and aberrantly hairy, like a testicle. Eating his eye boogers when no one is looking. A dull stink emanating from him, the sour, putrid stench of chronic loneliness. One middle finger upturned and pointed at me as he sneered through poopy teeth.

Flinty McGee sees no hope for the human race and no reason to care for any of its particular members. He is the hate manager within, and his portfolio is broad. Flinty would refuse Anne Frank and her family his empty attic. *Sorry,* he would say, closing the door, *I just can't do anything for you people right now.* Flinty McGee once secretly recorded my younger brother confessing to acts of self-love and then played it for friends for laughs. That was Flinty, not me. Flinty McGee used to call my mother "meat hook" during our nastiest fights. (What did that even mean? Ask Flinty.) These days, Flinty McGee carries on elaborately bitter conversations in my head with peers that I am too afraid to confront directly. He wastes hours and hours of my time on the meditation cushion this way.

Flinty hates a lot of things these days, including tweens who act like infants and expect to be treated like adults; snarling, pig-hearted Republicans and self-righteous liberal weenies; and virtually anyone working at the post office. Flinty McGee hates reality TV almost more than anything on earth. In fact, the only thing he hates more than reality TV is the fact that he kind of likes reality TV.

My big illusion when I decided to move to the monastery was that I would leave Flinty McGee behind after I ascended the mountain, as though the ugliest parts of me could not survive at such lofty altitudes. Bullshit. They've thrived up here, sadly, thanks to the warmth and comfort I've provided them behind the cover of my robes. Hate, rage, cowardice: they lie latent within me, like herpes, waiting for just the right conditions to manifest so they can burst through my skin and infect everyone I love.

Your spiritual practice is not tested all at once, in some Big Moment, à la Christ on his cross or Buddha under the Bodhi tree (those two spiritual show-offs). It's tested every day, again and again, in stunningly average situations, where no one is watching—no one except, hopefully, you. Spiritual work doesn't elevate us to a higher plane than other people: it gives us perspective on ourselves. And from this vantage point we occasionally glimpse ourselves behaving like total assholes. Spiritual discipline opens up a space within wherein a formerly unconscious pattern now becomes a choice: Do I really want to change? Can I turn the tide of bad habits? Or deep down am I secretly okay with being the same old high-end primate I've always been, as long as I have everyone else, along with myself, more or less fooled most of the time?

And so I whispered a solemn promise to myself: *I will keep you locked up today, Mr. McGee.* Flinty had been clawing around inside me lately, desperate to climb out, to rape my life and eat the flesh of my unborn hopes and dreams. He wanted something. I could tell. He was making more appearances than usual: the odd temper tantrum (always sublimated, so that I hollered at someone only in my head), or an unexpected surge of disgust for a new Zen student's innocent human failing. Yes, Flinty McGee wanted out. Out of me, out of hiding, out into the world. He was trying to turn me into that guy who has a meltdown in a public space, making everyone within earshot ashamed to be a human being. (*"I ordered this steak medium rare! You call this medium rare?"*) But this would not pass. LAX would be the test, and I would nail it, remaining calm, clear, and in perfect control of myself. I was going to go all Dalai Lama on that airport! Activate the iZen!

Monk up! I shouted within, hoping to scare the Flintster back down into the black basement at the base of the brain, where I kept him in chains. Flinty would not see the light of day. I would see to that. I would hold that fucker's head under the dark waters within until he stopped kicking, motherfucker.

It was time to fight Flinty with Flinty.

Hour One

I pulled into LAX—that dim, massive horseshoe of pig-gray terminals—with all the enthusiasm of a PETA vegan arriving for her first day of work at the sausage factory. The sun grinned brightly overhead with monochromatic SoCal ubiquity, but Flinty Mc-Gee cursed it within me as if it were just another overexposed celebrity. I parked, dodged an angry taxi outside the arrivals level, and approached a goateed TSA worker with tattooed tendrils of blue fire rising up his neck. He looked like the hulking motorcycle thug-stud Jesse James, but his voice was pure Fran Drescher. He was waving his cigarette like a cross between a classical music conductor and a short-order cook, holding forth to a group of coworkers, none of them working.

I *so* did not want to talk to him, to step out of my comfort zone, to make this whole lost iPad situation a reality that I would then have to rectify. But I bucked up, interrupted his story, introduced myself, and explained my situation. A problem! Someone needs us! His peers scattered. Meanwhile, my interlocutor's eyes glazed over, as though a very powerful sleeping drug called Work had taken effect. He checked his watch. His eyes rolled back in his head.

"It's only eleven in the *mawning*. I ain' even had my *cwoffee* yet," he squeaked.

I had forgotten! TSA, the wing of Homeland Security designated to handle flight check-in security, actually stands for: Totally Sick of Airports.

"For real dude, this is not my problem," Franny James whined, leading me to his boss, a much older manager with a certain tarnished elegance, like the king's butler forced into a doorman's old coat.

The older man frowned at Franny James, who skedaddled, and then turned to me and frowned more completely, with a deeper commitment to hostility, as though it took someone like me, with my stupid pressing little problem, to really bring out his true gift for enmity. Immediately, I felt that tension particular to interactions with service-sector seniors, wherein you want to behave respectfully toward the tribal elders, for they have won world wars and petted the heads of their great-grandchildren and came of age in a time before child beauty pageants or sexting. But you also need something from them, and dammit, isn't it their *job* to provide you with a service?! It's not your fault the economy has gone to hell and they've had to compete against their grandchildren to get a job that requires them to wear a name tag and take random drug tests and pretend like bottles of shampoo and shaving cream larger than a baby carrot are potentially lethal terrorist implements.

There ensued a short discussion about my problem, which he made clear was my problem, which is what he called it, "*your* problem," as in "It certainly isn't *my* problem." "Do you see this mountain of bags and suitcases and that little yipping diva-dog there?" He thumbed his bushy mustache and pointed to the poodle in pink barrettes trapped in the portable dungeon at his foot. It seemed to be wearing its cage rather than stuck inside it. Its black nose stuck out the front, its tail poked out back, and fur poofed out from the mesh metal cage in between. Little triangles of teeth were locked around the silver bars in a gum-slobbering rictus of pure animal rage.

"I have *enough* problems!" he declared, hoisting the fluffy, cubed monster by its handle and disappearing into the burgeoning flow of flight check-in foot traffic.

I stood there, temporarily adrift and sinking, like Wile E. Coyote run out of cliff, until the crowd parted and there appeared a new TSA manager, looking tall, dark, and alert, as though ready to repel anyone who might need him. He had the green eyes of a beautiful reptile. They found me and read my intention. When he tried to dodge me like a football fullback, I grabbed his shoulder and cried "I've *lost* something!" in a high-pitched voice. I felt that I was sharing some far deeper truth about myself.

As if he cared: "Is it human? Do it have a heartbeat, son? Then I don't wanna hear about it." He just laughed and walked away, swaying his long arms behind him. I could hear him still laughing long after the crowd had swallowed him up again.

"Hugga hugga hugga *haw!*" went his laugh.

I felt like a superhero who suddenly wakes up on a planet where his powers no longer work. LAX had mindfulness-deflector rays! TSA was Zen Kryptonite! This is the single most disconcerting thing about transitioning from monastic life back into the "real world," even if only for an afternoon. Living at a Zen Buddhist monastery is like training in a martial art, only instead of learning how to take down your opponent, you're learning how to make peace with *all* "opponents"; you're learning how to remain unruffled by life by fully engaging in it. You practice this skill in the contained milieu of a monastery and then come down the hill expecting to be able to put it to use, only to find that you get your ass kicked by the first guy off the street. *What have I been doing at that monastery this whole time?* you wonder.

Karl Marx called religion the opiate of the masses, but spiritual practice earnestly undertaken does not numb you. It opens you up. What does it mean to be open? The outside comes in and the inside goes out, freely. Where before there was a gatekeeper—your self—between these two worlds of inside and outside, now there is an open door. Though it often feels more like an open wound. As a monk, you continually put yourself under the knife of wisdom for open-soul surgery. It's sensitive work, often leaving you achingly raw and vulnerable. When you're at a monastery, everyone's in this heightened state of feeling and awareness together, and there is some respect for the process whereby it is cultivated. But the workaday world has its own rules, geared mostly toward the survival and success of its institutions and not the personal or spiritual growth of its members. And so, staying truly open and soulful—plugged into your spiritual practice 24/7—can be downright agonizing when you're not safely ensconced in your monastery, temple, or church, with its bells, incense, and special rules.

A boisterous family, all six of them identically overweight and looking like the same Mr. Potato Head doll with different body parts stuck on, thundered by, clipping the back of my knees with a rolling suitcase.

"Watch it, Slim," the father barked at me.

He paused for just an instant to see if I would defend myself, and when I didn't, he swaggered on, grinning with the taste of fresh blood on his lips, a tiny chunk of my soul sliding down his well-worn gullet. You could have fit two marbles inside my flared nostrils just then.

Cocksucker! Flinty McGee shouted up from my depths.

His voice actually didn't sound that out of place at the airport. All around me people were unleashing their own inner McGees. There was Pissy McGee, Prickly McGee, Bitchy McGee, Cocky McGee, and those ass-scratching, finger-sniffing twins: Sneaky and Greedy McGee. LAX—hell, planet Earth—was the McGee family writ large. As I tried to summon some patience, compassion, and fellow feeling for those around me, I began to suspect that my spiritual resources would be of exactly zero help when it came to actually getting the damn iPad back. Spiritual values are fine for spiritual environments. But it is a religious fool who tries to rewrite the world according to the rules that govern his spiritual refuge *from* that world. Why do you think they call it a retreat center, I asked myself? You're retreating *to* your center from a world in full-on *attack* mode.

Was Flinty's energy actually appropriate for a dark and hateful world, both a kind of immunization against it and a tool for navigating through it? *Let me off the chain,* Flinty moaned up the staircase of my inner basement. *Why do you think I'm tearing you up inside? I belong out there, in the world. You suffer for your repression of me, for then I turn on you, motherfucker.*

Release me. Let me protect you.

Hour Two

Eventually I found myself at TSA's off-site location, seated before a skeletal, sallow woman. Celebrity she most resembled? Emily Dickinson after a bout of dysentery. She was crammed behind a tiny desk in a windowless office cruelly outfitted with once-white

1980s furniture now the sad, stained brown of an old smoker's grin. The room's centerpiece was a glass case displaying dozens of actual "weapons" confiscated from LAX travelers by stalwart TSA employees. There was a "hand grenade" cigarette lighter, some neon-green squirt guns, a dozen identical Swiss Army knives, a shaving can with a false bottom, and a lipstick holder that, when turned, produced a weak little blade the size of an overgrown toenail.

I know all of these vicious appurtenances of housewives and Boy Scouts by heart because I stared at them for an edgy eternity while the woman behind the desk chewed on her silky black hair extensions, hitting return on her keyboard every once in a while with one hand and dipping into her bag o' breakfast—bagel chips—with the other. She looked pretty good for forty-eight. The problem was, she was in her midtwenties. Her skin was the cloudy color of water that's boiled too many hot dogs. Hers was a sweet face, worn free of expression or hope. She studied her ebony fingernails—each of which was host to a tiny plastic jewel—impervious to the waves of wrath rolling off me, which then receded and washed back over me as self-loathing, leaving on my face an expression as though I'd been sucking on a 9-volt battery.

In polite, civilized society we cut our entrails out to keep from being aggressive, desperate, foolish—but it always shows on our tight, pinched faces, which suck inward to fill the chasm where our guts used to be. Nothing triggers me more than being treated like a number, a useless nuisance, a horsefly begging for his morsel of poop. Sitting before someone I rather dismissively labeled a bureaucrat, waiting for her to acknowledge me, I had an insight: in modern-day hell realms we are not burned to the bone. We are slowly drained. Ours is a scientific age, not a religious one, and so we have no pitchfork-wielding demons haunting our inner lives per se—just the psychic mosquitoes of culture, industry, and state, swarms of them, which alight upon our souls, stab inward, and suck and suck and suck. American hells fill not with the screams of the damned but with the anonymous sighs of the resigned.

I thought these insights were pretty creative and longed to share them with this young crone. I tried to stare her into looking at me, but she was miles away, sitting on a porch in the moonlight, sipping absinthe and getting her shoulders rubbed by a young male vampire she hoped might sexually conquer her. Without asking who I was or what I wanted, the scowling daydreamer printed something out and attached it to a clipboard, which she then passed to me along with the Bic ballpoint she'd been chewing on this whole time, her eyes never leaving her computer screen.

As I hunched over my three inches of counter space, scribbling on her form, feeling like a hateful little troll, a cheerfully obese man with a tremendous pair of what I can only call male breasts walked behind her desk and with his tinkling key ring jiggled open a large metal cabinet.

My jaw dropped.

Its rusty innards were a mass graveyard of abandoned electronic items—Droids, laptops, cameras, iPods, and one Tickle Me Elmo doll, his mouth open; his arms spread; his round, oversized eyes bulging, like a bright-red child trapped in a kidnapper's lair. The girthy man deposited a handful of MacBooks and slammed the door shut before I could scan its contents for my teacher's iPad.

My eyes locked with the sepulchral desk jockey's. I slid her the form. *I have met your petty requirements. Now show me what's in the cabinet.*

I didn't actually say this, of course, because I somehow knew that if I mentioned the cabinet, all was lost. I had fallen down the bureaucratic rabbit hole. Color me logical, but looking in a cabinet filled with lost electronic items seemed like the most reasonable course of action given my problem of a lost electronic item. And so I instinctively knew that by the reverse rationale of this mad TSA universe, it was the one option least available to me. She followed my eyes to the cabinet and stayed conspicuously silent. It felt like a test. I was afraid that if I even mentioned the cabinet, the floor would fall out from beneath me and I would plummet into a cage of starving lions, her dark figure hovering over me through the open square of missing beige government-building carpet above.

"You shouldn't've mentioned the cabinet," she would say, Man Boobs shaking his head behind her as my soft flesh succumbed to the jaws of the ravenous cats.

Finally, after determining that everything was in order with my filled-out form, this young, female Alice Cooper was able to tell me that she wouldn't be able to tell me if they had the iPad or not. All she would tell me was that she would be able to tell me tomorrow if they had it. And even that seemed a little uncertain.

"Anything else?" she said, and then turned back to her computer and completely ignored me before I could answer.

But I did not leave. I stood there and tried to disembowel her with my eyes. Flinty McGee was rattling a tin cup across the bars of his cage behind my clenched teeth, trying to get her attention. *"Listen, Morticia Addams,"* he cried, *"you don't even have to get up out of your little miniature chair! Just turn around, open the cabinet, and I can see for myself if you have the iPad!"*

I was bottoming out emotionally, and like every fed up airline customer at one time or another, I thought about posing a false terrorism threat to get a little attention. *"I need to get that iPad back to LAX,"* Flinty roared between my ears. *"The iBomb is scheduled to go off today! I'd be doing your whole office a favor if I blew up this awful* Miami Vice–*era Barcalounger!"*

Finally, after having passed a sufficient cloud of invisible hate gas that my noxious presence might linger long after I was gone, I stormed out the door.

Hour Three

I hopped into my escape vehicle and burned rubber back to LAX. Something shifted in me after this encounter, and not for the good. It was as if *I* were trapped on the inside now and Flinty had taken the controls and was manifesting freely in the world. I wound up nearly throttling a TSA worker on the departures level whose sole job seemed to be to unclip the zippy cord thing and let people bypass the totally empty line to the X-ray detectors. She whipped out a phone and very quickly hot-potatoed me to another TSA guy, let's call him Jesus, who appeared out of a door that appeared out of a wall. It was as if he walked right out of the center of the building. His smooth Chicano face teemed with heart and diligence. *There is a way of doing things here,* his body language said. *Respect that.*

A decent man: no just receptacle for my spasms of rage. And so my rage stayed in my body: I thrummed with it. Suddenly I felt myself almost crying—tears were the very next thing around the corner from all of this wrath. Airport Jesus listened to my whole rambling story, nodding intently, gradually tuning my mood to his frequency. "A vital person vitalizes," Joseph Campbell said. So, too, a poised and purposeful person spreads calm. I took a deep breath, cooled off a little, and allowed myself—*forced* myself—to notice something about this savior of mine, anything. His muscled forearm, freckled like soup broth; the blueness of his shirt, short sleeved despite the ocean fog blowing in through the hissing automatic doors. His pits were dark-wet. I could smell his deodorant working. It had the smell of dignity.

I straightened my carriage—turning my spine into a lightening rod—and allowed myself a few physical sensations. And so, in that moment, practiced Zen. Left to its own devices, my mind is like a piece of raw meat slabbed on a rock in the afternoon sun: the maggots of overthinking chew through it in no time. When I shift the flow of energy from my brain to my breath, however, my neurotic and energy-wasting thoughts transform into sensory awareness, and I wake up to the world around me instead of being obsessed by the world within. My *hara*, or breathing center, becomes like a pot-bellied stove, sucking down and torching stray thoughts, so much brain confetti, turning them into fuel for the fire of consciousness.

With my lung bellows working, I gave myself to LAX and exhaled. Then with the in-breath I took the airport in: its crisp bleachy smell . . . the blood-red airline banner with its curly white calligraphy . . . that heinous Muzak rendition of Eric Clapton's already pretty heinous "Tears in Heaven." And in the infinitesimal in-between, where one breath ends and the other begins, there appeared, as a gift from who knows where, a more favorable version of myself, one less consumed by rage and self-pity, by inner heat and hate.

Consciously doing something that I'm supposed to just do naturally, like being present and breathing, often has the effect of making me realize how rarely I actually *do* do it. In crowded public places, for example, I almost always unconsciously regulate my breathing. It's as if I don't want to fully take these places in. But if I remain open to all the filthy and aggravating details on my journey's way, if I breathe them in, make them part of me, from the snooty stranger's cloying cloud of Samsara perfume to the slight menthol of a pube-bewigged urinal puck, I inoculate myself to their hellish aspects. Whatever you become one with cannot harm you.

Hour Four

With Jesus's help (TSA also stands for Totally Sometimes Angels), I finally discovered that today's fresh hell actually had interconnecting levels, à la Dante's *Inferno*. I was dealing with two bureaucracies: TSA and the airport police, which are separate entities with separate lost and founds—separate entities, that is, working in tandem.

"Which is to say," a policewoman told me with a fleshy grin, as though repeating an official motto: "creating double the confusion for half the effectiveness!"

She was one of those people who try to tug you into their orbit of extroversion, usually against your will. This made me feel shy, which in turn made me irate all over again. So much for the progress I'd just made with airport Jesus! The policewoman—let's call her Sergeant Girthy—was shouting at me from her desk behind a great sheet of bulletproof glass in a police bungalow on the airport's outskirts. In her massive man hands was my teacher's iPad. The device had just hit the market, and she was treating it as nothing less than the Second Coming of Christ.

"Why you ain' got no e-books on this thing?" she said.

It was an accusation. She tapped the iPad and stared at me. Her peers, a flock of short, skinny men all armed to the teeth with that Los Angeles police-officer staple—a plastic coffee mug with spill-free top—fixed me with their collective gaze. This woman was tremendous in every way, an airport cop goddess with her he-harem of minicop minions. The sheer scope of her forehead alone exerted such a gravitational pull on my attention that I was momentarily thrown off balance.

"Uh, it's not my iPad," I stammered.

"Whose iPad is it?" She held the device a little closer to her epic bosom, as if answering her own question.

"It's my teacher's."

"You a little old for school."

"I'm a Buddhist monk," I said, for the first time that day.

She looked me up and down. I was found wanting. "You don' look like no Buddhist monk."

My knuckles found their pissy place at my hips: "And what's a Buddhist monk *supposed* to look like?"

"Asian! Japanese or Korean or some shit," she said, not missing a beat. "Not no Opie Cunningham with an iPad, tell *you* what."

Did she just call me Opie friggin' Cunningham? I fumed. *Totally inappropriate! Especially given the fact that . . . well, that I look like Opie Cunningham.*

Suddenly I felt as if I were trapped in one of those classical Chinese koan stories where the neophyte monk gets shown the true meaning of Zen by a wise and irascible old tea lady. With her burly biceps, gang tats, and no-nonsense attitude, it was more like a "Mr. T" lady in this case, but still. In honestly and cheerfully insulting me to my face, Ms. T held up a mirror to my own petty preconceptions and prejudices, which I had grouped under the name Flinty McGee as though they were wholly separate from me and then compulsively indulged in all day. Flinty McGee, I very briefly realized, was like a sock puppet that I gave life to. Without my voice, my energy, my fingers up his butt, he lay limp and lifeless within me.

Ms. T eyed me warily, then looked back at the iPad lovingly. "Oh—" she said, gently tapping the screen. The iPad had reverted back to its sign-in box. Her eyes, big as crab apples, narrowed to slits. "What's that password again?" She stared at me. Everyone in the room stared at me. I'd called her office just minutes before with the four-digit code, but now I was drawing a total blank.

"C'mon now, I'mma need that password, honey." She crossed her arms and began laughing. The whole room practically shook along with her—a regular girthquake. "Maybe it's your birthday or your mama's birthday," she offered. "What was the name of your childhood pet, how 'bout that?"

They all nodded and agreed that this was probably it, the name of my childhood pet. "That's *my* ATM password," a black Barney Fife said, as though this sealed it.

The name of my favorite childhood pet was Green Bean. I loved that lizard. I got him when I was six. "That little guy actually had *personality*," my dad had confirmed, taking me into his arms after Green Bean escaped from his cage and shot off into a heating duct for good. And no, the iPad password *was not* the name of my childhood pet—I couldn't think with these overcaffeinated cops yakking at me.

"Shuddup!" Ms. T cried, "Y'all makin' him more nervous."

There was instant silence, and in the womb of this charged, trusting hush my eyes slipped shut. . . . "Lookout, this monk's in the *zone!*" Ms. T said, making some kind of face that was supposed to indicate enlightenment.

"Oh four oh eight," I cried. "My teacher's birthday. And the Buddha's birthday."

She entered the password and the device glowed back to life, and she and her peers cheered and leaned into its light and cooed and giggled proudly at this marvelous little bundle of freshly delivered iJoy. She looked up at me and gave me a grin as big as half a paper plate. It was an invitation. We were to have a moment together, all of us. We were to worship this sacred tablet, handed down to the American people by Steve Jobs, that modern secular saint with the holy trinity of qualifications: an outside-the-box individual, a major contributor to our material well-being, a one-of-a-kind personality.

Her smile waited for my heart to catch up. She had the patience of a young mother, of a large black woman from a hard part of town who'd grown bigger than her surroundings, her setbacks, the hand she'd been dealt. This was my chance to rejoin the human race through a moment of shared tenderness with a good woman having a great day. Could I get over myself and throw the old girl a bone?

It is amazing how Flinty seems to take me over sometimes. He possesses me from within, from every angle, and there is just nothing I can do about it. If I figure out how to practice with anger, he goes underground and reemerges as a kind of disgusted misanthropy wherein I can't even be bothered to fight with people. Whenever I defeat him, sooner or later he comes back even stronger, in a new form. It's as though I had some basic badness as an integral part of me and no amount of spiritual practice would ever dissolve it into my bloodstream for good.

Ms. T slid the iPad through a thick slit in the bulletproof glass. "Take care now, honey!" she shouted, still waging her indomitable grin campaign.

She gave me one last chance to smile back. She was the Michael Jordan of smilers, able to hang her grin out there in the air for a miraculously long time. So I let her. I took a good long look at

her, held her eyes with mine, waited for her smile to slowly drop
. . . every last trace of it . . . and then I turned around without so
much as a good-bye, leaving her a little worse for having met me,
the thought of which made me smile broadly, finally, to myself as
I gave her my ass on the way out the door.

Booyah! Flinty roared within.

Hour Five

I crossed a vast expanse of sun-spangled autos, tucked myself into
a quiet concrete corner off a queue of taxis, and devoted several
quality minutes to deeply resenting the high-tech tablet nestled
in my lap. *We have inventions to see into the furthest reaches of our
cosmos down through the heart of the heart of the heart of the atom,*
I mused, *but when it comes to looking into ourselves—to seeing the
I—our greatest technologies fall short. Only the human heart can
see into the human heart.*

And looking into my own heart through the endlessly serpen-
tine coils of traffic on the honking, cursing, bumper-to-bumper
crawl back home, I didn't like what I saw.

I saw Flinty McGee doing a victory dance.

There is nothing worse than riding through long stretches of
traffic in silence with Flinty McGee in the passenger seat. I feel
like the college girl who got drunk last night and slept with a particularly distasteful slug; let this person empty himself inside me,
for I was too weak willed to fight him off; and now I have to spend
the day shooting darts in his filthy apartment or running errands
with him as he gloats and belches and winks.

Here's a fair question to ask a monk: Has your practice touched
that deepest, most vile, hateful, hideous part of yourself—has it
thrown the curtain on that demonic inner rodent and given it an
ultimatum? Or is that part of you still alive? Is it underneath all
of your *zazen* meditation practice, all of those years of retreats
and private meetings with your enlightened teacher? Have you

simply, through your spiritual work, found a way to live with that worst part of yourself, the dark and filthy little shit stain in your soul that you first sought to scrub a luminous white when you took up spiritual work? I get some version of this question time and again from new students and the Zen curious: What is the point of spiritual work if it doesn't make you a better person in some way?

One of the most disheartening things about being a full-time monk is watching your peers refuse or remain unable to change, grow up, and transform as the years go by; watching them stay the same and move higher up in the monastic ranks; and knowing that if you take away their robes, their position, their title, they are, underneath it all, the same rotten person they ever were. They've just been hiding from the world behind robes and religion all of these years.

And the most devastating thing of all is when you realize that people feel this way about you.

Hour Six

Blacktop became icy gravel as I swung into our driveway, where I was greeted not by conifers quivering in a cool quiet breeze but by a boisterous orgy of invaders glutting on snow play. It was parking-lot-a-palooza. A man was, no lie, juggling three lit torches. The stink of sizzling hibachi meat farted through my cracked window. I leaned into the horn, and dozens of sledders scattered as I skidded around the icy uphill corner. I slammed on the brakes, leaped from the Toyota, unlocked the chain, laid it down, drove forward a little, got out again, stretched the chain back out over the driveway, and reset the padlock behind me. Then I hopped into the truck and accelerated forward.

That's when I heard a sickening snap—and felt a tug at the truck.

I threw the Tacoma into park, jumped out, and sprinted around back—where an unnerving phalanx of faces was aimed at me. Some sat in a circle, playing cards and smoking, while others put the finishing touches on a snowman. This snowman was not like other snowmen. He had a rather enormous icicle for an erection.

I looked down. The chain lay in two limp pieces in the slush at my feet. The poles on either side of the driveway were bent and half pulled out of the earth, mangled and defeated looking. I'd been careless in reattaching it, and somehow the chain had gotten caught under the trailer hitch when I pulled forward.

And that was the end of the sole barrier separating our monastery from the outside world.

I sort of stood there and surveyed the situation, rubbing my chin thoughtfully while flushing red, trying to pretend that this sort of thing happens a lot and for a very good reason, which only a spiritual VIP like me can fully understand. My arms were tightly crossed, and I made eye contact with no one. Yet no one was fooled. There were snickers in the crowd. A few people were speaking in Spanish about me. (A gringo always knows.)

World: 1, Flinty: 0.

In my experience, you get the lessons that you need in this life. You put something out into the world, you manifest an energy through your intentions and actions, and then the world sends you back a message. The deeper you engage in a spiritual practice, the sharper these messages get. Sometimes it's almost comical how sharp they get. Like, you know, when you've spent all day trying to flee LAX back to your monastic hideaway, where there is a crisp distinction between the worldly and the spiritual, with a nice chain fence separating the two—and now that distinction lies in two useless pieces at your feet.

What was the world trying to tell me?

"Hey bro, Snow Buddha loves you," a voice called out.

I looked up. A smart-ass teen was stroking Frosty the Snow Pimp's priapic icicle, which now sported two strategically positioned snow balls.

This got a big laugh from the crowd.

I took a deep breath—*be calm, goddammit!* My knees soaked in a soup of frigid slop as I tried to yank the broken chain halves together. I wheezed with effort. My struggle was incommensurate with the shrieking frivolity around me, and people stopped to watch. I was angry. They could tell. I was unable to unite the broken chain halves with the padlock. I released them into the snow with a low animal groan.

There was another burst of laughter from the peanut gallery as I struggled to my feet. "Hey, now!" someone shouted. The smart-ass teen's lips had found their way around Frosty's frozen phallus. "Damn that shit's cold," he cried. He flicked his tongue over the tip of the icicle, his eyes straining to meet the various digital devices capturing him for posterity. No doubt his Facebook page would host the picture tomorrow, with the caption *"Suckin' off Frosty at Mount Alcatraz Monastery! Check out that monk beeyatch with the poo face in the background! Snow ho ho!"*

Peels of laughter halved in volume as I slammed the truck door and spun my wheels to the other end of camp, kicking up snow the whole way. I felt big and strong and powerful in my V6 4x4— until the front end heaved one way, the aft slid oppositely, and the entire vehicle crashed down over a brilliant mountain of white and stopped.

I got out. Thick heavy flakes were falling in the headlights, as if a sky-wide down pillow had suddenly burst over my head. I studied the hilly cleavage between which the monastery driveway curves. Hadn't really noticed this when I'd pulled into the parking lot . . . nope. It had snowed a good two feet up here since I'd left for the airport that morning. The truck looked like a beached whale. Of the four massive tires, none were touching ground.

I was genuinely fucked. Snow would continue to dump, foot upon foot, and a week would pass before my monk peers would return from up north to help dig the truck out. I was totally alone, with only the worst parts of me to keep me company. That is,

Flinty McGee, who had just opened his trench coat inside me. He was wearing nothing underneath. His old, unused love organ swayed by his kneecaps like a pendulum as he hissed at me and flicked his filthy gray salamander of a tongue.

The Final Hour

I hiked through the blizzard, temporarily losing one of my slip-on shoes as an overhead bough waited until I was directly below it to release a cascade of snow. Soaked and furious, I invaded the cabin of the student from whom I had been stealing cigarettes and stole one more. I torched it in the cloudy moonlight as squeals of laughter echoed throughout camp. Emboldened by my failure to fix the chain barrier, invaders had begun to explore the monastery proper. They were like a legion of zombies skulking toward me through the black-and-white night. Soon the armies of unconsciousness would find places to smoke pot and form drum circles and make love; they would stack Budweiser cans in front of the *zendo* and crookedly urinate their names in the snowbanks by my teacher's cabin.

Here we go again! I thought, as a procession of invaders loudly tromped up the driveway. Every winter a fresh crew of them gets the exact same brilliantly original idea: to go on a "spade raid" and pilfer plastic shovels from our tool shed with the vain hope of using them as impromptu sleds. "Over here," a rowdy teen barked at his peers, waving one of our brand-new, top-shelf red shovels, which a kindly monk had gone out of his way to purchase on a recent trip to Colorado. Plastic shards of it would litter the mountainside in the morning.

I had a memory then of the most stolen book at the Either/Or Bookstore, site of my first retail job in LA more than fifteen years ago. Was it *The Anarchist Cookbook*? Something by William S. Burroughs? *Steal This Book* by Abbie Hoffman? No, no, and no. It was the *King James Bible,* by a margin so wide believers should be wincing right now. People felt it was their God-given right to help themselves to spiritual knowledge, just like they felt perfectly justified in snatching up and destroying the monastery's shovels.

That says it all, I concluded. Even the most spiritually ambitious among us are basically shits, with laypeople nicking bibles to get their religious fix and Zen monks looking on while smoking bitterly and cursing the human condition and all of its constituents.

There was a bustle of activity down by the oak tree where our driveway forks toward the student cabins. I saw cigarette lighters flash for light as a clot of invaders surrounded the monastery truck. I could see them peering through the windows. It occurred to me then that the iPad was still in the truck.

Which I hadn't locked.

Those spade raiders are going to steal my teacher's iPad!

I felt a bolt of fear shoot through me. Then there was a blank space within, followed instantly by a surge of pure unalloyed rage. This one-two punch of fear, then fury, was instructive. Not that I noticed just then. I began quivering, my breath short and sharp, a rapid-fire hiccup. I could feel Flinty McGee trying to burst through my chest like the slimy penile space creature in *Alien*. I'd wasted the whole day pursuing that ridiculously overvalued iBauble, and now, with its theft imminent, I had officially arrived at the crossroads of wit's end and going postal.

Yet somehow, after nearly a decade of Zen practice, I had enough presence of mind—no, that wasn't the organ: presence of *lungs*—to hold my rage in my body, to cradle it in my meat and bones, instead of letting it go to my head. I breathed deeply and felt the thick reds, the waves of bottomless black undulating beneath the surface, the great heaving molten substrata of self, amorphous, oozing, white-hot.

I tried to stay with the raw physical sensation of the experience, to keep it flowing, circulating, instead of letting it harden into emotion and assume the Mr. Hyde–like features of Flinty McGee: the beast blood; that smashed windshield of a furrowed brow; his black, cavernous anus, from which a diseased, oily turd of a hateful deed or word would inevitably come rocketing out into the world, plopping into someone or another's punch bowl.

I worked my lungs and followed the fire down, a plunging energy trail halting in my guts: the foundation. *Taitoku*, this is called in Rinzai Zen Buddhism: "to apprehend with the body." Beneath my compulsive surface self-conversation there was a story line, beneath the story line there was emotion, beneath the emotion there was feeling, beneath the feeling there was physical sensation and then bodily awareness. This was the stopping point. In the lower brain, upon which the upper one rests. When you're spazzing out and people tell you to "*get ahold of yourself!*" this is usually where they expect you to find the handle: behind your belly button.

"Can't I think *at all* during *zazen* meditation?" I once asked my mentor. "You can," he said, touching my gut, "but only *right here*."

And this is ultimately where I found Wimpy McGee. Right in the pit of my stomach.

He appeared just then on the heels of an insight—*Behind my anger is fear: the two go hand in hand*—looking frail and hairless. Shivering. Glistening with afterbirth that he will never quite clean off. Terrified; his eyes shooting left-right, left-right. You got the sense that he could feel the very photons that landed on his skin and that he felt guilty if he didn't personally introduce himself to every last one.

Wimpy McGee is that most vulnerable, precious part of myself, every inch of him as sensitive as a sexual organ or an eyeball. He lives within me and grows younger by the second. Wimpy McGee (not me, of course) wet my bed at least five nights a week until I was eight years old. Jason Anitch once duct taped Wimpy McGee's hands, feet, and butt to their respective components on my Huffy Thunder Trail bike, then set it in motion and cackled as I pedaled furiously in circles and eventually toppled over from exhaustion. (You can laugh. It's kind of funny in retrospect.)

Taken separately, Flinty was horrifying and Wimpy was pitiful. But when I saw these two McGees together, felt them huddled inside me at the bottom of my breath, they each made sense in light of the other. My anger and aggression, I realized, came from fear, a fear of getting hurt. Wimpy needed Flinty to protect him, and the uglier, meaner, and more bizarre Flinty was, the better he did his job. No one would go near Wimpy as long as Flinty was blocking the way, passing wind while whispering in sexual tones to an old doll with missing limbs, occasionally turning to one side and spitting bloody teeth onto the sidewalk.

Just being able to see these two parts of me clearly in that moment was enough to give me peace. I didn't need to not be angry. I just needed to stay with my anger long enough to see what it actually was and how it arose (or co-arose with my chicken heart). This kind of big-picture thinking, where things make sense as a whole when taken in relation to each other and not as unconditionally separate parts, is the spiritual project in a nutshell. Spiritual work is not the same thing as self-help. It is not meant to "everlastingly improve" or fix you. It's a means to help you see clearly what's been there all along, beneath the surface, both in the larger sense and within yourself. You don't have to change things. Just see them properly, bear witness, and they fall into place. Attention, not intervention, leads to true healing. If you spend all of your time and energy trying to become a better person or "change the world," you miss a profound opportunity to see how all the imperfect, muddled, fucked-up things in our world come together, find their place among each other, and then form something far greater.

More shouting from the driveway—fresh packs of teenage zombies were arriving from all directions, coalescing around the truck, a hullaballoo that I was helpless to ascertain without my glasses. I was forced to listen, then, and it didn't sound good.

Shouts of the worst kind sounded, young men amped up, that chorus of testosterone that usually climaxes as a duet, with some other—a scapegoat, a victim—screaming.

For so long I had lived within the monastery walls and kept the world at bay. Now the world had gotten in. So I pinched out my half-smoked Marlboro, that false prop, took a deep clean breath, and set out to meet it.

Once I made the decision to act, I ceased to be terrified and enraged and grew stronger and lighter with every snow-clogged stride. It felt good to finally be taking steps toward the kind of real-world fray that I had been fleeing all day. I thought about putting on my robes, which always drives these invaders away in droves. They would see me stumbling along, with my huge sleeves swaying, and like the Sand People in *Star Wars* when Obi-Wan appears, they'd croak menacingly and scatter. But I opted against it. I didn't need them. Like the cigarette, robes would merely be a false prop.

I was finally starting to pick up on the hints that the world had been dropping all day. I'd moved to the monastery nearly a decade earlier to pursue a path out of my confusion and suffering. But over the years I had made an "identity" out of that path, when the point instead was to become its *embodiment*. Ultimately, like an iPad, monk's robes are a tool, a spiritual technology. They can be used either to hide from or to enhance genuine human interaction. They are an outfit, matched perfectly by the monastic setting. But what happens when the costume comes off, I descend to sea level, and I'm nowhere near a meditation cushion or a Buddha statue? Who am I then? If that day was any indication: a pale-skinned schmuck with a stiff back and a bug up his ass.

Ultimately, the true monastery is something you carry inside you, wherever you go. It is not some groovy, magical place you gain access to with a couple layers of intricately sewn black fabric. It is not the creation of new special spiritual surroundings, and with them, a new special spiritual ego, the monastic ego. It is the art of dissolving your ego into your surroundings, *wherever* you go. The true monk stands at the point where all of his many identities and energies and inner McGees converge and cancel each other out, what Zen master Rinzai called "the man of no rank."

There were more of them than I had thought. Close to a dozen. Maybe they were digging a shallow grave to dump my body into after they had their way with me. I heard the *clink* of shovels hitting something hard . . . like the windows of a truck. I squinted and broke into a snow-befuddled jog. The human heart is the opposite of eyes: the closer it gets to something, the more perspective it has. I thought I was charging down there to kick these invaders out. As it turned out, I was arriving to help them help me.

The whole scene fell into place as I came upon it, shovels pitching high and low. *Aw hell,* I realized, *they're digging my truck out.*

"Great of you to join us," said the wise-ass teen who had pleasured the snow Buddha earlier. He handed me one of my own shovels. The world, that old punster, was sending me one final message for the day: *Whatever we take from you, we give back in spades.*

As I took the shovel, I felt Flinty and Wimpy embrace within me, and for the first time that day I manifested their love child, Smiley McGee. Earlier, as I had tended to the monastery alone, the mountain had felt haunted. We see demons all around us when we refuse to face the ones inside us. Now my surroundings felt not haunted but alive. If I carried the true monastery within me, that was also where I found the true mountainside upon which it rested. I was my own foundation: I carried it within. Beneath both Flinty and Wimpy was solid ground.

My movements were smooth, fluid, and natural as I hurled all of that whiteness back toward heaven. I could not tell the difference between me and the mountain as I swung my shovel into it, the snow at my feet sparkling in clouds above, the moonlight above splashing from the silver hubcaps at my feet, the whole world turned upside down and inside out, and everything perfectly out of place and in order.

13

Hugging Whoooole World!

It is the final evening of Rohatsu, the most intense retreat on the Zen monastic calendar (the "monk killer," Japanese practitioners call it), and we are taking a drive down to the sutra hall, where the following morning we would perform the traditional Jodo-e ceremony in honor of the Buddha's enlightenment. For the first time in anyone's recollection, our teacher would not be attending.

"I coming diiiiiiiificult," he'd said in his broken English. "My body ooooold." His face, ancient yet lineless, bloomed into one of those buoyant expressions that the elderly and infants have in common.

Body old, check. Going to the sutra hall difficult, check. And yet here we were at 11 P.M., loading him into the old Lexus. *He should be resting at this late hour,* I thought. *What does he want to show us?* Exhausted and ornery, I was in no mood for a lesson. Which is to say, I was ripe for the kind my teacher excels in providing.

I crouched on the driver's seat, and a nun guided our teacher from his wheelchair down onto my upturned palm. Not five feet tall, this man is nonetheless profoundly dense. I heaved and strained until he was comfortably positioned in the passenger seat. Have you ever felt the butt of an impossibly old man? Well, there's not much of it to feel. It was as pliant and yielding as over-chewed bubble gum, and my fingers went straight to the bone. I could feel his skeleton. He is that exposed to the world. "There is just the thinnest membrane separating him from death," my mentor told me recently.

"Okay, Roshi?" I asked, using his honorific.

"Yeahhh," he sighed. He was cocooned in two cashmere blankets and a massive scarf that went around his tiny yet rotund body three times. He wore an enormous fur hat that towered on the top of his head. He looked like a Mongolian warlord. He pursed his lips and blew through them. *"Ooooook."*

I carefully drove the length of camp through fog that becomes clouds when seen from below the mountain. We passed two cooks heaving steaming silver cauldrons up the driveway. It was time for *tempatsu,* the tradition of eating udon noodles in a thin broth on the last night of Rohatsu.

"Tempatsu, Roshi," I said, and was overjoyed when he seemed unconcerned that we would be missing it. The Japanese like to slurp their noodles; apparently it is a culturally accepted way of expressing culinary approval. And so naturally all forty of us Americans sit there in our Southern California *zendo,* pucker our lips, and inhale our noodles as noisily as possible, looking for all the world like delegates from the First Annual Japanophile convention. My first year here, the slurping apparently wasn't of a sufficient volume, and so one of the *zendo* officers felt compelled to break the silence and announce: "Slurping okay."

When my teacher dies I will have many such memories of Americans engaging in formal Zen practice. Fortunately, I will have other memories too.

I wheeled Roshi through the weather-warped double doors of the sutra hall, which was in various states of preparation for the following day's ceremony. Roshi's eyes slowly traveled right, then left, taking in the scene. One of the priests produced her Blackberry and began recording our teacher on video. I watched this old master on her high-tech screen as she dictated the date, the time, and the people present. Most of what our teacher does now is accompanied by this kind of hullabaloo. We can't take for granted that he'll be around much longer.

In many ways this ancient man has become like a child whose every breath and bowel movement we must monitor. This isn't sycophantic hero worship: the guy is a living relic, as if someone performed incantations over a classical koan text and out he crawled, flinging teacups and shouting non sequiturs. He is literally the last of his kind, a pre-WWII-trained Rinzai Zen monk with core Buddhist principles hardwired into the very marrow of his bones. Every teaching he gives is like a piece of fruit fallen from a tree that is about to go extinct from this planet.

Be that as it may, I was exhausted and, frankly, annoyed by the proceedings. Let me ask you something: How many times do you think a Zen monk bows during an average morning of full-on formal practice? I once counted. We're talking forty to sixty bows here, and that's not including the nine full prostrations you perform variously in sets of threes. You bow when you enter the *zendo,* bow to the tea server, bow to get up and sling the *kesa* portion of your robes over your shoulder, bow to the "*zendo* guardian" on the way out to your private meeting with Roshi, whom you will then bow four times to, twice before you even say howdy.

"If you're ever in doubt about what to do," I tell new students, "just bow. You can't go wrong."

Earlier that day I had taken a controversial bathroom break at a time not normally allowed for such bodily functions. I entered a stall and slumped on the toilet seat in my underrobes, only to discover that in fact I didn't have to go at all. I guess I simply wanted a moment away from formal Zen practice and subconsciously drifted to the only place in camp where I was assured of one.

Hell, I think I just wanted to escape all of those bows—the bows and the punctilious and heavily policed *oryoki*-style meals and the cloying and ubiquitous Kyo-nishiki incense and the weighty forced silences of the *zendo* and our American mispronunciation of the Japanese mispronunciation of the Chinese mispronunciation of the Sanskrit mispronunciation of the original Pali chants—and the googolplexian other contrivances that make monastic Zen life what Chögyam Trungpa Rinpoche once called "the biggest joke that has ever been played in the spiritual realm. But it is a practical joke, very practical."

Sitting on a toilet I had no intention of using, I whispered my sacred mantra, given to me by my very first teacher, which was pop culture, mostly MTV, mainly eighties new wave, specifically the Vapors single hit: *"I'm turning Japanese / I think I'm turning Japanese / I really think so!"*

At eleven that evening, I was still sour on all things Zen. Roshi must have smelled the nastiness oozing from the bald pores of my febrile skull, because he immediately banished me to a tiny crawl space behind the altar. He did this in the name of choreographing tomorrow's ceremony. To reach this place of exile, I had to climb over the white-sheet-draped altar with its ceremonial pound-cake platters and towering tea and fruit stands, and I felt very foolish standing in this dark stuffy space in my elaborate "seven-layered" robes. Though what I quickly discovered is that sometimes feeling foolish feels very, very good. It breathes air into that dark stuffy crawl space between your ears.

Every time I tried to poke my head around the curtain, Roshi would point at me and laugh. *"Ha ha ha,* Shozan-san." I felt like the hapless protagonist in a Beckett play, consigned to some ridiculous fate by a mad taskmaster. *"A-hahahahahahaha!"* Roshi cried, jiggling askew that hat that looked like a small television made out of fur. "Shozan's in his little cage," said the nun I'd been fighting with all week.

Roshi turned next to the priest who would be pinch-hitting for him at tomorrow's ceremony. "More on floor!" he cried, gesturing for the priest to put his *hara,* or diaphragm, flat on the carpet while performing his great bows. This particular priest, with his eggheady Ken Wilber glasses and inexhaustable penchant for mischief, knows Zen form inside and out and has a unique talent for tweaking it just enough so that you know he's doing something wrong but you can't quite figure out what it is. He sprawled on the floor, looking like a gunshot victim, trying to mash his *hara* into the carpet, doing some abomination of the break-dance move the Worm.

"No, no, no," Roshi cried, and began to rise up out of his wheelchair in that time-slowing way of his. Dealing with an extremely old person is like dealing with an extremely drunk person: they can tip in any direction at any time. People scrambled to box him in and grab a limb. The great thing about Roshi, I realized, as he stood, balanced, and then produced possibly the longest flatulence I have ever heard in my entire life, followed by, "*Ohhhhhh,* gas come out," is that he allows you to see both the "great and powerful Wizard of Oz" manifestation and the "wrinkled old man behind the curtain" manifestation. Both are equal. To favor the spiritual is to be "too in love with heaven," he claims. "And the problem with heaven is—no toilets and no restaurants there."

"Oh, no, uh-oh," the nun murmured as Roshi descended to his knees before the dragon-embroidered bowing mat, his joints sounding off like confetti poppers and all of us gasping and groaning in sympathetic agony.

First he crunched into what's known as child's pose in yoga, his hands outstretched before him, his shins flat on the carpet— the most prostrate stage in a Zen great bow. But then he began to slowly, impossibly, stretch his legs out behind him one nano— and much-argued-against—inch at a time, until he was lying flat on his stomach with his face pressed into the bowing mat. It was really quite extraordinary, like watching someone suddenly do a double backflip while waiting in line at McDonald's. He balanced on the fulcrum of his tight, rounded stomach, arms and legs outstretched like a kid pretending to fly.

From my confinement behind the altar, I craned to catch a glimpse of "The Roshi Show" over a votive candle and practically set my *koromo* sleeves ablaze. Surely some mind-blowing lesson awaited us at the end of all of this significant effort! But then, maybe the effort itself was the lesson.

"This . . . how Tibetans do it," he grunted.

The priests looked at one another, pens paused over their notebooks. "What, Roshi?" someone asked. "This . . . how Tibetans do it," he repeated, his face muffled on the bowing mat.

"Apparently in the Tibetan tradition they go all the way down and lie flat like this when doing their full prostrations," the priest with the Ken Wilber glasses explained.

That was the big lesson.

But already Roshi was rising, and the two priests and the nun were scrambling to help ease his rickety, tendon-trembling ascent. Now he was going to show us how full bows before the altar and the Buddha statue were done in the Zen tradition. Whatever. I was over this little lesson, mentally downshifting as I often do when I privately figure that my teacher is having a senior moment.

I was studying the bloody end of a cuticle I'd been nervously gnawing all week when I looked up and saw my teacher staring straight at me—straight *through* me. He was at the top of the bowing mat, squared off in front of the altar, looking very samurai, his hands passing just over his heart, that invisible sword. Behind me was the Buddha statue he was ostensibly addressing with his momentum-gathering gestures. He looked ever so slightly past me to it. And so I saw how he sees the Buddha.

I have never been looked at this way in my entire life. It took me completely off guard. Have you ever been fixed with a gaze of total love that was not a smile? He was, in fact, utterly expressionless. *How do these Zen masters do it?* I thought. *Catch you so off guard with something so simple?*

I watched him find his balance at the top of the bowing mat; I watched him extend those tiny, withered hands, the fingerprints worn smooth, out in front of him; I watched him open his arms and widen them in a looping circle, hands meeting at the palms in a prayer gesture or *gassho*.

"Taking whooooooooooooole world into your arms. Hugging *whole world*," he said.

For that's exactly what he did. He took the whole universe into his frail gray arms and brought it back into his chest like a great samurai sheathing his sword, unlocking for me in a single phrase and motion what had for nearly a decade been a largely meaningless gesture, repeated by rote, day upon day. "Turning Japanese"— aping the customs and rituals of a spiritual tradition so foreign to me—didn't seem like such a bad thing now. Watching my teacher in action, it hit me all at once what a tremendous container the rituals and customs are for a truly enlightened mind and what a profound opportunity they afford for a cathartic gathering and releasing of group anxieties and energies.

"*Etai—etai!*" Roshi suddenly cried, Japanese for *ouch*. A few simple movements. The result—utter agony. The wheelchair appeared behind him, and as he collapsed into it, my heart sank along with him, for I finally realized what I had witnessed that evening: certain crucial aspects of a tradition—and so, a whole way of life—literally dying before my eyes.

Rinzai Zen customs and rituals don't come naturally to us Westerners, but in our *sangha,* our community of practitioners, we heartily participate in them because in the context of this great teacher and his powerful manifestation, they make sense. But what, I wondered, will happen to these customs and rituals when he's gone? Will we have learned what's really behind them, or have we just been blindly participating in them, riding on the coattails of our teacher's understanding? I don't think most of us will truly know the answer to this until he's gone. A great teacher is what an old friend used to call a quality problem. Sometimes it's hard to get out from under his or her enlightenment and learn to think and practice for yourself. But we will all have to, and soon.

When he sighs deeply and stares out his window, past the snowcapped mountain peaks, retreating deep within himself, Roshi looks like a great mythical animal who knows its time has come and who must soon go off into the forest to die alone. His tenuous health is like a bubble shifting under a carpet: one day his blue-veined feet are swollen but his back is okay; the next, his sciatica is on fire but he "came out"—got unconstipated—that morning; then his eyes are dried out and his mucus is green, but his energy is *genki*—good, strong.

Where his reach once extended to every aspect of *sangha* life, a gulf of responsibility now opens up behind him that we must fill. But the question on everyone's noodle-slurping lips is *how*? Change a tradition and you change its meaning: this is how traditions die. But follow it to the letter and you become its slave: Who wants to be a spiritual company man, a bean counter of the cloth?

About a year ago Roshi got the flu, which can be lethal at his age. Three of us bore him down a flight of stairs to the Town Car, folded him into the front seat, and sped him to Cedars–Sinai, where his attendant and I stayed with him for a week, sleeping on the floor and in chairs upholstered with, it seemed, large slabs of granite.

I saw him naked for the first time. I helped him urinate and defecate. I spoke to nurses and doctors on his behalf, and he and I watched trashy medical dramas on the TV together, which he interspersed with relevant dharmic commentary, usually revolving around the figure of a pretty nurse. The standards of formality significantly lowered, and a new intimacy developed. We even joked around. "White rice, white flour, and white sugar," he proudly stated when I asked him his secret to living a long life. "And sake!" He reminded me of how my grandmother used to say she felt as we braved icy parking lots to her favorite diners: newly game for life with this whippersnapper at her side.

More important, watching Roshi in a nonmonastic setting gave me new insight into just how seamlessly he had made the Zen tradition his own—and vice versa. An uneasy tension had always existed between my free-spirited self and the hyperdisciplined, even militaristic conventions of formal Zen practice. But that week in the hospital I began to see that the proper relationship between an individual and a tradition *is* one of tension—healthy, creative tension. This is what produces spiritual growth, both in the individual and in the tradition itself: not the individual's solo efforts nor the tradition's overarching forms but the two locked into a single struggle/dance, from which a new kind of person—and practice—emerges.

With the full force of the tradition behind him, my teacher searched within himself (the "backward step," as Dogen called it) and eventually broke through, turning himself inside out and taking the outside in. The tradition became personal and the personal universal. As the religious historian Karen Armstrong has pointed out, the tendency in our age is either to reject the traditional and remain isolated, secular individualists or to cling to religious forms and ideals and become fundamentalists. But the truth, like all truths, lies somewhere in between: We can't do it on our own, nor can the tradition do it for us. When the individual and the tradition are perfectly wed, intermingled and indistinguishable, a spiritual heavy hitter—a genuine master—is born, and an institution is revitalized.

In short, the tradition must be dissolved within the individual, and the individual must dissolve within the tradition. That's the middle way.

Toward the end of our strange, harrowing "vacation" in the hospital, I opened an Odwalla juice, poured it into a paper cup, delivered it to his bedside, and flat-out asked my teacher, who was swathed in a nest of blinking lights and wires and looked, with his soft pink skull and silvery hairnet (though of course he has no hair), like an alien life-form preparing to return to his home planet (the "space fetus," I dubbed him that day): "Roshi-sama: are you afraid of dying?"

It didn't take him long to answer: "Not afraid of dying. Afraid I die and no one understand my teaching!"

Over the next two days I watched him literally come back from the dead. "Hospital where people go to die!" he shouted at us, the formerly charmed nurses now exchanging nervous glances. "I not die till I one hundred twenty-eight!" *Resurrecting,* he calls it: "There is no true religion without resurrection." I have watched him do this time and time again. Get sick, slip into an exhaustion coma, loiter on death's door—and then a day later he is reborn, fresh life rippling through him as he waves his gnarled manzanita stick in our private meeting. *This is why I stick around, don the robes, participate in the rituals, put up with this abuse,* I would think, ducking. *Because some teachings transcend tradition.*

Roshi has often said that he will not die until true Buddhism is born in this country, but what will an American Buddhism look like? What *does* it look like? If my practice is the proverbial raft to the other shore, then which of the customs and rituals will I take with me when my teacher dies, and which will I heave overboard?

These questions were haunting me on the final evening of Rohatsu, as I drove Roshi from the sutra hall back to his cabin. But my worries cleared when the clouds briefly parted above and below and a twinkling vista of stars and city lights opened up. I studied Roshi's one exposed hand, liver-spot marbled and gripping the handle above the door for support. Is there anything more beautiful than old, banged hands that have been put to good use over a lifetime? A tradition, I thought, is like an old man: it must be taken care of, taken with a grain of salt, taken for what it is: precious, limited, a window into the past and, properly plumbed, a door to the future. There we stand at the hinge, making it all happen—or not.

When the time comes, I decided, *I'll leave off noodle slurping but bring with me every last one of my bows.* Noodle slurping I can live without, but the practice of taking the cosmos above and the metropolis below—"the *whoooooooooole* world"—into my arms and sheathing them in my heart?

That is nonnegotiable.

14

On the Road with Roshi

The Great Vehicle

It is high noon. I am power jogging across a sandstormy restaurant parking lot. The sun is baking the top of my bald head: I can literally feel it pinking. Soon it will go orange. Then red. My skull has become an airport terrorist-alert warning.

Almost there . . .

I yank open the door to our recreational vehicle, and the mechanical stairs drop down to greet me. I feel as if I were boarding a rectangular metal whale—rolled over on its side—through its blowhole. This thing is massive, and like many things massive—Kanye West's ego, for example, or Dolly Parton's rack—it is tacky but lovable. My arms curl around white plastic bags fat with Denny's takeout. *Let's eat!* screams my hunger-drunk grin.

But something's off.

My eyes dart left-right. Four people are assembled on RV furniture: the eyes of three of them fix me firmly as I hobble into the mini-living-room lair of the great whale's belly. Only my teacher, the Roshi, looks off—seated with his feet up on a big square cushion (to soothe his shot sciatica nerves) by the window, staring beyond the white crosses of a nearby dirt cemetery into the Mojave Desert, which is colorless and aggressively blank, as though nature were still thinking about what it wants to do with itself in this particular place.

"The plan has changed," Roshi's *inji*, or attendant, says, grinning.

Myoshin is petite, adorable, fierce, single, and roughly my age. She and Roshi share a special bond, along with a common ancestry (they were both born in Japan) and spotty English. I have seen them shake their fists in each other's face. I have seen them touch each other's cheeks while smiling. I have seen them banter back and forth like a vaudeville duo: "Roshi, you very old." "Not old! I will live one hundred twenty-eight!" "Nooo, thank-you!"

Her dark eyes sparkle at me: she loves delivering exciting news. "We're not going to the monastery. We're going the other way. Roshi wants to take us to Las Vegas."

We are between *seichus,* formal training periods, traveling from one Zen center to another in a forty-foot-long turf yacht/RV (the only comfortable means of transportation for our teacher these days). I call it the Great Vehicle. It has a bedroom, bathroom, living room, an analog clock above the dashboard with dried-out sea horses and sand dollars for numbers, and a steering wheel nearly the size of a hula hoop. It can comfortably carry a dozen people. Incidentally, the style of Buddhism we practice at our monastery is called *mahayana* in Sanskrit, which translates as the "great vehicle." In the Mahayana school of Zen, we seek enlightenment for the benefit of all beings. The Great Vehicle of Mahayana Buddhism refers to the size of one's heart and its ability to carry others.

Roshi's heart is huge but his body is small. And either he's getting even smaller, especially around the neck and jawline, or his ears are growing a little bigger every day. We're talking about a man who will never have the strength in his legs to stand up fully straight again. (He comes up to my sternum when I help him walk; I have the orange basal-skin-cell cancer spots on his bald head memorized.) Yet the years seem to be refining, not diminishing him. He is being reduced to his essence, which is the very definition of aging gracefully. This morning, lying in bed on his side, his pink body slightly cupped, the RV rumbling sonorously beneath him, Roshi looked fetal—not like a man approaching annihilation so much as one growing organically toward death, doing a metaphysical Nestea plunge backward in slow motion, out of time, out of being, his eyes open and holding mine the whole way down.

Yet looking at his schedule, you'd never know that he has lived to within fifteen years of his namesake—a legendary Zen master who passed away at one hundred twenty. Fifty years ago Roshi arrived on American shores from the Myoshin-ji temple complex in Kyoto, and he has taught nonstop ever since. He is in a state of near constant motion, going from one Zen center and set of disciples to the next. In reality, however, it is more that he moves several feet, from one seat to the next. The older he gets, the less he moves, and the more things move around him. He is at rest most of the time, while his monks and nuns are in constant motion on his behalf. In an average year he travels thousands of miles, meeting with as many monks, priests, and students, while having walked only a grand total of a hundred steps. Roshi is like the battery of our *sangha,* or community of practitioners: you put him in place and then everything lights up around him.

"Las Vegas?" I whisper, dropping the plastic Denny's bags on the fold-out dinner table. "He wants to go to Las Vegas? Why?"

Myoshin shrugs and can't stop grinning. "He wants to see the lights."

Roshi has only 30 percent hearing in his good ear, and we are in the bad habit of carrying on full-blown, half-whispered conversations about him in his presence. Typically he slits his eyes and pretends that he's backdrop, and then every once in a while he shifts slightly when something is said, and we all go silent and study him out of the corners of our eyes. Sitting there, he looks like a mountain, stony and settled. *But these mountains have ears. . . .*

Perched side by side on the RV couch, like two oversized lovebirds, is a pair of married Zen priests. Lew and Hattie are like a dharmic aunt and uncle to me, and I have grown immensely fond of them during our three (and counting) road trips together.

"Really? Vegas?" I moan.

"I'm afraid so," Lew says.

His head is cocked, his eyes turned upward, and he, too, is grinning. Everyone in this vehicle is grinning, I now realize, except me. A pretty big dude, Lew nonetheless has the metabolism of one of those hundred-pound high-energy Korean women who are always winning professional hot-dog-eating contests. He is bespectacled, with thick German features, including Brillo Pad eyebrows and a pair of enormous feet, which he is in the habit of sheathing in colorful pairs of those foot-glove socks that are popular now, each toe bulging forth brightly in a manner I find either cute or obscene, depending on how I feel about him that day.

Hattie speaks quickly, with half a smile, and is always checking our coordinates on the road with her iPhone, which she says is never working. Once, after I suffered from a life-threatening illness, she had me form a circle with my thumb and forefinger. Then she closed her eyes and stuck her own finger in the circle and began jiggling it around while chanting to the internal organ that had recently broken down: "Accessing pancreas, accessing pancreas! Requesting permission to speak with Shozan's pancreas!" She is a trained acupuncturist and a modern-day medicine woman, with short-cropped gray hair and a sly, comical shamaness quality, both lightening the mood of the trip and proving to be its anchor in many ways.

On the road, Hattie and Lew work as a team. Lew does the doing, and Hattie does the redoing.

"Nope, nope—turn here, Lew. You missed it, go back."

"Oh, dear, sorry, dear, hang on to your yarmulkes," Lew cries, yanking the massive steering wheel and sending all the drawers on one side of the RV shooting out.

These are great people to be traveling with. And I haven't been to Vegas in ten years and would actually love to see what the city has done with itself. So what's my problem? Why has the color drained from my cheeks? Why is my expression broken seeming, as if someone dropped the fragile equanimity inside me and it shattered on the floor of my face? The truth pricks me in the guts: I have become one of those people who, when faced with the sudden and unexpected prospect of having fun, immediately begins to worry incessantly about all the important and useful things that a day of spontaneous levity will preempt.

Vegas? Not an option! I think. *I have to call Quality Septic and get the lower chemical toilets pumped before our* seichu *training season begins!*

I start to worry obsessively that I left the rearmost burner on in the monastery kitchen before embarking on this road trip. *The entire camp has probably burned to the ground by now, and these fools want to take a detour to sin city?!*

That's when my thoughts leap to my knapsack just a few short feet away at Lew's Sasquatch-sized, ten-toed purple feet. I am drawn to it like someone who has just quit smoking is drawn to the telltale square bulge in a passerby's pocket. My feet stay planted but my mind grabs the bag. I mentally unzip it, rifle through my dirty underwear past a couple of unread Zen classics . . . and open a sunglasses case, where I have hidden a tiny scrap of toilet paper. It is wrapped around three identical pills: Vicodin, a heavy-duty opium derivative used for killing pain—or if you abuse it, for feeling really, really good.

This is what addicts do: they want to celebrate by indulging in their vice when times are good, and they want to escape bad and boring times through their addiction, which pretty much leaves no time when they don't want to be high.

But wait a minute—I'm not a drug addict . . . am I?

Stabbed from Within

Four years ago, toward the climax of the most difficult *seichu* training season of my life, I escaped during a lunch break to the Owl's Nest, a cabin filled with books, movies, and a TV. In the thriller film I subsequently watched, the compound of a legendary crime figure is invaded by rivals, who put a gun to the head of the criminal's beloved young daughter and begin making demands. The crime magnate, who has drawn his own gun, then does something that struck me at the time, inexplicably and uncomfortably, as a metaphor for Zen practice. Instead of giving in to the demands of his rivals so that they will release his daughter, he shoots his daughter in the chest and kills her. Now his enemies have absolutely nothing to hold over him. He is completely free of them. He turns to them, smiling. Carnage ensues. One witness is left alive to tell others of what he saw that day, and a legend is born.

Zen, I concluded, is like crime: If you want to succeed in this practice, to be completely spiritually free, nothing can hold you back. See: Shakyamuni Buddha, who, while not a child murderer, did abandon his wife and child in the dead of night to embark upon his spiritual journey solo. Like the Buddha, I figured, you must give up all attachments, even seemingly healthy attachments to those things you truly love. You must hold the pistol of discipline and fortitude to whatever is most dear to you and pull the trigger, or inevitably you will be beholden to it and your practice will contain the seed of its compromise and demise. This is the true poverty of a monk: he empties his heart of all unnecessary things. By force, if necessary.

I didn't close my eyes once that night. And all the nights thereafter that winter I slept like a rock—and awoke exhausted every morning. Something snapped in me that afternoon in the Owl's Nest. I grew up a little; a little *too* much. Ask around: Zen students started calling me the Little Kaiser around this time. I became a lot more serious and a lot less fun, and then I awoke one morning at three o'clock with a pain in my side as though I were being stabbed to death—but from the inside. My pancreas had begun to excrete digestive enzymes onto itself, essentially eating me alive from within (the pancreas is one of those organs you cannot live without). I was alone at the monastery and vomited and shat myself into unconsciousness just after dialing 911. I spent the following week in the San Antonio Community Hospital, where nurses (or if you prefer, pharma-pimps) introduced me to Dilaudid, an opium-based painkiller.

It seemed okay to get high in the presence of medical professionals. And get high I did. Every time I pushed the call button, a nurse's aid materialized with a pain chart that featured little circle-faced caricatures. It was then my job to wince and point to the cartoon face that demonstrated the most anguish. I came to identify with him. Four teardrops spilled down his simple round cheeks. To his right were five different versions of him, telling his story, beginning with the well-adjusted and eager innocent, who gradually morphs into more startled and agitated forms, until finally he looks like Charlie Brown in the grip of a nervous breakdown. This, I felt in my high state, was a sextych of self-portraits depicting my physical and mental devolution at Mount Alcatraz.

The week blurred by in an aching opium haze, and then I left the hospital behind but not my fondness for opium, a bad romance that I prolonged through ongoing Vicodin liaisons. Meanwhile, after interminable blood tests and urine tests and stool tests—yes, I pooped into a little plastic jar and FedEx'd it to a lab in Sacramento—I finally sat down with a silver-haired general practitioner in my hometown of Brookfield, Wisconsin.

He shut the door, crossed his gray slacks, and gave it to me straight.

"The pancreatitis that nearly killed you? We're calling it idiopathic."

Tall, angular, and in possession of the brownest teeth I have ever seen, such that it looked as if he had a mouth full of bunny droppings when he grinned, he spoke slowly and quietly and communicated mostly with his eyes, which were to be reckoned with, magnified as they were behind thick spectacles.

"Which means we don't know what happened to you. The case is unsolved, as it were. We've ruled out alcoholism and gallstones. Maybe you have parasites? Scorpion venom can cause it, too." I watched the dandruff float from his Count Leo Tolstoy beard as he stroked and stroked and stroked it. "I don't know. No one knows why you . . . went nutso in there," he motioned to my gut. "Hopefully it won't happen again—right?!"

He rearranged a few books on his old-fashioned oak desk in silence. I took this as my cue to leave, but when I stood up he brought his fist down on the desk and exclaimed, "Tell me, sir, are you happy with your life as a monk?"

I knew this was coming. When my mother, who mistrusts the medical profession, recommends a doctor, it is a sign that the doctor is unconventional.

I finally said, "It's a good life."

I was too uncomfortable with his question to answer honestly. I didn't want to implicate my spiritual discipline in my illness, as though I literally couldn't "digest" Zen practice, and all the pressure of being a Rinzai Zen monk had swelled up, finally causing one of my internal organs to implode; as though I were too strong willed or stubborn to quit the Zen life on my own and so my body and unconscious mind conspired behind the scenes to give me a face-saving exit strategy: a mortal illness, fallow now, but potentially reoccurring.

After all I'd been through, who could blame me if I never went back to the monastery again?

"I have a brother-in-law who is a rabbi. *Was* a rabbi. Nobody knows where he is now. He ran away *twennn-tyyy-fiiive* years ago," the unconventional doctor said, drawing the syllables out while scribbling on a prescription pad. "We never figured out what went wrong with him either. But my experience with people who live the religious life is that at some point you get tired of *being* good and never *feeling* good. That's when the trouble starts."

He tore out and held forth one last scrip for Vicodin: "You know something is wrong with your life when the only way you can get both the rest that you need and perspective on yourself is in a hospital bed."

Eventually my four-month convalescence at my parents' home concluded, and though I felt a little better physically, I had no psychological closure on my illness. I flew back to the monastery, where I spent the subsequent summer *seichu* training season largely whacked-out on Vicodin. That is, until I took eight pills before lunch one Sunday, accidentally slathered myself in baby oil instead of sunblock, passed out on a large flat stone in the afternoon sun, and awoke with a face bubbled and brown. My skin was baking like a sheet of cookies. Inside my head there was a faint but perceptible sound, as though someone had tuned a TV to static. My brains were literally frying. I took this as a sign. No more Vicodin for this Zen monk!

But drugs are like old lovers: you think you're completely over them, and then the two of you find yourselves alone in a room together once more, and a rush of lust sends your stomach through the floor as your tongue glides from your mouth to greet the forbidden fruit all over again. Indeed. I would fuck Vicodin if I could. Even now, any time I'm in someone's bathroom, I cough loudly and simultaneously snap open the medicine cabinet above the sink, *just in case*. I do it out of habit, so to speak, even though I supposedly swore off Vicodin that day my baby-oiled face tumesced in the sun until I resembled the Elephant Man.

Then, a few days before setting out on this road trip, I opened the chest above a friend's sink, absently read the label on a transparent orange prescription bottle, and felt my nipples instantly harden: *"VICODIN® (hydrocodone bitartrate and acetaminophen tablets, USP) 5 mg/500 mg CS-III."*

This never happens. Usually when I snoop for drugs in other people's homes, I find heart medication or something for erectile dysfunction. People tend to hide their Vicodin. My heart was pounding like a bedpost against the wall of an hourly motel. I didn't know what to do, which is a bad sign. Instinctively I pocketed three pills, coughed again, quickly shut the medicine cabinet, and saw me glaring back at me in the mirror, each of us filled with hate for the other.

Attached to the Enemy

I am at the wheel. The great vehicle is hurtling forth. I hate driving this thing. It has hips. These hips stick out, they want to hit pedestrians and small European cars. I feel as if I were straddling the shoulders of an elephant and trying to coax it down the narrow isles of a glassworks shop. It takes an act of total meditative focus just to switch lanes. But after we get to Vegas and I park it for the night? I'm getting *so* fucking high.

I-15 stretches before me, an infinite tightrope needling into the horizon yet magically widening to exactly our size as I hypnotically eye travel it back to the RV windshield. My mind drifts. . . . Why did that six-inch slab of meat, coded to the core with my DNA, turn on me and douse itself with its own deadly digestive juices that night? Perhaps because the self-denial of my spiritual discipline had gone too far, become an unhealthy denial of the life impulse itself, and so my body called my bluff. *You want to deny every single last desire? Deny this one: the desire to live.*

Having Vicodin on hand is bringing back memories of my life-and-death struggle with pancreatitis, and I'm not sure if the faint ache I feel in my side right now is simply my body remembering that era or a warning cry that those dark days are about to return.

"*Ooooooh!*" Roshi suddenly shouts from the back.

All four heads spin his way.

"Eyes on the road!" Myoshin yells at me.

"Yes, Roshi?!" Lew hollers.

To put it bluntly, we live in constant terror that the old man is going to throw a gasket and the great vehicle of his heart will suddenly clank to a halt. His eyes are slits, staring at nothing and everything. He points out the window.

"A cactus. Yah, thank you, cactus," he intones, making a half bow from his seated position to the cactus whizzing by.

Well . . . okay.

We settle again into our respective seats and daydreams, when Roshi suddenly cries out once more.

"*Ooooooh!* A stone! Thank you, stone," he cries, pointing out the window to the craggy red-rock mountainside, and again with the bow.

This is Roshi screwing with us, and I'm not sure what it means. I feel that he's lampooning the seriousness with which we are taking this Voyage to Vegas. He's a hundred and five. He doesn't want to "go see Vegas lights," as he put it. He's seen them. He's seen and done everything. It's a burden for him to travel a couple hundred extra miles to the land of opulent overstimulation and cheesy magic shows, especially considering that he's been constipated for five days now. He's doing this for us. He wants us to have a little fun, and yet we've deluded ourselves into thinking that he brought the whole idea up because he wants to escape to Vegas for a little R & R himself, and so we're plotting the trip out in painstaking detail to best accommodate him. Our fun hinges on making the trip fun for him, and his fun is contingent on our loosening up and having a little fun ourselves. The result is that no one is having any fun.

The laughter in back proves me wrong, however. Everyone is having fun but me. Story of my life lately.

Roshi is a mass of cotton and wool and silk, with blankets and pillows propped at his back and strategically sandwiched between his limbs and swirled all around him, so that his head looks like a tiny bobber amid a sea of fabric. Myoshin remains ever vigilant on his behalf; his comfort has become her instinct. She jumps up onto the couch behind him, balancing on the balls of her miniature, perfect feet, and pulls him up by his armpits, sliding new pillows beneath him and behind him and between him and the window, checks in with him—

"Okay, Roshi?"

"*Yokunai* (not so much)!"

—and so new pillows appear and old ones go flying as she keeps propping and adjusting and tweaking. I watch the proceedings in the RV's circular rearview mirror with a troubled grimace as this quest for comfort seems to be going more and more awry, and just when I think Roshi can't possibly be any more miserable, he says,

"Okay. Good."

He stays in this unbearably tense and awkward lying/half-sitting position for the next couple hours, as the sky goes from blue to gray-orange and then blackens in my windshield. Gradually I get used to the new configuration as Roshi settles more and more into place, and just as I think *Wow, that seems cozy,* Myoshin appears out of nowhere to begin the readjustment process all over again, leaping onto the couch behind him on those tiny perfect feet. . . .

Myoshin drops her lightweight frame into the passenger seat beside me with a smile. She reads the expression on my face, and the one on hers registers the realization that she has just gone from one high-maintenance man to another. She is eating Pringles potato chips from a tube, her one vice. I frown disapprovingly. She points the tube at me.

"Just this once," and I relieve her of a fistful. I am never so cranky that I can't indulge in a little moralizing. "You know, I saw you back there fretting over Roshi," I murmur.

"What's 'fretting?'"

"Be careful that you don't get attached to caring for our teacher."

She laughs lightly and then crushes me with: "At least I am attached to caring, Shozan-one. You are attached to yourself."

This Is True Love

"*OOOOH!*" Roshi cries.

This time something really does appear to be seriously wrong with him. He raises a wrinkled finger to offer what will surely be his last words . . . gradually turning it . . . pointing out the window to: "Vegas! Thaaaaaank you, Las Vegas!"

We have arrived. The Strip is spectacular in the great vehicle's movie-screen-wide windows. Tens of thousands of tourists swarm the sidewalks. The breathtaking hulls of two ships are docked in the middle of the city, in front of a hotel. Pirates with sabers and poofy pants are blasting canons at each other, complete with orange cauliflowers of pyrotechnic plumes.

Vegas has even colonized the sky: fireworks pop open the black desert night, a rainbow of fire pouring out.

Lew is at the wheel. I'm relaxing in back. And what a strange sensation! To be cruising past fifty thousand tourists in a vehicle this cushy and colossal, as though you had put wheels on your living room. I am lounging on a La-Z-Boy that is floating down the street.

"Guess how many miles we drove today?" Lew cries out. No one does. "Seven hundred!"

He bangs his cantaloupe-sized fist on the steering wheel, and I give him a thumbs-up from the recliner. Hattie is riding shotgun and looking for hotels on her iPhone. She and Lew exchange a few words, and then Lew shouts to me, very tactfully, over his shoulder, "How will you explain to your board of directors that you and Roshi spent several hundred dollars on a hotel in Vegas?"

He's read my mind.

"So this trip is on us," and he and Hattie spin around and smile in unison.

"That makes Shozan very happy," Myoshin pipes up. "He is veeery cheap."

"What 'keep?'" Roshi shouts, a hand to his ear.

We all turn his way, surprised. You never know when Roshi is suddenly going to tune in to a conversation.

"Cheap!" Myoshin shouts back. "Cheap!"

"Keeping not good! Attachment not good! *Yokunai* (bad news)!" He makes a fist. Shakes it. Opens it. Looks at his palm like a baby examining a rattle. Laughs. Points at me. "Understand?"

Whenever she wants Roshi to hear something, Myoshin simply repeats the word but draws every last syllable out: "Chee-aaa-uuu-pppp!" she cries, jabbing her finger my way.

"Ah," Roshi nods, and then adds, apropos of nothing, "Shozan very handsome, yah?"

Everyone laughs at this, a little too hard, if you ask me. Roshi could lift two fifty-pound dumbbells with the corners of his mouth, so strong is his mischievous grin, which I recognize from our countless encounters during *sanzen* practice or koan study.

During a three-month *seichu* training season, a monk meets privately with Roshi two to four times a day to present an answer to the special paradoxical problem or koan that Roshi has given him. These meetings are terse and formal: you are to manifest an answer with your whole body. A purely logical, verbal response will not do. Far better to give a shout than an explanation. We practice samurai Zen, and Roshi is the master. If you want to learn from him, you must swing your sword of wisdom, however dull and flimsy, and swing hard. Roshi then steps out of the way and puts you on your ass. This is how you learn exactly where you're at—and stuck—as a Zen student.

If you're not clear in your intention and execution, however, *sanzen* can digress into a kind of performance where your aim is merely to please Roshi, as though you were auditioning for the role of good monk instead of actually being one and answering your koan as if your life depended on it. "Anything goes in sanzen," my mentor once told me. "*Anything.* Just don't physically hurt Roshi." Roshi is not a therapist, spouse, daddy figure, or close friend. He is not a guru. He is not going to solve your personal problems. Nor will your personal problems just solve themselves as long as you are in close proximity to him, as though his mere presence were enough to make everything right in your life.

A mere teacher merely teaches, but a master manifests a principle and a practice, both through the environment he trains you in and in his very being, and then you must teach yourself. You will spend 95 percent of a *seichu* training season away from Roshi, cleaning toilets, chopping kindling, sitting in the meditation hall, eating formal meals, and chanting, and 5 percent of *seichu with* Roshi. And during that 5 percent sliver of time in the master's presence, he will be looking at you to see how you've been using the other 95 percent of your time. Roshi doesn't teach you how to practice Zen. You bring your practice to him, and he tests it.

The paradox is that the older Roshi gets, the more powerful he grows as a Zen master and yet the more fragile he becomes physically. He towers over us. He hobbles beneath our bowed heads. This poses a unique problem for those of us tasked with intimately caring for him. There is the danger that we will infantilize him or treat him like a little baby to subtly get control over him and lessen his considerable influence over our lives.

"Sure, he may ring me out of *sanzen* shouting '*Yokunai!*' (you suck)," I think, "but look at the poor thing! He can't even stand without my cupping him under his armpits and hoisting him out of his chair. Who's *really* in charge here?"

When I'm feeling too lazy or frightened to practice sincerely, I unconsciously diminish Roshi to the proportions of his age-decimated physique and then dismiss him as adorable but dotty, a kind of enlightened toddler: the "indigo senior."

Big mistake.

His body may be going, his mind slipping into simpler gears, but his spirit is stronger than ever, and his intuition is otherworldly. This is a man who is somehow still coming into his own at age one hundred five. He will stop at absolutely nothing to teach you Zen. And this is what scares me.

What are you up to, old timer? I think, studying Roshi out of the corner of my eye. *Everything is a teaching opportunity for you, so surely this journey to Vegas is about seeing more than just the lights.*

Then again, one thing I've learned from koan practice is that whenever Roshi is trying to get you to see something, it is always right under your nose. I usually waste months coming up with wildly forced and unnatural answers to the koan he is giving me.

"More normal," he smiles, dismissing me.

Then one day something finally clicks, and I realize that he was showing me the answer all along. It was so simple and organic to our interactions that I took it completely for granted. Here I thought that all of our simple exchanges were adding up to some greater spiritual truth. But instead, each handshake or hug was yet another simple and straightforward manifestation of the wisdom at the very heart of Zen Buddhism.

Over and over, after I finish giving some harebrained or half-assed answer to my koan, Roshi says, "No need thinking, no need talking. Just . . ."

And here we take each other's hand, or hug, close our eyes, and dissolve into a deep simultaneous sigh, the kind that seems to have no end and no beginning and from which I emerge several moments later feeling renewed, even reborn. Then he utters the homemade idiom for which he has become world renowned and continues to move our entire lineage forward:

"This is *true love.*"

Really? That's it? I think. *But we were just . . . sharing a moment.*

Exactly.

At which point I always make the mistake of deciding, *Okay, now I must answer my koan again, correctly this time.*

But that *was* the answer. A little bit of the hug or handshake, of the togetherness, is inside me now, and it's coming out in my bright and happy face. I am manifesting love.

"Understand?" Roshi asks, looking both about fifty years younger *and* older than he actually is.

I pause, and he rings me out, indicating that I've overstayed my welcome. An instant is an eternity in Zen, and eternity is an instant. We're on heart time in *sanzen*. Wait for a second, and the whole universe appears between you and the truth, or between you and the other half of yourself: the person before you . . .

"Shozan!" Myoshin cries.

This nun has a genius for yanking me out of whatever reverie I am drifting into by thrusting a dirty adult diaper into my hand or scolding me for not performing some task that, upon being scolded, I discover for the first time that I am supposed to be performing.

"Do you expect me to read your mind?" I asked her a few days ago.

She paused in the doorway of her cabin, cutting a tiny but formidable figure in her black underrobes: "Yes." A statement that she then qualified: "Read the air, please."

Strangely, I agreed with her. We have a working relationship that borders on paranormal. We are uncannily in tune with each other and, as caregivers, serve as one body to meet our teacher's needs.

She points to the roller coaster extruding from the side of a hotel right over the street. It is magnificent and frightening, like thick tubular links in the steely spine of some alien air serpent.

"Amazing," I concur.

"Roshi, look!" she cries. "A jet coaster!"

He does not turn his head. He does not twitch a muscle. It's night, but his sunglasses are on to protect his sensitive eyes from the glitter blast of the Vegas lights, which scroll across the black lenses of those supercool shades, below which his lips are like a cryptic subtitle chiseled from stone. He is unreadable behind those badass sunglasses, like a *yakuza,* a Japanese gangster.

He says, in perfect English, "I am not. Your kid."

True Love versus the Beatles

As I push Roshi in his wheelchair past columns of flashy slot machines, which sing like sirens on all four sides of us, beckoning us to the financial shoals, I realize that I should be wheeling him into his cabin on the mountaintop right now, crickets chirping all around us in God's own moonlight. Instead of taking him home, away from all the noise and nonsense of the confused human world, I am leading him deep into the brightest burst of sheer shimmering nothingness in this vast waste of a desert—otherwise known as the Mirage, our quarters for this evening.

It is midnight on the summer solstice, the longest day of the year. Not that you can tell inside this hotel-casino, where it is always day and there are no clocks. I have never been out this late with Roshi. Nor, in our nearly ten-year relationship, 90 percent of which has taken place in that tiny bare *sanzen* room, have we ever shared sights like these.

A flower garden with lush greens and blues rims a Japanese restaurant nestled in an indoor bamboo forest.

Behind the row of concierge computers is a twenty-thousand-gallon fish tank the size and shape of several semitrailers, with thousands of rainbow-colored miracles floating and darting and bobbing, their fish eyes permanently saucer sized and their lower lips forever jutted out, sea foliage swaying slowly in the water as though in wind.

A boutique tattoo parlor: rich rebels flashing their arms in a long line on what looks like dental chairs. They look like a row of people giving blood. The very last two people getting tattoos on their forearms are a bride and groom, he in his ebony tux and she in a glorious white gown that flows past her feet and pools in endless folds on the floor all around her, completely covering her chair, so that it looks as if she were floating.

The bride has caught Roshi's eye.

This breathtaking young angel—hovering—her arm held forth to a burly, bald, ink-gun ogre, black lines appearing on her soft skin; this ancient monk in his traditional *koromo* garment slowly gliding on his little chariot across the marble floor . . .

Who needs Vicodin when you've got Vegas?

If I could inject this city directly into my veins, I would be an addict. It is the perfect delivery system for the most powerful drug known to man: fantasy. *The deck really is stacked in your favor. Sit down at this blackjack table and prove it. Play the game! Buy in!*

In other words, Vegas is the exact inverse of a monastery. It is Mount Alcatraz's doppelgänger. Where Vegas is painstakingly manufactured to heighten illusion and hide suffering, Mount Alcatraz starkly minimizes illusion so that suffering comes to the fore and you must face it. If Vegas is one big glittering surface from which you cannot tear your eyes, Mount Alcatraz is defined precisely by a lack of sensory stimulation, so that you must look inward.

Buddhism's First Noble Truth: Life is suffering.

Vegas's First Noble Truth: Life is fun!

Before me in the hotel lobby is a sign: the very embodiment of the difference between a Zen monastery and Las Vegas. It is huge, 3-D. Chunky, psychedelic, groovy-colored blocks advertise the hotel's nightly live performance of selections from the Beatles catalog. It is simply, beautifully, four letters: LOVE.

A Zen monastery is about manifesting true love.

Vegas is about LOVE: *the show.*

I should be saddened and disgusted by this orgy of empty spectacle. Instead, I am enchanted. Monks are supposed to be highly disciplined spiritual warriors who can resist any temptation, right? Well, in reality we are quite often like primitive mountain-dwelling tribespeople who, upon being exposed to bright and shiny things, begin to drool and squawk mightily, popping erections and vomiting from overstimulation.

Yes, the monastery is becoming a distant memory. Unfortunately, I still look like a monk, though I'm not in robes. I'm wearing bright-blue rubber shoes and my "goin' out" shirt, the button-down I wear for every single goin' out occasion, with its ketchup stains and wrinkles sharper than used tinfoil; and my pants are paper-thin khakis that I commandeered from the monastery's lost and found. In the right light you can see through them to my bare legs, a sight that does nobody any good.

No, you wouldn't know it by looking at me, but I'm feeling very rock 'n' roll tonight. Vegas baby, Vegas!

It occurs to me that Vegas is an entire city designed to foster the illusion that suffering is not real—but you can *leave* Vegas. Drugs foster the exact same illusion but in a much more insidious way. They do it from the *inside*. It's far more difficult to leave a state of mind than it is to simply drive beyond a city's limits.

This fact strikes me to the quick, and all I can say is . . . how friggin' awesome is Vegas going to be, high? Drugs are more Vegas than *Vegas*!

A plan is taking shape:

- Wheel Roshi to our hotel room on floor eighteen.
- Get the ball rolling on the complex nightly ritual of putting him to bed, which involves taking his blood pressure, heart rate, and oxygen level; holding the bucket for him while he brushes his teeth at the edge of the bed, splattering me with electric-toothbrush spray.
- Convince Myoshin to complete the process (details still to be worked out) and excuse myself to go out for a walk.
- Get high, stay out all night, and party!

It is a great plan not because it is so brilliant or original but because it has behind it the insurmountable momentum of a man hell-bent on pushing the line between extreme pleasure and self-destruction. Such plans always succeed, and the authors of them rarely fail to pay the price.

There is only one obstacle.

She is walking a few steps ahead of me in her shuffling manner (which Western women foolishly mistake for obsequiousness), with a wide grin (plush lips, big teeth), her head turning left to right . . . right to left . . . taking in the panoramic hotel splendor yet not *taken in* by it.

The world's most reliable nun.

I will have to get past Myoshin first. No small task. The game is deception, and I am both the coach calling the play and the quarterback executing it. I think I'll try for a straight-up fib down the middle, for I will not be able to break free this evening for any reason other than a falsely altruistic one.

I try the words out in my head: "So, I'm going to go get some stuff for Roshi."

"What are you going to get?" she will ask.

Cataloged alphabetically on her iPad is everything that Roshi has ever owned, ever will own, ever needed, or ever will need. If on a lazy afternoon in 1942 he mended his robes while listening to a crackling radio broadcast of the American siege of Guadalcanal, she knows the color and make of the thread he used.

"Kleenex?"

"We have ten boxes. He blows his nose an average of six-point-three times per day. I think we are okay," she'll say, her eyes narrowing.

"Hairbrush? Jujubes? Chia Pet?"

No, it'll never work. We've been working side by side for four years now. She knows my whole repertoire of irresponsible tics and tactics, which always merit the same response, her war cry in the ongoing campaign against my immaturity.

One small hand on her hip, and with a deep sense of shame on my behalf, she will sigh, "You are almost *forty.*"

Sex, Celibacy, and the Marital Monastery

It's time to come clean. Myoshin and I have a history. That's a euphemism for, We've fucked. We've kept our complicated relationship a secret from our community (that is, until the start of this paragraph), but of course, in a community as tight-knit and socially claustrophobic as ours, there really are no secrets. Everybody knows what everybody's doing. Always. (Unless you're the monk in charge. Then you have no idea, because everybody, in a rare display of total solidarity, conspires to keep you in the dark.) Yet if it ever goes public that we are an item, I fear I will have to own the relationship, which means marry her and get on with it or break up and move on.

Neither option feels right.

If I am keeping her in limbo, it is because that's honestly where I am too. Yes, I have serious questions about Myoshin and me as a couple. There's a thin line between two very different people perfectly complementing each other and those same two people having absolutely nothing in common. But the fact is, we probably have as much going for us as any twosome. No, my problems with women and commitment run deep, much deeper than my more localized problems with Myoshin, and go back an awful long way.

At the risk of drifting from our A-story line, which includes drugs and deception and irresponsibility and, most horrifyingly, blue plastic shoes, I'd like to share a personal anecdote to shed some light on my issues when it comes to intimate relationships (before I lose all of my female readers). Before I moved to the monastery, I dated a series of women I met online, and one of them particularly struck me. After having lived on the streets for much of her life, she worked her way through fashion school and became an up-and-coming clothing designer with her own company. She had been so deeply sexually and physically abused as a child that she walked with a slight limp. She was inked and pierced from head to toe, but she was no Girl with the Dragon Tattoo. She was incredibly kind and vulnerable; she had a clear, straightforward heart. Despite everything that she had been through, she was not, unlike 99 percent of the women I dated in Los Angeles, fucked up in any way. She was, and still is, a genuinely good person—one of the few I've ever met.

We had a real connection, and things got serious fast. And just as we were about to take it to the next level, where she would have become a bona fide girlfriend and potential wife, I broke up with her, as per my pattern. I had broken up with a lot of women by this time, and while it was never easy, I was able to escape with most of my limbs and organs intact. But Tina Trash (as she called herself) got inside me, like a fishhook, and the distance I put between us drew the line taut. After our breakup I went home and took a shower. Something came over me, a dark cloud I have never been under before or since, which still haunts me, and I began to sob. The sobs wracked every inch of my body and got louder and louder and reached a hysterical, animal pitch. Pretty soon I was scream-sobbing and clutching at the handicap bars in the shower. I couldn't even stand up.

I was not, at this time in my life, what you would call the picture of self-awareness, but I remember thinking with total clarity, *Something is wrong with you.* As a youth I had always been a loner, but something had changed in me over the years. Or not enough had changed. Youthful shyness became teenage sullenness, then twenty-something angst and rebelliousness. Now I was thirty. Misanthropic, lonely to the core, and unable to connect intimately with others.

What will I be like at forty? Fifty? Sixty? I thought, sitting on my futon, now fully dressed, my hair long dry, and still sobbing—a thoughtful sob now, sob-thinking.

At that time I had a nasty little line that I used at the close of my stand-up comedy routines. I would smile at the stone-faced audience and give them a fake "please, please, enough applause" gesture before saying, by way of a blessing, "Thank you all, yes, thank you—may you die alone and be instantly forgotten." I realized now that with this line I had actually foreseen my own fate.

I'm gonna die alone in this run-down apartment, and when the landlord sniffs me out, he'll shovel my sloppy remains into a trash bag, pitch me into the Dumpster, and that'll be it. A burial in the belly of rats.

Two of my previous girlfriends from that era, upon our break-ups, had offered the exact same words of tear-stained advice that Tina Trash had just given me as we hugged in her bed one last time: "*I hope you find what you're looking for.*"

What are you looking for? I asked myself.

I genuinely wanted to know. I was shipwrecked off a distant inner island after being tossed in a sea of stormy sobs. I was a very long way away from my normal self and could survey the far-off shore of my character with some objectivity. This moment of self-diagnosis, where you distance yourself from the illness within, is crucial for someone who is seriously screwed up, for it is the first moment when you can finally reach out to others for help.

A few months later I moved to the monastery.

Here at last, I thought, I can escape the pressure that society puts on guys to settle down and start a family and instead embark upon a Really Important Spiritual Quest—that is, I turned my problem with women into evidence of a higher calling. But as it happens, I lined up with the most marriage-driven teacher on the planet. Not only can monks marry in our tradition, but Roshi has said, "Marriage is the only true monastery in the West."

You would think he'd want to keep his monks around so they can continue training seriously with him. But one of the first things Roshi does after ordaining someone is get to work trying to marry the person off. He can't help himself. After all, is there a simpler way to negate the ego than by giving yourself to someone else? It works a hell of a lot better than directing all of your energies toward self-improvement or self-transcendence or self-mastery, that is, all of those masochistic/heroic loner-guy "spiritual" schemes that always end up pumping the ego full of steroids while emptying the heart of all meaningful content.

The self can't cancel out the self. Only someone or something else can complete you. "Having a wife completes you," Roshi has said. "Take care of that which completes you." Marriage is the perfect spiritual practice: it's strenuous, sexually frustrating, the ultimate illusion killer, filled with dark nights of the soul, and a flawless antidote to the idea that your life belongs to you and you alone. Yes, marriage is the perfect practice. And this is no accident. According to Roshi, the activity that gives rise to the whole cosmos consists of two mutually opposing yet complementary functions that are constantly uniting and separating, a gazillion times in one second, so we don't notice it, or there's no "we" to notice it, for we think that a consistent human self persists from one moment to the next, when in reality we are disappearing and resurrecting again and again within every instant of our lives. We are continually dying and being reborn in true love.

Did you get all of that?

Every time Roshi talks about this stuff, either I get a headache or it puts me to sleep (he occasionally looks out at our bald heads bobbing in sleep during a lecture and remarks that they look like eggplants in the wind). Well aware of the somnambulistic effects of too much Buddhist philosophy, Roshi caps off many a talk by saying, "Words are lies." Much better, then, to shut your mouth, fling open your heart and arms, and—

"No talking. No thinking. Just . . ." Roshi repeats during our private meetings, cutting off my verbal koan answer and wrapping me in a hug—and we dissolve our respective individual positions into one activity. Then we release each other and have a look. We were one, now we are two. In order to become one again, we will have to give up our new separate positions and come together once more, entwining each other in another boundary-breaking embrace. And from that unity, our separateness will arise yet again, that is, the two of us pulling away, looking at each other and smiling, our glowing faces expressing the fundamental prayer: *Ain't it grand!*

As strange as it seems, if you're exposed to this idiosyncratic style of teaching for long enough, it begins to take. It works on you in ways you never imagined. For if you can experience the love at the heart of the universe in a five-second hug with your teacher . . . imagine what's in store for you in the intimate arms of a lifetime partner, that ultimate of reciprocal opposites. You go to bed one night firm in your commitment to never under any circumstances get married—you're a free bird; ain't no cage gonna hold you in— and suddenly you wake up the next morning with an egg in your gut. The egg hatches. A downy little insight hobbles out. This is what happened to me around a year ago. The insight squawked and noodled around inside me all morning until I finally listened. The little chick had a point: for the past nine years of Zen practice I had been trying to conquer my ego—a battle that arguably resulted in a physical crisis that nearly killed me and a subsequent drug habit. Anyone who claims to have conquered his or her ego has been thoroughly conquered *by* that ego. To paraphrase Alan Watts, you can't wash blood off your hands with more blood.

The ego is sneaky. It's like the house in Vegas. As long as you're playing its game, it always wins. Just because it wins by a slight margin, every time, does not mean that you're about to win. You'll never win. You'll always *just* lose.

But how do you not play ego's game? How do you walk away from the high-stakes table that is your self?

Give yourself away, the little chick chirped. *Make a gift of yourself to another.*

This is why marriage is always sacred in religions and is consecrated with vows and rituals. It is the act of love as a committed spiritual journey, the bringing together of two halves to make one complete whole. It is the human embodiment of the cosmic principle of true love. When you truly "make relationship," as Roshi calls it, that is, give yourself fully to whatever is in front of you—marry your present circumstances—the ego is not conquered. It disappears. It is fulfilled. It dies in love. And from this union a fresh self is born, as vibrant and sparkling as a newborn. And its first job? To make relationship all over again. To give itself away.

Zen, as Shunryu Suzuki said, is the path of no turning back. Is there a better description of marriage?

I have it all worked out, don't I.

So what's my problem?

What am I still looking for?

Why can't I get on board with the dharma activity and make some fucking babies already? Why, a year ago, after I finally had a little insight into the profound joys of the long-term male-female union, did I introduce a new factor into my relationship with Myoshin, a wedge that has put more distance between us than ever: *celibacy*?

What kind of a monk am I, to deny a fellow nun a good rooting?

Is it any wonder that upon being taken out of my safe and predictable monastic routine and inserted into the real world, which is to say the glorious fantasyland that is Vegas, all of my issues with Myoshin, sex, and women are coming up, and I simply want to escape them by getting ripped on Vicodin? If Vegas is Mount Alcatraz's doppelgänger, then the issues it brings up and flings in your face are the ones that you've been able to repress in the monastic environs—and this is why it is so important to, as the monks in Japan put it, "jump the wall," escape the dimly lit monastery for the bright lights of Vegas and see what comes up . . . see what's been there, right under your nose, all along.

Which brings us back to the koan of the moment: *to get high or not to get high.*

Nothing turns Myoshin off more than me on drugs. It is a deal breaker. For a few months a few years ago, during my prescription-pill era, I fooled her into thinking I had chronic back pain, and she shared with me a bottle of Vicodin left over from Roshi's excruciating bout with shingles. When she found out I had been lying to her—after I stole the whole bottle from her drawer—we got into our first real fight. And something in me knows that if I get high again, it will be our last real fight.

That is to say: she'll dump my ass. For good. As she probably should.

Shi Shi Shi Shi Pookoo De Gozaimasu Gets His Ass Handed to Him by the Dragon Lady

"Shozan-one I am really worried about Roshi."

"Me too. I'm really, really worried." I yawn.

We are settling into our suite. It is unforgettable, with elegant Japanese-themed duvets and pillow covers, and bay windows stacked on top of each other, a whole wall of glass opening out to a brilliant desert sky that is all but invisible above the heart-stopping twinkle-sweep of Vegas seen at night from a height. After effusively bidding us good evening, Hattie and Lew have departed for their room. I can hear their loud happy voices disappearing down the hall. Roshi is in his wheelchair before a glass coffee table, eating a cheeseburger. Kind of. The top of the bun is off, and he has his traveling chopsticks and is picking at the grilled onions and mushrooms as though the meat patty were a little brown plate.

"He has not had a bowel movement in five days. I think it is time for suppository."

"Of course. Good luck with that. In the meantime, I'm going out—"

"But I cannot give it to him . . . *quite yet.*"

She bites her lip and squints, as though cracking this constipation case were tantamount to solving the riddle of the sphinx.

Here she launches into a disquisition on the suppository, how it simply helps to release the looser lower portion of the agoraphobic bowel movement, which refuses to come outdoors, but does not affect the plug.

The plug.

I have heard a lot about the plug from Myoshin. In Zen practice, you finds koans in the strangest of places—especially if you're the *inji*. Inji/full-time attendant is not the kind of job you will find an advertisement for on craigslist. An *inji* is like the Navy SEAL of nuns. You must have an intimate knowledge of terrifying topics and be willing to act decisively when the moment of truth comes.

You must be willing to "pull the plug."

I once dropped in to visit Myoshin as she cared for Roshi in his cabin while the rest of us attended a picnic outside. Her voice was even and she was wearing a big grin, but she had just spent the better portion of an hour on her hands and knees six inches from our teacher's bare posterior, where she had been tactically implementing a toothpick to extract a vicious plug and free the hostages that had been held captive behind it for nearly a week. I stumbled onto this scene and then quickly bolted for the door.

"Hold on," she said, washing her hands, "I'll come with you. I crave for some barbecue."

Her ability to care is intimidating. If it gives her energy, it often exhausts me by proxy, and then I am doubly drained by the self-hatred I feel as I compare myself to her—and then I'm triply tired by the blame I place on myself for playing the very non-Zen game of compare and contrast in the realm of spiritual practice. It seems that I don't want to care *for* her. I simply want to be more caring *than* she is. Yet most of the time I care about nothing and no one at all but myself. It's exhausting, being so selfish. Poor me. I begin to pity myself when—

"Shozan, come on!" she cries.

She is trying to hoist Roshi's red suitcase—"the ladybug"— onto the bed. It is more than half her size. Typical! I am having a conversation in my head about how I should be more caring toward Myoshin, and she's right in front of me in desperate need of very immediate help—

"Hello?" she cries again.

I cross the room to help her. Yet I don't feel good about it, for it was not my decision. I feel like a henpecked husband. My feet ache, my dick stinks, and it is past midnight. And I am not high. And I am not twenty-five anymore. And so I shouldn't be getting high. When a kid gets high, it's to expand his mind. When an adult gets high, it's to escape it. And so I feel terribly guilty about the Vicodin I've just surreptitiously slipped from my sunglasses case into my pocket.

My nerves are frayed from the long drive. I have the taste of dust from three different states in my mouth. I haven't been laid in a year, during which time I have also withheld the dubious pleasure of my sexual company from someone I love. I am a horrible monk. And a shitty person, and not much of a man to boot.

You are almost forty!

"Sho-*zan*! I need your help," Myoshin shouts one last time, at a Roshi-audible pitch—which means it is now up to me to stop the fight that she has been valiantly fending off entirely by herself for the past six hours.

A task at which I choose to fail.

"So I really wanna go take a walk. In the lobby."

My words are like sharp steps taken right in her direction. They are fighting words, and I have initiated them. It is I who has tilted the evening's tensions irrevocably toward separation.

"I really wanna go take a walk in the lobby. . . . Did you hear me?"

"I heard you," she says.

"I wanna go take a walk. In the lobby." I grab my wallet.

Out of the corner of my eye, I see her gather herself, coiling inside. She is about to go Dragon Lady on me.

"You are going? When Roshi needs help? You are just going to leave me here?"

"Help? What help? Me sitting here is help? Me sitting here waiting for Roshi to crap is somehow helping? What the fuck?"

It does help our fights when I swear. It adds a layer of aggression to the interaction regardless of whether or not the curse is directly aimed at her.

Roshi is sitting in his wheelchair, chopsticks down, hands in his lap. Eyes shut. Or half open. I cannot tell. He cannot hear us. I don't think. He is facing the windows, the birth of the cosmos before him, Vegas style: infinite pinpricks of vibrating light—and blackness.

I am worked up now; I cannot stop. I need her blood on my teeth.

"I just wanna go for a *walk* in the *lobby.*"

"You *think I don't*?"

"I have been *driving* all day."

This is a tactical parry. She has never had a driver's license and feels guilty about not being able to pitch in and take the wheel during these long road trips.

It backfires.

The Dragon Lady strikes.

"Just go! Four years I have put up with this. You not knowing what you want and then apologizing. Always apologizing. I am sick of it."

"Why don't you try apologizing?"

"For what? Caring for you? Being so stupid I trust you? Four years. *'I don't know what I want, I don't know what I want—I am so sorry, I am so sorry. . . .'*"

"I know what I want." I overpronounce each syllable like a three-year-old throwing a tantrum. "I-want-to-go-for-a-walk-in-the-fu-cking-lo-bby."

"Four years you never want to be with me. You are always trying to get away. Always! Do you know what that feels like? With me you never know what you want. But when it comes to getting away from me? You are always very clear."

For a second there I think she may . . . but she then she doesn't. She does not cry, thank God. "My tears are all dried up," she told me recently. "You cannot have a single one anymore."

She has moved effortlessly from our fight to our teacher. With her help he is now lying on the bed, looking almost like a little creature, his lips flat across his face and his eyes open but not open, his hands folded at his *hara* in a kind of mudra, his belly strangely bulbous and his lightly freckled arms fleshy and frail. Myoshin slides his socks off (beige toe socks, if you must know, compliments of Lew). I join her in silence at our teacher's feet. He is in no way gross. No old-person smell. Myoshin takes far too good care of him for that. I remove a blob of calamine-infused beeswax from a tiny silver jar and begin to rub the oily wonder sludge into his feet, getting between the toes, working those tiny toenails, no bigger than the smallest word on this page; feeling the sharp flakes of his peeling heels, trying out what little reflexology I know; closing my eyes and giving myself completely to the parts of his feet that ache on my own, so that I can almost feel a kind of sympathetic relief . . . and my asshole finally begins to unclench for the first time in about forty-eight hours.

I take great pleasure in stroking the sharp angles of his shinbones, roving my fingers across the precious dollops of just-enough muscle where hearty calves once bulged. At his age, the physical textures of his body have taken on new qualities, and the physical qualities have taken on new textures. He is like a skeleton clad in some kind of extraterrestrial flesh: ultrasoft and smooth, clean and hairless, glowing. This morning, as we had tea, I looked for some part of him that has not aged, and after making a full circuit of his body, wound up gazing past the deep wrinkled folds of his eyelids and into his eyes, which are timeless. He held me with his gaze for several moments. Then the light caught what appeared to be artificial dents where he had cataract surgery. Now his stare seemed weirdly robotic. There is no part of him, inside or out, that age has not touched. My teacher is ancient. All land this ancient is uncharted, and I feel deeply privileged to travel the length of his body with my eyes as I rub his feet.

Myoshin is smiling at me. I didn't mean to look at her. I'm supposed to still be mad at her or something. Typically, I begin our fights. And they end when she wants them to end. Like an unskilled sword fighter, I often feel a slight sting after provoking her, look down to the sight of my own glistening entrails, and realize that she has disemboweled my entire argument before the fight even began.

"Shi shi one," she whispers to me.

She has her own private language that she uses to communicate with, in this order, small animals (specifically cats), Roshi, and me. A cat that has found itself in her favor may get an extended bit of this wondrous gibberish, "Ooooh shi-shi-shi-shi pookoo de gozaimasu!" "I am not good with words," she has told me. "Not like you." But between the two of us, we have learned to articulate some of the deepest feelings known to man. Weirdly, our relationship often seems to work not *in spite of* the fact that it is hanging in the balance but *because* of it. She doesn't get what she wants, I don't know what I want: it's unnerving, unpredictable, unconventional, and we're in it together.

"You are like the mystery of a cat," she once told me. "You take affection completely for granted, but I cannot stop giving it to you." It's a statement that goes a long way toward explaining our strange symbiosis. She is not merely a victim of my irrational Sagittarian fear of commitment. She is also, in so many ways, my master, and I am deeply dependent upon her. If I never stay for long, I never stray for long. I need the milk.

I'm not saying it's ideal, folks. But I am deeply grateful that no matter what happens between us, I have been able to experience half of my time as a monk in training with a partner. How many of us can say that?

"Shozan, where sleep?"

"Floor, Roshi."

"Not comfortable."

"Comfortable, Roshi."

"Bed better."

"Which bed, Roshi?"

"Yah, floor too many spiders."

Our otherwise intrepid Zen master has a terrific fear of arachnids. It's bedtime, and I'm positioning myself on a sheet I've draped on the carpet between Roshi's and Myoshin's beds. Myoshin arms herself with a pee bottle in case Roshi has to urinate tonight. She takes off her sweater, smells it, seems satisfied. Takes off her socks and smells those too.

She catches me looking at her. "What?"

"Good night," I tell her.

"Good night, Shozan-one."

"Good night, Roshi!!" I scream.

He doesn't hear me. I take a deep breath and relax into the floor, a position that suits my bad back. It occurs to me that I did not hug Myoshin good night. From the beginning this has been our custom, to dissolve the day's differences in an embrace. No matter what, every single night. "I am simple," she's said in my arms. "With this, I can forgive everything that comes out of your mouth." As with my other master, during our private *sanzen* meetings, so with Myoshin: there's no problem when I open my arms. The trouble starts when I open my mouth.

I am drifting into dream with a smile . . . when Roshi's voice suddenly cuts through the darkness.

"Yah, good night."

Banzai in the Bathroom

I awaken to a stinging sensation and instinctively clutch my side—*is it my pancreas*? No, I just have to pee. With utmost care I stealth-step to the overlit, echoey bathroom and whiz against the side of the bowl to minimize splash noise. I don't flush, carefully tiptoe back to my floor bed and slooooowly slip one of three quilts over me.

Suddenly I freeze in terror—I see a shadow flash.

I hear Roshi moan.

Someone is blasting across the carpet on hands and knees.

It is Myoshin—super-*inji*—or: the Ninji.

She pauses to stare into the depths of my soul—and then punches right through my soul and continues glaring into the gaping hole that she has gouged in my very being with her penetrating black eyes . . . just for good measure.

"You. Woke. Him. Up," she finally says.

"Myooooooooooshin," Roshi cries. "Shoooooooooooozan!"

We help our teacher out of bed while conversing about the hotel art on the wall. Myoshin thinks it's cheesy and wishes she'd continued her career in Vancouver as an artsy photographer.

"I could have made much money. Look at this crap."

"I'm sorry about last night. I can be a real douche bag," I tell her.

"What's douche bag?" she innocently asks.

We wheel Roshi into the great pristine bathroom, barely edging his wheelchair through the door. He offers his hands and Myoshin gently pulls him to standing, jockeying his body a bit so that I am now holding his soft hands and helping him turn around, feeling the tensions and jolts in his body in my own and responding accordingly.

"Completely I give myself to you," he says, chuckling.

Myoshin whips down his diaper at the speed of light just before he lowers himself onto the toilet. Fifteen minutes later she returns from the bathroom. I am in front of the TV.

"Yeah?"

She shakes her head no. "Just pee."

I study Roshi in the unforgiving bathroom light, sitting on the toilet like a man slumped on the electric chair. His face is gray and funereal. The shit is turning to poison inside him, and there's nothing we can do about it. It is devastating.

I lean over close. "Okay, Roshi?"

He looks up. His eyes fasten to mine. His jowls are sagging. A tiny line of saliva has found its way down his chin through a rare wrinkle.

Suddenly his fist shoots up.

"*Banzai!*" he roars.

This is one of Roshi's pet terms. The literal translation is "ten thousand years!" When Roshi says it, he means . . . hallelujah? Amen? Booyah? Fuck yeah? It is the ancient Chan-legend Gu-tei raising one finger whenever a student asks him a question; it is Zen master Joshu crying "*Mu!*" (no) when asked "Does a dog have Buddha nature?"

In other words, I don't know what it means, but it makes sense when you hear it, and it does me good to hear it now.

Feasting at the Cravings

The plan is to stuff Roshi so full of breakfast that the pressure from above pushes down on the plug and releases it. Anticipation is high as the five of us wait in line at an upscale cafeteria entitled . . . Cravings. A row of twenty suspended TV screens—ten on each side of us, creating a tacky tunnel of sound and fury—displays floating strawberries, a martini tinkling with ice, penile champagne bottles ejaculating corks. . . .

"What's the Japanese word for *buffet*? I ask Myoshin.

She thinks about it for a moment. "Buffet," she says.

Roshi is in good spirits, all things considered. A staggering amount of sheer physical pain seems to be the daily toll that this hundred-and-five-year-old man has to pay in order to stay alive. And why does he stay alive? He has appointed no successor to take his place as a teacher, and so there is no one waiting in the wings to show us young men and women how to love one another. I honestly think it's that simple. (That, and the fact that he's eaten a lot of nutritious fish and seaweed—plus, as he's said, "I did too many bad things my whole life. Now I have to stay alive as penance." This latter statement is probably the truest of all . . .)

The line is going nowhere. "I think I just heard my own stomach growl," Lew says, cocking an ear the size of a croissant toward his belly.

"He is one hundred and five years old!" Hattie suddenly tells everyone within earshot.

The jet-black-haired woman behind the cash register—from Brooklyn, her nametag tells us—lights up. A conversation ensues.

"Well, he doesn't use microwaves, for one thing," Hattie carries on. "He is very positively charged on every level. I call him the auracle! Say, did you know that water molecules can hear music?"

Lew gets in on it: "One hundred and five!" he shouts, and puts a meaty arm around his wife.

The woman from Brooklyn cries, over and over, "He's a hundred 'n' five. I cain't believe it. I just cain't belieeeeeeve it! He don't look a hundred and five, he just don't."

We are stopping traffic. A manager glides up and is trying to figure out how to move us along when Lew jubilantly roars, "This man . . . is one hundred and five! And a Zen master to boot!"

The last part goes over the manager's head, but one hundred and five she gets. She is a ropey old girl with legs like stilts, midsixties, peering out from a stern face that looks like it's been worked over a bit by the Las Vegas life. She is a kind of pleasant cop policing this line toward ever greater gluttony. We all suddenly desperately crave her approval. We don't want to be scolded, even politely, by a consumption cop when we are having this very human moment together.

But the manager—"Dusty," from Houston, Texas—is caught up in her own astonishment. Several cafeteria worker bees are gathered now, to see what the old battle-ax will do, and she'll be damned if she isn't going to show them that she's not good people too. The moment is suspended in my memory: I still love watching Dusty's face open up with respect and glee. On a deeper level, she is teaching herself once again how to burst at the seams with pure joy. It is grounded human ecstasy. She is no longer an overstressed cog in the vaguely sinister Vegas pleasure wheel but a respectful member of our vast human family, paying her respects to a senior member of the lineage.

"Wonderful," she slightly bows her head. "I wish I had his skin."

Roshi looks at me. I shout-whisper in his good ear. "She thinks you are a very handsome old gentleman."

He nods and smiles and bows with one hand from his wheelchair. "Yahhhhh, thank you, thank you!"

He is positively glowing. I look at Myoshin. There are tears in her eyes too. We will do anything to keep this man alive. Dusty ushers us through. I slowly wheel Roshi, the crowd parting. Everything is helped back into its proper place around a Zen master. By virtue of who he is, how he's lived, Roshi creates a space around himself into which people can move and come alive. Part of his gift is to attract what I half-jokingly call "*hai*-men" (*hai* means "yes" in Japanese; that is, Roshi has to break his *hai*-men) who will do his dirty work, sing his praises, and take care of business for him—all while making sure he doesn't neuter us in the process. More and more I feel devoted to what Roshi is devoted to, rather than to Roshi himself, a fact that makes me more devoted to him than ever. He's helped me see—beyond him.

But even the coolest Zen master is no match for a really stubborn plug. I've been so caught up with his constipation this morning that I have yet to obsess over whether or not to pop my pills. Like most koans, the Vicodin Crisis (remember: the Chinese characters for *crisis* mean danger and opportunity) seems to be unraveling of its own accord. I simply have to hold the heat of the question within me, not act on it and not *not* act on it (not acting can be a way of acting), and my inner climate changes, and the problem passes, even if the question remains.

If I get high or I don't get high, it doesn't really matter. I'll be waiting for me on the other side of the buzz—fuzzier around the edges. Whatever life problems I had before I got stoned will be well rested and ready to rumble afterward, only I'll be slightly less equipped to face them. Do I really wanna go there? Is it worth it? Besides, a morning buzz is so much less thrilling than a nighttime high.

For the life of her, Hattie cannot get her iPhone camera to work. "I don't need a picture of this. I will never forget it. Thank you all for being here," Lew says. We raise our steaming coffee mugs. On the table before us: a stunning vista of edibility. Waffles with whipped cream, bacon, eggs, oatmeal—the good kind, cooked in milk and butter, not water—hash browns, sausages, bagels with cream cheese and lox and salami, eggs this way and that, sliced avocadoes plus rock salt, fruit salad with more whipped cream. . . . We are the center of a circle of a hundred tables, ringed at the perimeter by 360 degrees of food stations: Latin, Italian, Chinese, Middle Eastern. . . .

We dig in.

"Have a little meat too," Myoshin jokes.

My plate is a small graveyard for pigs and cows. During formal training we eat vegetarian, but there's no hard-and-fast Rinzai Zen rule about never taking meat. (Near as I can tell, there's no hard-and-fast Rinzai Zen rule about anything.) Yet I've been trying to go vegetarian in the off-season. So much for that. I would guess that 90 percent of Buddhists worldwide are vegetarian, and would probably rather see me occasionally do drugs than dine on swine. Sadly, this thought gives me a perverse thrill as I decide against drugs and heartily hoover the pork on my plate.

In the Belly of the Beast

But the meat has weakened me. It always does. Now I want meat *and* drugs. (Perhaps the other 90 percent of Buddhists in the world are on to something.)

I'm heading into three solid months of hard-core training. I deserve it!

I just want to feel good!

Here's the thing: Rinzai Zen monks are great, unparalleled in my opinion, when it comes to letting go of attachments in this life. The training disabuses you of the notion that there is anything you can cling to in this world that will save you or make you unconditionally happy or fulfilled. But then there are those things that make you feel good. Those things you have a weakness for. And the practice is so damn hard that feeling good is oftentimes what you need, lest you become hard too, hard inside. And so you indulge. And instead of becoming attached, you become *addicted*, a different thing altogether, and something that all Zen monks are vulnerable to: addictions, be it to sex, drugs, money, adulation. . . . Perhaps this is why you get monks who are amazing people on the one hand, titans of self-discipline, compassion, and clarity, with these pathetically human flaws on the other: they become fuck fiends, gamblers, alcoholics, pill poppers, chain-smokers. They are a mess of contradictions, perhaps because they're trying to hit a tricky internal balance between not being attached to the things of this world and yet also not being dead inside. They funnel their flaws down to a single indulgence and then completely give themselves over to it without any discretion, which often ruins them.

The Greeks, of course, called this the Achilles' heel, that tragic defect that brings our hero to his knees, and right now I can feel mine like three tiny precious jewels against my thigh in the thin pocket of my cheap khakis . . . into which I am slowly reaching.

Who did I think I was fooling? The second I stole these pills I knew this moment would come.

Suddenly I feel a sharp ache in my side—that *other* Achilles' heel.

Roshi, Myoshin, and I are riding the Mirage elevator alone back to floor eighteen. Lew and Hattie are in the oversize-vehicle parking lot warming up the RV. Roshi claims he has a number two in the queue and refuses to release it anywhere but back in our hotel room. Myoshin apparently has some clairvoyance in these matters and doesn't believe him. She is furious and waves off my suggestion that we think optimistically.

Roshi chirps something to her in Japanese. He does seem to say it with the faintest hint of a grin. She replies to him in their native tongue at twice the necessary volume. He follows with an equally sharp retort. And suddenly the elevator explodes with clashing dialogue as though I were trapped in the climax of a Kurosawa samurai film. The cadence of the Japanese language, as stunning and elegant as it is at this pitch and intensity, is not my foremost concern right now. I slowly inch to the other side of the elevator. Breathing heavily. Hand moving from my pocket to my left side.

Roshi's words halt in his mouth—his eyes shoot from Myoshin to me.

How did he catch that? I was trying to hide my pain from him.

But now I see that I am gripping my gut.

It's happening again.

You get this every now and then. . . . Don't worry . . . the pain always subsides.

But this time it doesn't. This time it's bad. It feels as if a dark hole were opening up in my flesh—as if I were being invaded through the portal of my own private self.

I breathe heavily . . . wait for it to pass. It doesn't. I've been here before. The ache is growing up very quickly inside me. This is how it was that dark night when I nearly lost my life. Around 4 A.M. I realized what it means to be dying. Instead of the pain leveling out and getting better, it goes from bad to worse to critical. You try to bargain, you try to will the pain away, you pray like a motherfucker, and it only gets worse. You can feel something inside coming for you. Everything is being taken from you, from within. Somehow even that is not yours—from your puddle of guts to the electric juice in every fold of your brain—not even the inside of your body belongs to you.

Et tu, *body? I spent my whole life thinking I owned this dancing carcass . . . but it was a loaner . . . a loner, just like me. . . . I thought I was precious. Protected myself, all these years. What a waste. I had nothing to lose and everything to give.*

It is all coming back. I remember lying on the floor in Roshi's cabin, which I was watching that evening while he led a retreat in Los Angeles. I had just dialed 911. Then hung up—*if I dial 911, that means this is real.* The operator instantly dialed back. I wasn't coherent. She said they were coming and could I stay on the line? I couldn't hold my body upright anymore, so I lowered myself to the floor before Roshi's altar, where we do *sanzen* practice. Long ago a student did a simple, fierce wood print of Roshi that hangs on the wall above his chair, and through it, I felt my teacher's eyes on my body from many miles away. I was failing one of his koans, again: *Stay alive! Resurrect!*

The pain goes from bad to worse to critical, and you go from denying it to fighting it to waiting for it to overcome and be done with you. This is what it felt like for me, to be dying for the very first time in my life. It was new, inevitable, and pretty much the worst thing imaginable. Toward the end of this struggle, you give up that one last thing you've been clinging to, which you now realize is all you ever really had: your desire to live. At this point, if you do live, you will be sick for a very long time and recovering for much longer. Being able to truly contemplate your own death is a gift that comes at a great price—I was paying that price. I wasn't particularly upset. I figured I was just getting a jump on what was ultimately everybody's fate. I didn't feel cheated out of the forty, fifty years I would miss; those years were not meant for me. They were not mine and were never meant to be. A life, I realized then, has a shape. It is shaped by time. A beginning, a middle, and an end. I'd come to the end, and it almost had a face, a face I could look into, a face I'd never seen or even properly imagined before now. All at once I was undergoing the dying process that I'd been watching, with fascination and dread, slowly consume my teacher for several years now.

I remember gazing up at the old wood print of Roshi above his soft, padded chair. Ferocious; implacable. And young! *I can't believe that bastard is going to bury me instead of the other way around* was my last thought before going unconscious.

PING ... PING ... PING ... The elevator passes floor after floor.

Both Myoshin and Roshi are speaking to me, their lips moving in the morgueish green light of this oversized steel coffin, but I can't hear a word. My entire inner life halts—the breath disappears from my throat; my heart rate doubles; all of my awareness narrows down to the single pinpoint prick of pain in my side ... and I wait ... wait and see whether that pinprick will swell into a stab, as though all of my guts were being dragged out of my belly through a dime sized slit in my side, from the same spot where the crucified Christ took that Roman's spear (extreme pain always brings me back to my Catholic youth).

"*Ha!*"—a voice suddenly cuts through the tunnel of death I am plunging down.

I look up.

Myoshin flashes a wicked smile. "You just ate too much—especially too much *meat!*" She bursts into laughter.

I snap out of it.

I want to kill her! How dare she. ...

Hmm, the pain does appear to be intestinal rather than pancreatic.

It is usually the case, when I get one of these postpancreatitis scares (every six to eight months), that in fact I have either had too much to eat or too much coffee or both. Idiopathic indeed.

"Was that you?" She sniffs the air like a bloodhound. Her face contorts. "Shozan-one, that's really bad."

"It wasn't me!"

She's really laughing now. "We're gonna go back to the room and *you're* gonna shit your brain out instead of Roshi!"

"*It wasn't me!*"

"Stinky one shi-shi-shi de gozaimasu!"

"*Oooooh!*" Roshi cries.

"Whatever," Myoshin rolls her eyes.

"*ooooooH!*" Roshi cries again.

Myoshin's nostrils flare. Her head whips downward about a foot. She breathes in sharply. Her eyes light up.

It's on.

PING—the elevator doors open—an older couple waiting to step in, all smiles, leap out of the way as Roshi's wheelchair blasts between them and I speed wheel him down the hallway.

Hugs Not Drugs

Thirty minutes later we're all feeling a little bit lighter, especially Roshi. I won't drag you into the details, because frankly, I'm a bit tired of finding spiritual metaphors in shit. Sometimes a dump is just a dump, man. . . . Well, maybe one more.

"Doko ni iru no?!" Roshi cried out as we lowered him onto the toilet.

"What's he saying?"

"*'Where are you?'* He's giving us a dharma teaching," Myoshin said.

"Now? Why now?"

"Why not?"

We hunkered down over Roshi, and she grabbed my hands and guided them around his side by his ribs right over the hips and showed me where and how to push, massaging my hands into his waist and lower back.

"Do it with his thrusts. Do you see? *Hard*, Shozan; you gotta get in there, you sissy!"

He was moaning. It sounded pretty horrifying. "Is he all right?"

"This is just natural." Myoshin shrugged.

"Like I give birth!" Roshi cried. He let loose a long, low groan. Myoshin groaned along with him. I joined her. We all groaned.

"What is the true activity? What is the true coming out?" Roshi asked.

We groaned mightily together, and I pushed on his midsection, sliding my hands and syncing with his thrusts while Myoshin perched in front of him, gently rubbing his belly in circles, like a snake charmer calling the snake out into the lake.

"Goooooood!" Roshi cried.

I was down there pushing on his sides with everything I had when the plug popped free. There was a tremendous release, felt by all in the room.

"Okay?" Myoshin asked me. I think she thought I was about to faint, like the father in the birthing room when the baby slides out.

"I've had my head up my own ass for so long, it feels like a tremendous improvement having it up someone else's."

I got it then: *This is true happiness. Head in a toilet and you're smiling.* We moved Roshi to his wheelchair, stared into the bowl victoriously together, and then I furtively dropped the three Vicodin pills along with their promise of fake happiness into the toilet and flushed the whole glorious mess away.

Roshi is sitting in his wheelchair before the big bay windows. Two massive pools coil through nonindigenous tropical trees eighteen stories below. Replicas of the Roman Colosseum and the Eiffel Tower loom in the distance, twice as big as the originals. Roshi takes in the view. Or doesn't. Are his eyes open or closed? Does it matter?

Vegas, you big phony, I think. This detour has been fabulous, but now I'm ready to return to the monastery. Like all addicts who are finally done with their addiction, I feel better now for not having taken the drug than I would have felt high on it.

Myoshin approaches me with a troubled expression. I figure I forgot to do something important again and brace myself for a scolding.

"We did not hug good night last night," she says.

I take her into my arms. "Good night, shi-shi-one de gozaimasu," I say. I squint. . . . In this light, at this angle, I can see Roshi's reflection in the window before him. Faint, spectral, like a spirit hovering over morning Vegas. I can't tell if he's staring out the window or staring back at Myoshin and me as we embrace. I decide it doesn't matter, close my eyes, and practice the principle that he taught me.

Banzai into the Blind Spot

I am at the wheel of the Great Vehicle. Roshi is riding shotgun. He is legendary for so many things, one of which is making his drivers (like Myoshin, he's never had a license) navigate traffic at dangerously fast speeds. When the inevitable police officer pulls you over, Roshi lowers the corners of his mouth into a kind of reverse smile, stares silently ahead, and lets you try to talk your way out of a ticket. Then, about a week later, he will ask the *inji* to get his satchel, pull out a wad of large crisp bills, peel a few off, and hand them to you without a word.

As in the driver's seat, so on the meditation cushion: when it comes to the Great Vehicle of Mahayana Zen practice, if you have a blind spot, chances are Roshi is encouraging you to steer into it while punching the gas. He is always trying to get you to collide with those parts of yourself that you cannot or refuse to face. And he often goes about this by giving you a little push so that you will collide with your peers, through either conflict . . . or those other ways that people collide.

The romantic ones.

It is often at the extremes of love and hate that you finally break down and see yourself and others most clearly. Then the middle way opens up before you, opening you up too. And so, I half-jokingly think, what could be better for your spiritual practice than if the person that you love and the person that you hate are one and the same, so that you can collide all day long, in every way imaginable, through sickness and health, for the rest of your lives? In an attempt to unlock the secrets of Roshi's matchmaking and to figure out how his methods could possibly be so consistently flawed, resulting in so many fraught unions, some have concluded that he simply matches people up by their height. Lew and I got into a heated discussion about this as we crossed the California border around noon.

His take was, "Look—if it wasn't for Roshi's encouraging people to marry, some of us might never find anyone."

"We didn't know each other at all when we tied the noose," Hattie chimed in with a wink. "It was a real leap of faith."

"We're still learning!"

"And leaping."

The fact that Roshi has more or less left Myoshin and me alone, with only the occasional hint that we would make a winning pair, gives me hope that we really are compatible—and not just height-wise. If Roshi is not actively trying to hook you up with someone that you are attracted to, it is probably an indication that the relationship actually has a shot at working out.

"*Hai!* Shozan-san," Roshi says.

He is wearing his badass gangster sunglasses, an elegant black *koromo*, and his monk's traveling cap, which is perched on the top of his rather large skull like a little fez. He jabs his finger and motions for me to switch lanes. Between my daydreaming and his thirst for danger, we make for one very bad driver.

"*Hai*, Roshi!" I shout, and punch the gas, and the RV, big as it is, goes nowhere but simply moans at a higher pitch. The single time Roshi has ever become truly angry with me was the day that I refused to take his directions while driving.

"Yeah, yeah, Roshi, my way okay," I had said, waving his suggestion away.

He flew into a rage, shouting at me in Japanese until I pulled off I-10 in downtown LA, did a U-turn, got back on the freeway going the opposite way, did another U-turn, got back on the I-10 freeway going the right way, and then merged onto I-110.

"Okay, okay, okay, Roshi, your way okay."

It is the only time he has ever told me exactly what to do, and he was right. "*Ah so,* Roshi," I said, as we shot past about forty minutes of traffic. He just looked at me and laughed. "Fifty years I live in America. I know the way."

"I can't believe Roshi never gets angry with you," muses Myoshin, who seems to get into rip-roaring tonsil testers with him bimonthly. She thinks it's because back when I had pancreatitis he saw me lying in the hospital bed, and something passed between us. She was dating someone else at that time, and Roshi, Myoshin, and her boyfriend were visiting me at San Antonio Community Hospital. But that didn't stop Roshi from telling me, "You need *Japanese* wife take care of you," and then looking around the room until he found Myoshin and resting his eyes on her until her boyfriend finally went over and put his arm around her.

I was so high on Dilaudid, all I could say was, "Sure, man, sure!"

High, I was not myself, and I remember looking right into Roshi's eyes in a way that I never would have sober. I looked at him, pleading for help. I wanted the tiniest morsel of support, of motherly nurturing. I wanted him to just hold my eyes for a second and smile. And what did he do? He turned away. This is why he is the Roshi, or great master. And this is why, after four months of convalescing, unsure about both my health and my commitment as a monk, I left my parents' home in Wisconsin and returned to the monastery. This is a hard thing to explain. It may sound masochistic or cold, but I wanted to learn love without attachment, love without pity, love without human sweat and stupidity. I wanted to learn a love that includes and is not averse to, but is not limited to and defined by, fear, want, frailty, clinging, lust.

I wanted to learn true love.

What I have learned is that there is no true love without love down here in the human trenches, and down here in the trenches, there is no human love but the greater love that gives rise to our flawed, needy, wonderful man-made hearts. To this day, four years later, Roshi will ask after my health and point to my side, and no matter how much I annoy him or screw up those post-retreat financial reports, or limp into *sanzen* and blithely give a lame answer to my koan, he will not manifest Angry Zen Master with me. But that day, when I thought I needed him the most and I tried desperately to hold his eyes with mine, he gave me nothing. He looked away.

I thought I wanted his love, but really I wanted his pity.

I wanted to quit.

But he wouldn't let me.

"A good doctor can cure your illness, but only the greatest doctor can show you you were never sick," Roshi has said.

Is someone firing up a chain saw in the back of the Great Vehicle?! No . . . it is just Lew forty feet behind me, lying down in the bedroom area. All I can see in the rearview mirror are his immense purple-socked toes pointed toward the ceiling. His snore is louder than the RV engine, and it, more than anything, seems to be propelling us toward our destination. This is a snore that says: I am a powerful man, and I am on your side.

Hattie is supposed to be finding us a place to eat. Instead she is performing incantations over her iPhone, which refuses to function. The day they come out with a smartphone made of all organic materials, which responds to water, sunlight, and love, she will be the first in line to trade Reiki treatments for it. In the meantime, I trust her intuition and know that when the time's right, she'll holler at me to exit the freeway, and low and behold—a Denny's!

A tiny hand appears with a plate of cold grapefruit. It has been peeled and parted into segments. All I have to do is pop them into my mouth, one by one, which I do. Myoshin takes a seat on the floor between Roshi and me. She is on map duty. She has no idea how to drive but always knows exactly where we are and where we're going, which is good, because I am always more or less lost.

"Slow down!" she tells me.

"*Yoooooosh!*" Roshi roars, jabbing his finger and motioning for me to speed up. There are at least three feet between the RV and the Honda in front of us—way too much space as far as Roshi is concerned. I punch the gas, swerve across two lanes, and a little VW Jetta shoots around us, angrily honking its horn.

"That's the exit we want!" Hattie shouts from the back, waking up Lew.

"Oh, dear, hold on to your yarmulkes," he cries.

I grip the steering wheel—there is no time to think.

"You're clear!" Myoshin shouts, and without looking I crank the steering wheel and all five of us lean into a hard . . . right . . . turn.

Holding . . . holding . . .

"*Banzai!*" cries the old master to my right.

"*BANZAI!*" we shout in reply.

Epilogue

MOUNTAINS ON THE MOVE

I am alone: my monk peers have traveled to Northern California for a retreat. I stroll the monastic grounds, touring the arid, stony terrain as though for the first time. Tears arise as I sit atop an enormous boulder I have cursed countless times after smacking into it in the black of night. The sun is setting, and with the help of a great deal of smog, the sky looks lit as if by cinders from God's own campfire. Every corner of this property throbs with meaning for me—as only a place can that you are about to leave for good.

I duck into cabin one, the site of my first night on this mountain (*more than two presidential terms ago!*). Mouse turds speckle mattress covers; a student's self-massage implement is abandoned on the floor like a murder weapon. Nonetheless, for me this is a sacred shrine. I inhale the rickety shack's musky aroma, my nose pressed right up against its olfactory fingerprint. Memories flush in—that dream, the night of my ordination, the one I'll never forget, the whole thing but a single image: a skeleton puts his hand on my shoulder as I weep in a corner.

But how can I leave the monastery now? I think. *Not now, not when these mountains have finally become my home!*

I sit down on one of four bunk beds and gather myself. A student has left a book by his pillow, *Zen Mind, Beginner's Mind* by Shunryu Suzuki. I flip through and pause on Suzuki Roshi's observation to the effect that living at a monastery is like walking around in a mist. At first you merely feel dampened by the monastic structure and rhythms. But if you stick with it long enough, eventually you discover that you're soaked to the bone in formal Zen practice. You have become this new way of life, only it is no longer new. Where before you were only full of yourself, now you find you are also full of Zen—that is to say, emptiness (*sunyata*). Zen practice is learning to allow ourselves to conceive of the inconceivable: that these two are really one and the same.

You breathe in the monastic customs, the form, those rituals and teachings and practices—all of that rare mountain air. Over time they become part of you, negating and completing you at once. And now it is time for you to breathe them out, into the world around you.

In other words, right around the time you stop desperately wanting to leave the monastery, it's time for you to go share what you've learned there with others.

I reach into my parka pocket and pull out "the letter"—the one causing me so much consternation, with the signatures squiggled in different colors of ink by eight of the seniormost teachers in my lineage. The news is about me: It's good. Flattering. Terrifying. For some reason, pretty much out of nowhere, my teacher recently set in motion the process of my "promotion." *Surely someone will stop this madness,* I'd thought. But no. The letter in my trembling hands states otherwise. The community has agreed, in its uppermost levels, that I am to be made an *osho,* or priest.

Are you ready for this? a voice inside me demands. Becoming a priest, moving off the mountain, and starting a city temple somewhere is not the end of my training, I assure myself, but the beginning of a whole new phase of it. No one stays here forever; it's a place for people like me to grow up, not grow old.

But I have *grown old at the monastery,* I sigh. *Or at least middle-aged—which is to say:* newly *old.*

I am touching the hemline of forty, a gown—more of a mildewed old bathrobe, actually—that I will slip into next year. While not ancient, I am no longer a potential housemate on *The Real World*. Exhibit A: my wee gray gut, flopping slightly over my belted robes like the chin of a child peeking over a fence. Plus, my hips have little jowls. When did that happen? Professional athletes and cops are now younger than I. Cops! "The Man" is my junior!

I should've had kids, I conclude. Kids can be young for you. They've got your back like that. They give your age context. When you have kids, you're old "in comparison." Without them? You're old in a vacuum.

But I'm still twenty-five, aren't I? Haven't I always *been twenty-five?*

Every adult I ever ignored warned me that this day would come. But I didn't listen. I couldn't hear them for the blood pumping in my ears, that drumbeat hammering out its rhythm in my heart, sending me out into the world to search for some way, some means, some work, purpose, or destiny to free the music. The drum pounds and pounds and pounds. It stretches you from the inside out, all the years of your youth, and then settles and disappears somewhere inside your flesh, now wrinkled and flabby for the work it's done containing and expressing your song.

There's only one consolation for getting old, I decide: *becoming wise*. Am I wise? A wiseass, yes. But *wise*-wise? Am I nascently wise, at least? Wise lite? I realize you can never field this question yourself; the answer has to come from others, and to prove it true, you can never believe them.

So I try for some lower-hanging fruit and conclude that I'm certainly stupider in all the appropriate Zen ways since arriving at the monastery. I will probably have to settle for that. Wise will come much later, if at all, when I become stupider still. And then, finally, as my stupidity ripens: simple.

Simple is key. If you lose simplicity as you accumulate years, then you begin to look and feel very old indeed. After my first summer training season, friends asked what I had learned from my Zen master—himself now a hundred and five, though not a day over three years old at heart. During our private meetings, I explained, my teacher shook my hand or hugged me, over and over. It was so basic, but what I learned was how to embrace and how to let go. This is the secret to life, I tried to explain. When to hold on and when to let things pass.

I went on and on and on. . . . But I didn't actually hug any of my dear friends to make my point. That's where I went wrong. To paraphrase the novelist Zadie Smith, young men have the answers to everything yet know the meaning of nothing. Now, instead of having a staged environment to support my practice, I would have to actually *do* what I had learned at the monastery in the Real World. "Just make yourself master of every situation, and wherever you stand is the true place," Zen master Rinzai said. Almost a decade ago I left the world and made a spiritual home at the monastery. Now it was time to leave the monastery and make a spiritual home in the world.

I stand outside the *zendo* under a light night snowfall and perform some heavy breathing exercises, the kind that help me relax. Which is to say, I have a cigarette. I'm not a smoker, mind you. I quit that habit years ago. Yet here I am again, back where I started, puffing away and staring off into the same set of fabulously snow-capped mountains that greeted me when I first arrived at the monastery nine years and a full head of hair ago.

The moon is a cosmic fingernail, hooking the topmost peak as if slowly lifting the entire mountain range into the sky. There is no sound anywhere. The cold night has ears, and we are listening to each other.

Just yesterday the stooped septuagenarian at the post office tilted her head up like a bird and shook her little freckled fist and exclaimed, "This mountain range is one of the fastest growing in the world, you know." She's told me this seven or eight times now. I always nod and grin and look around at the bank of post office boxes, as though surveying the vastness of our shared mountain home.

"Amen!" I cry.

Yet I never know what she means exactly. How can a mountain "grow"? If a mountain is growing, what *isn't*? Is *grow* really the right word? I decide now that it is. It feels right to me. I can relate to these mountains. I feel their seismic shifts within. I know what they're going through.